Capital Projects and Healthcare Reform

Capital Projects and Healthcare Reform

Navigating Design and Delivery in an Era of Disruption

Robert D. Levine and Georgeann B. Burns, Editors

HAP

ACHE Management Series

Your board, staff, or clients may also benefit from this book's insight. For more information on quantity discounts, contact the Health Administration Press Marketing Manager at (312) 424-9470.

19 18 17 16 15 5 4 3 2 1

Library of Congress Cataloging-in-Publication Data

Levine, Robert D., author.

Capital projects and healthcare reform : navigating design and delivery in an era of disruption / Robert D. Levine, Georgeann B. Burns.

p. ; cm.

Includes bibliographical references.

ISBN 978-1-56793-716-9 (alk. paper)

I. Burns, Georgeann B., author. II. Title.

[DNLM: 1. Health Care Reform—United States. 2. Capital Financing—United States. 3. Health Planning—United States. 4. Healthcare Financing—United States. WA 540 AA1]

RA971.3

362.1068'1—dc23

2014043453

The paper used in this publication meets the minimum requirements of American National Standard for Information Sciences—Permanence of Paper for Printed Library Materials, ANSI Z39.48-1984. ♾™

Acquisitions editor: Tulie O'Connor; Project manager: Amy Carlton; Cover designer: Carla Nessa; Layout: PerfecType

Found an error or a typo? We want to know! Please e-mail it to hapbooks@ache.org, and put "Book Error" in the subject line.

For photocopying and copyright information, please contact Copyright Clearance Center at www.copyright.com or at (978) 750-8400.

Health Administration Press
A division of the Foundation of the American
College of Healthcare Executives
One North Franklin Street, Suite 1700
Chicago, IL 60606-3529
(312) 424-2800

I am glad to witness today the signing of this Medicare bill, which puts this Nation right where it needs to be, to be right. A responsive, forward-looking Congress have made it historically possible for this day to come about. . . . These people are our prideful responsibility and they are entitled, among other benefits, to the best medical protection available.

—President Lyndon Johnson, July 30, 1965

And yet, 50 years later:

For decades, few things exposed hard-working families to economic hardship more than a broken health care system. And in case you haven't heard, we're in the process of fixing that. . . . Already, because of the Affordable Care Act, more than 3 million Americans under age 26 have gained coverage under their parents' plans. . . . More than 9 million Americans have signed up for private health insurance or Medicaid coverage. . . . Because of this law, no American can ever again be dropped or denied coverage for a preexisting condition.

—President Barack Obama, January 28, 2014

Contents

Foreword

Joe Flower

WHAT YOU THINK becomes brick. What you imagine becomes steel and glass. What you visualize becomes technologies deployed, people hired, cars in the parking lot, lights on.

Across healthcare, organizations are changing shape, consolidating, affiliating, changing business models and revenue streams—and launching strategic plans, capital programs, and technology deployments to match. If you have not thought deeply enough, contrarily enough, questioning enough assumptions, you will end up with a capital program that fetters rather than launches your transformation.

Your assumptions about the nature of your organization, what you are actually doing to "make a living," what your "community of practice" is, end up baked into the steel and concrete and glass, the WiFi network, the heat recovery systems, the art collection—and the bond debt. You end up servicing your capitalized building stock and technology platform instead of the other way around.

What will your organization actually be like in five years or ten years? What tasks will it be doing? In what kind of environment?

Sure, we will still be doing surgery on messy compound fractures. But will we be doing as many amputations from sequelae of diabetes?

Sure, we will still need a neonatal intensive care unit. But will we be seeing as many preemies?

Sure, we will still have an intensive care unit. But when we step patients down, will we be putting them in a med-surg bed? Or sending them home with an electronic ICU tracking system strapped to their wrist, feeding back into our 24-hour monitoring system?

The future is impossible to predict. But it is not impossible to think about, because we know the broad trends that will produce it, and examples of what it will look like. As William Gibson (1999) famously remarked, "The future is already here. It is just not very evenly distributed."

What will the future of healthcare look like?

Cheaper. Prices, costs, and acute utilization rates can all be expected to drop over time, constraining healthcare budgets and the ability to support capital programs, but at the same time requiring dramatic rethinking of how healthcare can be delivered.

More distributed. Healthcare organizations will be dramatically reshaped under these efficiency pressures, not only consolidating but decentralizing, especially at the primary level.

More tech. New mobile technologies and "big data" will play a big part in reshaping what kind of care we give, when, where, with what kind of capital needs—which in turn will reshape the organizations themselves and the buildings and technological environments in which they work.

Less top-heavy. The center of gravity of healthcare has typically been giving the high-end specialists, particularly "the procedure guys," the machines, space, and support they need to do their stuff, to our mutual profit through the magic of fee-for-service billing. Any payment scheme that moves the provider from volume to value causes a revaluation and a re-evaluation of the need to build more resources for the primary care base of the institution and fewer for the top-end specialists.

Can you think through the implications of all this by yourself? Not likely. Think for a moment about how people think—indeed, about how *you* think.

Being more experienced does not necessarily exempt us from illusion, unless something in our process constantly and directly tests the results of our judgments (the way, say, a robust retail market does on price setting). Even if our judgments are correct, they are based on an environment that formed our skills: in the jungle or the savannah, in a controlled market or a retail market, in a risk-bearing business arrangement or an endowed business arrangement. When our environment shifts, our illusions, biases, and assumptions persist, even though they may be dangerously out of date.

We are in a rapidly shifting environment. Over the next several years, all healthcare leaders will be called on to make numerous strategic decisions and tactical choices that will be fundamentally different from decisions they are used to making. But they will be making those decisions with a mental apparatus formed in the old environment.

So thinking about the strategic future, and what that means for a capital program, is hard. We have to use those broad trends to think through the problem in detail, from C-suite decision making through financing, planning, and design to technological advances. That is what this book does, bringing together experts from a variety of fields to get down into the roots and soil of the question. This is the book you need to help you think through the question: How do we do capital planning that works in this rapidly shifting environment?

This is heroic work. It is boring to all except those who do it. Much of it is invisible to most of the people it affects. But all this study and thought, and turning the thought into actual capital programs and real buildings and technologies—hard, detailed, tough-minded, relentless labor—ultimately will save lives, reduce suffering, and make healthcare more available to all by reducing costs.

REFERENCE

Gibson, W. 1999. "The Science in Science Fiction." *Talk of the Nation.* National Public Radio. Broadcast November 30.

Introduction

Prediction is very difficult, especially if it's about the future.

—Niels Bohr, 1949

INTO THE STORM

Healthcare has had it pretty good for a long time. What other industry could stay in business without worrying about price or quality? Or, generally speaking, not even know what its actual costs were? Could you picture an automobile company or a computer company surviving for long in that environment? Wind the clock back 25 years, before prospective payments came into play, and you had a "cost plus" environment where providers were also paid to fix work that wasn't done correctly the first time (readmissions).

Furthermore, why does the same procedure being delivered in Albany, New York, have costs dramatically different from those for the same procedure in Charlotte, North Carolina, even after adjusting for local labor differences? It's simply because they're done differently. That would be like General Motors having a different cost for a car built in Michigan instead of Tennessee. Would they then charge differently based on where it was manufactured? Good luck with that.

Yet that described healthcare in March 2010 when the Patient Protection and Affordable Care Act (ACA) formally became law. No wonder everyone had that puzzled look.

A BRIEF HISTORY OF HEALTHCARE

Every once in a while we get reminded that healthcare is a regulated business. We don't mean regulated the way the Federal Communications Commission regulates communication, or the way the Federal Aviation Administration regulates the airline industry, or even the way the government regulates utilities. We mean regulated in all facets of how you conduct business. Regulated in how care is delivered (evidence-based medicine), regulated in how everyone gets paid (diagnosis related groups, or DRGs), and even regulated as to whom you can sell services (insurance). Fifty years ago healthcare was more or less unregulated and essentially delivered through the private sector. The private, not-for-profit hospital was either community based or faith based, and reimbursement was either self-pay or paid through private insurance. But in 1965, everything changed.

That, of course, was the year of the enactment of the Medicare and Medicaid programs. As a result of those programs, providers had to change the way they delivered services, not only to accommodate additional covered lives, but to do so in a growing public sector reimbursement environment.

Then, in 1985, with the advent of DRG reimbursement, everything was once again turned on its head, with hospital systems scrambling to adapt to the changed environment. Going from retrospective reimbursement (cost plus) to a prospective payment system challenged the financial capabilities of a large segment of the hospital universe.

In 1997, once again, regulation affected delivery of services, as the Balanced Budget Act dramatically changed the rural healthcare landscape with the advent of the critical access and sole community hospital designations.

Each of these laws had a major impact not only on the delivery of services and the reimbursement for those services, but also on the capital projects that followed.

Having lived through those three major regulatory ages when the ACA was enacted in 2010, healthcare professionals had every reason to assume the industry was again going to undergo dramatic changes, changes that would affect the healthcare landscape in ways that we couldn't imagine. But in talking to industry leaders then, we found dramatic disagreement as to what was going on, what changes would occur in both delivery and outcomes, and most important to us, how the buildings that house healthcare activities would change. In all areas of capital project development, from planners and designers to project and construction managers as well as public and private sector providers, no clear concept emerged of what those changes would be.

In our opinion, we were witnessing what is called historical determinism—living through a historical event without realizing it. Many people said they lived through the 1929 stock market crash as if they were aware of its historical significance, but few truly understood its impact. In 2010, although numerous pundits were offering opinions and numerous sources of information, there was no one source from which to get a grasp of the new reform law, no oracle to predict its true implications and how it would affect not only healthcare delivery but the capital development projects that would accommodate the industry going forward.

ENTER REFORM

This book attempts to look at reform and its implications for capital development projects through the eyes of the different participants in the industry, as well as within the context of a changed economic climate. We'll describe what the new paradigm is and why it exists, lay out a game plan for addressing that new environment, and identify what we believe the future will hold for capital projects. If you want to know why a bird flies, you don't examine the feathers—you look at the aerodynamics. We've done that with healthcare reform, concentrating on those components of capital development that will have the most impact.

While the ACA itself is comprehensive, this book is intended to address only that part of the bill that clearly affects capital development. We also examine related factors not specifically part of the bill that are forcing change. As Alan Yordy points out in Chapter 1 on the healthcare CEO's viewpoint, many of the issues being addressed in reform would've taken place without the ACA, although probably at a slower pace.

Although predicting the impact of the various dynamics within the reform bill is difficult, it is possible to discuss the potential for various outcomes. For example, coverage will be expanded, so we will look at both sides of this issue:

- With millions of additional people being covered, what is the potential that this covered population will enter old age in a healthier state, thereby lowering future development needs?
- Will state exchanges drive down reimbursements to the detriment of development, or will they support development resulting from broader access through affordable premiums?
- The potential exists for the loss of operating lease status. If all leases become capital leases, will they adversely affect a hospital pro forma and, ultimately, its bond capacity for new construction?
- With the dramatic shift from sick care to wellness, can keeping the population healthier add opportunity to development, or will it diminish use of facilities and therefore limit growth?

THE FINANCIAL CRISES

We've always looked at healthcare capital development as running counter to the normal economic cycle. Unlike development in the private sector, which is always tied to the strength of the private economy, healthcare development was a function of the twin pillars of demand and reimbursement, both independent of the economy. Or so we thought. On occasion, economic factors would affect healthcare development, especially when a strong economy led to rising interest rates. But even then, the availability of funds through variable rate products was always more important than rates, with the possible exception of double-digit rates in the 1970s.

The financial crisis of 2008–2009 challenged that thinking. A severe recession with dramatically high unemployment clearly affected healthcare as the unemployed not only lost their healthcare coverage, but the deleveraging that went along with the financial crisis put downward pressure on nonessential healthcare procedures and dramatically increased charity care. But the financial crisis challenged healthcare in another way through the tremendous pressure on the states as a result of lower tax revenues and higher social supports, such as unemployment payments and Medicaid. The states' mandates to have balanced budgets affected their ability to fund healthcare programs, such as Medicaid; Women, Infants, and Children nutritional support; and the Children's Health Insurance Program. So the thought that healthcare is immune to economic downturns is no longer valid.

Within that economic climate, enter the healthcare reform legislation of 2010. It's the most ambitious healthcare legislation since the advent of Medicare and Medicaid in 1965 and the introduction of DRGs as the basis of reimbursement in 1985. Notwithstanding the political ramifications of the reform bill, we believe the changes within the bill will impose a dramatic headwind to future capital development.

Although this book is meant to address the topic of reform, it's foolish to do it in a vacuum. We must consider what aspects of financing new development will change with reform as a result of a changing economic environment. The aging population, the lower workforce participation, and the widening income gap all put pressure on Medicare and Medicaid taxes, thereby putting pressure on

Medicare reimbursements. We've already seen what weaker economic growth can do to discretionary medical spending.

Thus the assumption that healthcare was countercyclical to the economy is no longer valid:

- The dynamics of the aging population seemed to have little to do with a slowing economy.
- Margin compression has occurred because of economic shifts primarily from unemployment levels.
- Philanthropy has dropped because of donor investment losses.
- The need to fund deferred capital improvements continues.
- Reimbursement has declined because of recent (and probably ongoing) federal budget cuts.
- Hospitals' nonprofit tax-exempt status has been challenged because of diminished charity care.
- Credit ratings have been downgraded because all of the reasons above are increasing costs and decreasing availability of capital.

Who was it that said the definition of despair is that it is always darkest before it goes black? We hope this book will show that all of the headwinds we mentioned can create opportunities for those who can see that there is much to gain on the other side of the ledger.

YES, WE KNOW YOU CAN'T PREDICT THE FUTURE, BUT . . .

By looking at past regulations as a way of getting a peek into the future, we identified three recurring themes. First, *major consolidation* followed the enactment of Medicare and Medicaid, most likely because the financial pressures of lower reimbursements were more dramatic than the offsetting of additional covered lives. DRGs exposed many hospitals unprepared to go from a cost plus (retrospective) environment to a prospective one. Once again consolidation solved the problem of the financially weaker hospitals.

We're already seeing the start of consolidation and acquisitions under the ACA. In 2013, the number of consolidations and acquisitions was more than double those in 2005. In fact, the consulting firm Booz & Company predicts that 1,000 of the nation's 5,000 hospitals will seek out mergers out of the next five to seven years (Creswell and Abelson 2013). The trend is all about efficiency. Despite some states' opposition to some of the mergers in fear of increased costs to consumers, for the most part the mergers continue unchallenged.

Second, we saw the *growth of investor-owned or for-profit hospitals and systems*. These barely existed before 1965, had substantial growth after that, and then saw a growth spurt after DRGs began. Although this book is not meant to provide the history of investor-owned systems, we do address them to the extent that their culture and delivery clearly flourish in a tighter reimbursement environment. And although these hospitals make up only 15 percent of the beds nationwide, they comprise 40 percent of the capital development dollars being spent. To ignore them is to look at only half of the market.

Third, *new legislation tends to evolve over time*, partially because new laws can be tweaked every two years with even a slight change in who is elected to Congress. Major legislation takes a long time to integrate into our lives to the point where it feels like business as usual. In spite of the 2012 Supreme Court decision (*National Federation of Independent Businesses v. Sebelius*), Medicaid coverage continues to vary state by state. Even though DRGs were enacted in 1985 with 467 different rate groups, the system has become more targeted over the years. The most recent International Statistical Classification of Diseases and Health Related Problems (ICD-10) addresses DRGs more strategically to allow for newer healthcare delivery methods and therefore lower reimbursement. We should expect the ACA to be no different.

To make matters more difficult, the ACA has established a series of pilot programs. These programs are tested nationally for a limited time. If found to be of monetary value, they can be inserted into the ACA without going back to Congress for approval. Currently 25 pilot programs exist, with 380 references in the ACA. Examples include the following:

- Tort reform (being tested in the Northwest)
- Bundled payments (which can ultimately include insurance)
- Payment for performance
- Increased payments for primary care physicians

Not only will the current law be modified through these pilots, but their inclusion will have substantial impact on reimbursements. Anticipating those outcomes adds to the challenge.

Clearly the ACA, with nine years to fully roll out (2010 to 2019), will undergo more changes. When you consider the fact that we attempt to design and build healthcare buildings meant to last 40 to 50 years, the importance of getting it right is critical, and that is the goal of this book. Nassim Nicholas Taleb (2005), in his wonderful book *Fooled by Randomness*, makes the argument that predicting anything with certainty is impossible. But it is possible to acknowledge change, anticipate the impact of that change, and embrace solutions that incorporate it. To do these things successfully, we must eliminate the preconceptions—conventional wisdom and confirmation bias—that we inherently possess.

A CULTURE CHANGE

It's one thing to make changes to processes when it becomes obvious that changes are needed. But it's another thing to change the culture within which those processes are delivered. One of the challenges all businesses face is how to grow while maintaining the company culture. Although approaches vary, some businesses choose to slow their growth so that it can occur organically and the company can avoid bringing new people in from the outside. For many companies, maintaining their culture is critical.

The ACA is challenging the very existence of our current healthcare culture, and therein lies a major difficulty. Asking a hospital to participate in wellness programs when its survival is tied to treating sick people is a small example of a dramatic culture shift. Forming accountable care organizations and patient-centered medical homes can drive down occupancy rates in hospitals at the same time that funding existing bond programs relies on maintaining bed occupancy and related revenue.

The culture is also changing for the physician. Smaller practices can no longer exist with the conflicting pressures of lower reimbursement and higher costs for electronic medical records and information technology (IT) mandated by the ACA. The resulting integration into healthcare systems is changing provider obligations to meet care delivery goals as systems look to benefit from that integration. Physicians are also being introduced to a more collaborative world as IT opens up the benefits of shared information between providers. And physicians are adjusting to a more informed patient as the Internet expands education and options for patients and their families.

Today's culture is changing for the patient also. In the past, insurance was most likely provided by our employer, the physicians we saw were dictated by our insurance coverage, and the hospitals we went to were dictated by our physician. That's changing. The ACA is encouraging more employers to underwrite employees' healthcare instead of providing it, thus driving them to the exchanges. In doing so, the choice of insurance is now in the patient's hands, and with that, the choice of physician. The patient must become his or her own advocate and be an active participant in the process.

And the culture is changing for the planning and design community. Sitting with the user groups to determine how they want to deliver services, and then designing based on those requests, is no longer enough. The design community must be knowledgeable about how healthcare must be delivered today—to address value, not volume, with a declining reimbursement environment. Yes, we know "form follows function," but as Winston Churchill (1943) said, "We shape our buildings, and afterwards our buildings shape us."

Each chapter in this book addresses this change in culture from the authors' unique perspectives. We've organized the book chapters in the chronological order we think a capital development project should occur, having nothing to do with the order of importance.

> Throughout this book, Georgeann and Robert will attempt to tie thoughts together in boxes introducing each chapter and in key takeaways at the end of each chapter. When you see these boxes, you will know it is us speaking.

REFERENCES

Churchill, W. 1943. Speech to the House of Commons, October 28.

Creswell, J., and R. Abelson. 2013. "New Laws and Rising Costs Create a Surge of Supersizing Hospitals." Published August 12. www.nytimes.com/2013/08/13/business/bigger-hospitals-may-lead-to-bigger-bills-for-patients.html?_r=0.

Taleb, N. N. 2005. *Fooled by Randomness: The Hidden Role of Chance in Life and in the Markets.* New York: Random House.

CHAPTER 1

Healthcare Strategy and Affordable Care

Alan R. Yordy

Finding information about the ACA and its implications is easy. Much has been written, and numerous information sources are available. But all of that pales in comparison with having a look from the inside, as Alan Yordy gives us in this chapter.

According to the Congressional Budget Office, the ACA will add $948 billion to the national budget, and $143 billion of that was meant to be offset by three things: lower hospital payments, increased Medicare taxes on higher wage earners, and additional premiums from young healthy participants.

Lower hospital payments will manifest in many ways, as Yordy points out. Hospitals are facing enormous payment headwinds. At the same time, they will need to increase patient satisfaction as healthcare culture changes from volume-based to value-based.

(continued)

(continued from previous page)

> Analyzing the perspectives of the other stakeholders within the chapters of this book is impossible without understanding what a CEO must consider as he navigates through reform. What stands out dramatically is the moving target that is healthcare reform.

Foresight turns out to be a critical adaptive strategy for times of great stress.

—Jamais Cascio

RUNNING OUT OF RUNWAY

By 2009 healthcare costs consumed 17.6 percent of the total gross domestic product of the United States—$2.5 trillion annually, or $8,160 for every citizen every year. By comparison in 1970 healthcare costs consumed 7.2 percent of the total gross domestic product—$75 billion annually, $360 for every citizen (Kaiser Family Foundation 2009). Projections in 2009 for the Medicare program were dire, suggesting that the program costs would outpace tax-supported funding by 2020. Many economists concluded that the international competitiveness of the United States would be severely compromised if the trend of cost increases continued.

The healthcare-industrial complex was in full bloom. The passage and implementation of the Medicare and Medicaid programs in the mid-1960s fueled much of the growth. More procedures, implantable devices, and pharmaceuticals had been invented in the 40-year period from 1970 to 2010 than during any time in human history. Life expectancy had grown from 70.8 years to almost 78.7 years (CDC 2011). During the same period, the US population grew from approximately 200 million to 325 million. From 1970 to 2010, obesity in the population of the United States grew from 17 percent to 34 percent (CDC 2011). All of these factors explain, in part, the rapid rise in healthcare costs.

In 2009, the Social Security Advisory Board issued a report concluding, "This Board believes it is necessary to offer our own perspectives, not because we are particular experts in health care policy, *but because we believe that the rising cost of health care represents perhaps the most significant threat to the long-term economic security of workers and retirees*" (Social Security Advisory Board 2009, emphasis added). The debate was on.

THE GRAND BARGAIN

The Patient Protection and Affordable Care Act (ACA) was a grand bargain: almost $1 trillion of payment cuts to providers and increased taxes in exchange for providing 32 million uninsured Americans with affordable health insurance. Physicians, hospitals, and other entitlement spending contributed $455 billion in payment reductions as part of the package (see Exhibit 1.1). Increased Medicare and other taxes contributed $349 billion in new tax revenue. It was the single largest tax increase since the Balanced Budget Act of 1997. On March 23, 2010—the day the bill was signed into law—the wheels were set in motion to fundamentally reorganize one-sixth of the US economy.

Expanding coverage to the uninsured was to be accomplished in two ways: expansion of Medicaid and development of healthcare exchanges. The exchanges would allow the public to purchase health insurance with associated federal subsidies for families with incomes of up to 400 percent of the federal poverty level for 2014—$94,200 for a family of four. Early estimates suggested that 33 to 50 percent of the expansion would come from increasing the eligibility for the Medicaid program to 138 percent of the federal poverty level. The remainder would come from individuals purchasing insurance via the healthcare exchanges, sometime called "marketplaces." The exchanges and the Medicaid expansion would

Exhibit 1.1 Overview of Funding Elements of the ACA

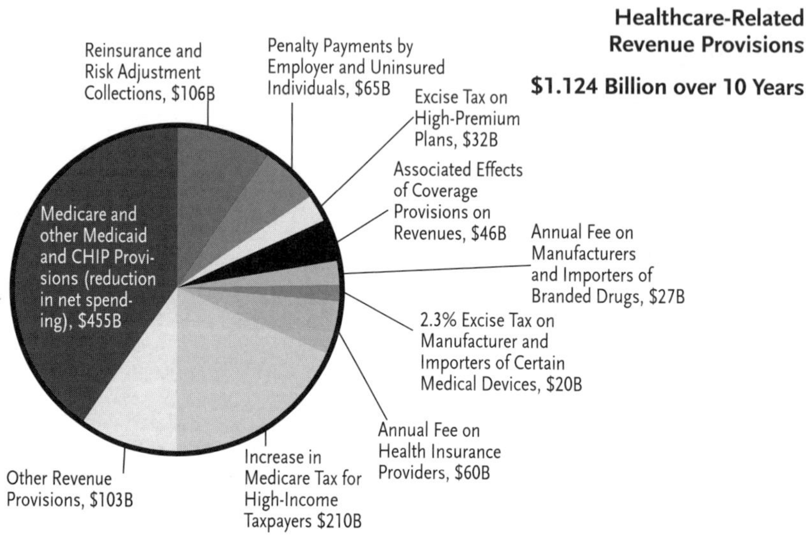

Source: Premier, Inc. (2011).

provide approximately 71 percent of the US population under the age of 65 with some level of subsidy to be entitled to or purchase health insurance coverage (Families USA 2013). Not since the Great Depression have so many Americans been entitled to a subsidy under a single program.

In exchange for the significant expansion in coverage, hospitals and physicians in the United States agreed to more than $155 billion in payment cuts over a decade. Most of these cuts were focused on Medicare payments and the elimination of disproportionate share hospital (DSH) payments to hospitals that serve a higher percentage of Medicaid and uninsured patients. A multitude of additional requirements, with much of the detail delegated to the secretary of Health and Human Services (HHS), was part of the legislation.

For instance, the secretary was given broad authority to establish rules for the exchanges and to work with states to establish state-operated exchanges. The rules under which the exchanges operate could either reduce insurance risk or increase the risk. Reducing the risk could be accomplished by spreading it over all the newly insured. One example of risk reduction was the decision to open exchanges for enrollment each year for a period of three months, similar to Medicare Advantage provisions.

Increasing the risk could occur by easing the enrollment criteria and causing the cost of insurance to go up. On the other hand the secretary adopted a rule requiring insurance companies and providers to cover 90 days of care when someone signs up for a plan through an exchange, regardless of whether she has paid her premium. If the premium is not paid, the policy is cancelled within 90 days. During the 90-day grace period, care must be provided at the expense of insurers and providers.

Additionally, the secretary was required to establish rules and provide funding for new exchange start-ups called consumer-operated and oriented plans or "co-ops"—community-based nonprofit organizations desiring to provide health insurance products (Hancock 2013). The secretary was also required to draft rules for Medicaid expansion and fraud recovery. All told, the secretary was required to draft and implement regulations in 1,120 specific areas under the ACA.

In the end, passage of the ACA came down to a single issue—funding of abortion and other women's healthcare services. During the debate in 2009 and 2010, the bill hung in the balance. For decades the Church Amendments had provided conscience protection for nonprofit hospitals that received federal funds but were morally opposed to abortion (HHS 1973). In 1997 the Hyde Amendment went further and banned federal funding for abortion services. Some argued that the language contained in the ACA would open the door to federally funded abortion. Because contraceptive coverage regulations and conscience clause protection were left to the HHS secretary to determine, there was also concern that the long-standing policy allowing organizations to opt out of providing these services would be revoked.

The Senate acted first, passing a version of the bill that most believed would retain both conscience protection and the Hyde Amendment, which required annual Congressional renewal. In the meantime, the Senate lost its filibuster-proof Democratic majority with the election of Republican Scott Brown from Massachusetts. The smaller majority of Democrats in the House meant that the House would have to adopt the exact version of the bill as passed by the Senate. A holdout group of pro-life Democrats, led by Michigan Congressman Bart Stupak, prolonged debate for months. After President Barack Obama signed an executive order reaffirming the Hyde Amendment, the group relented, and the bill narrowly passed in the House—219 to 212. The grand bargain was complete, but passed without bipartisan support. This single issue overshadowed the more profound changes to healthcare.

THE SUPREME COURT: CASTING THE FUTURE

Pay for Performance. From the beginning the ACA was a partisan debate. Unlike most major social legislation of the past 50 years, there was no central agreement on the tenets of healthcare in America. The ACA had the hallmarks of a debate that would have a long shelf life. A Supreme Court contest was inevitable from the beginning, and not just one. The complexity of the law made it highly likely that many aspects of the law would be tested. The first test went to the heart of the law on two issues: mandating Medicaid expansion and individual insurance purchase.

The major element of the Supreme Court decision in 2012 found that requiring Medicaid expansion in all 50 states was coercive. The court ruled that while the federal government may encourage states to participate in federal programs, it may not require them to do so. "When Congress threatens to terminate other grants as a means of pressuring the States to accept a Spending Clause program (Medicaid), the legislation runs counter to this Nation's system of federalism" (*NFIB v. Sebelius* 2012, 5).

The second and more fundamental constitutional issue was the personal mandate requiring individuals to obtain insurance or pay a federal tax. In some adroit constitutional hairsplitting, Justice John Roberts writing for the majority found that the federal government does have the ability to tax citizens to encourage certain behaviors. "The payment is not so high that there is really no choice but to buy health insurance; the payment is not limited to willful violations, as penalties for unlawful acts often are; and the payment is collected solely by the IRS through the normal means of taxation" (*NFIB v. Sebelius* 2012, 9). A new standard emerged—as long as a tax to encourage the purchase of health insurance is sufficiently reasonable, the tax may stand. For the ACA the tax is $95 or 1 percent of adjusted gross income in year one, rising to $600 or 3 percent of adjusted gross income by year three and thereafter (Healthcare.gov 2014).

The most enduring element of Justice Roberts' decision will likely be his reinforcement of the Commerce Clause of the Constitution: ". . . the individual mandate is not a valid exercise of Congress's power under the Commerce Clause and the Necessary and Proper Clause. The individual mandate thus cannot be sustained under Congress's power to regulate Commerce" (*NFIB v. Sebelius* 2012, 58).

In a single opinion, the Supreme Court fundamentally changed the underlying social contract in the ACA and raised doubts for many about the prospects of further expanding healthcare coverage. First, the requirements that the tax must be reasonable, not coercive, and that the Medicaid expansion could not be required made it unlikely that 32 million previously uninsured Americans would gain coverage under the ACA. Second, the ruling made it unlikely that the United States would one day have a single-payer system for healthcare requiring all citizens to have health insurance with some consumer responsibility.

Case law continues to rewrite the ACA. *Burwell v. Hobby Lobby* (2014) reinstated conscience protection for some private employers who find it objectionable to provide contraceptive coverage to employees. In conflicting opinions, the Court of Appeals for the

Fourth Circuit and the District of Columbia found that providing subsidies for purchasing health insurance through the federal exchange may be a violation of the ACA. The Supreme Court will continue to play a vital role as an interpreter of provisions within the ACA.

REWRITING THE BASIC RULES OF HEALTHCARE IN AMERICA

The debate over ethics and morals overshadowed three critical issues that, as a result, received little attention:

- Hastening the move from employer-based insurance to individually purchased insurance
- Moving from defined-benefit health insurance to defined-contribution health insurance, expanding individual responsibility for healthcare costs
- Vesting the Internal Revenue Service (IRS) with significant new regulatory power over healthcare in America.

Since World War II, much of the expansion of health insurance has focused on employer-based health insurance. It was provided as a benefit and could be considered as a pretax expense, making it an attractive way to provide coverage to employees. Employer-based insurance was widely accepted by the early 1960s as an essential employee benefit.

That benefit was often fully covered by employers. The norm was indemnity coverage, meaning that after the employee paid an often modest deductible, all additional medical expenses were paid by insurance via the employer's health plan. While the costs of health insurance remained low in the early days, employees often made few contributions to the premium payment; employers covered the costs.

The services were limited as well. In the mid-1950s a primary care physician would typically manage up to 20 common drugs, and hospitals had limited technology to apply to serious diseases such as cancer, heart disease, and stroke. Forty percent of the drugs prescribed in 1960 would not have been available in 1954 (Stevens 1996). With the inception of the Medicare and Medicaid programs in 1965, which paid doctors and hospitals for the entire cost of care, the rapid expansion of medical technology and treatments began in earnest.

The structure of the health exchanges places considerable emphasis on the individual. Tax credits are individually based. Purchasing is focused on the individual. And while small businesses (those with fewer than 50 employees) are also given tax credits, little attention is given to creating exchanges for small employers. With no penalties for small employers to drop coverage for their employees and significant tax credits for individuals to purchase healthcare insurance, the ACA has the potential to hasten the move from employer-based coverage to individual coverage. In fact, the Congressional Budget Office (CBO 2014) estimates that both employer-based coverage and non-group coverage will decline, shifting coverage to the exchanges.

The ACA also gives employers openings for creativity. Some large employers concluded that the $2,000 to $3,000 federal tax per employee is significantly less than the cost of providing health insurance. Some are seeking to establish their own private health insurance exchanges. Much like the public exchange, large private employers prompted by human resource consulting firms have established programs in which the employer provides a specific financial contribution to an employee. The employee can then select from a variety of options and pay the difference between what the employer contributes and the actual cost of insurance. The result of this second trend is that employees will now cover more of their own healthcare expenses and employers will limit their financial exposure for healthcare cost increases (Howard 2014).

These two trends that received virtually no debate in 2010 will ultimately reshape healthcare in the US. For hospitals and physicians it means that patients will have much higher out-of-pocket expenses and that collection prior to elective services will be essential. High-deductible plans will also encourage individuals to purchase basic healthcare services from low-cost retail vendors, leaving high-complexity services for hospitals and physicians. Employers will limit their increase in expenses to the rate of general inflation.

Yet to be fully understood by the public is the role of the IRS in ACA implementation. The IRS was granted broad powers to collect information regarding Americans' health purchasing decisions and assess taxes based upon that information. The executive branch has urged initial leniency in enforcement of these powers. Information related to health insurance and calculation of subsidies is now required as part of individual annual income tax filings.[1] But unlike ordinary tax obligations, the ACA eliminates the ability of the IRS to collect fines and impose penalties for those refusing to pay the tax for failing to obtain insurance. Only the US attorney general may file a civil action to collect overdue ACA tax obligations.

MIND THE GAPS

There is a growing gap between incentives provided by exchanges and the private sector and those included in public programs. Medicare and Medicaid, now comprising approximately 45 percent of total health coverage expenditures, have very different rules (Healthcare.gov 2014). Medicare is a federally administered program; Medicaid varies from state to state. While the federal government pays more than two-thirds of the Medicaid bill, many of the rules, payment rates, and coverage guidelines are set by each state.

The 2012 Supreme Court decision resulted in greater disparities in state Medicaid programs. Not only do states set the rates for provider payments under the Medicaid program, but each state establishes rules of participation. Over the past two decades, various states have been granted waivers to compliance with federal Medicaid regulations. Waivers range from an Ohio program to provide special services to seniors to an Oregon program to limit the provision of certain services when medical efficacy has not been demonstrated. Because of the waivers far more variations in state Medicaid programs exist than there are states.

Yet the programs all have one thing in common. Compared to employer-provided insurance and insurance exchange products, there is little patient participation in payment for the program. This lack of patient participation results from the fact that most Medicaid clients have annual incomes of less than 138 percent of the federal poverty level—$32,500 for a family of four (CMS 2014). Hence, there is less engagement by the Medicaid patient in the financial aspects of healthcare delivery.

Compounding this dynamic is the fact that the payment rates to physicians and hospitals established by states for their respective Medicaid programs are usually 60 to 75 percent of the cost of providing care to this population. Depending on the state's economic health, the federal government typically pays anywhere from half to two-thirds of the cost of Medicaid in each state—about 57 percent on average. The ACA established the incentive to cover the entire cost of the Medicaid expansion for those states that chose to expand the program. By 2019 the federal government will reduce its portion of the cost to 90 percent for the expansion population.

At the end of 2013 the federal government assessed the actual expenditures per Medicaid enrollee in each expansion state and set the payment rates accordingly. This policy tends to "bake in" the disparities in provider payment rates that vary widely from state to state. For instance, the Kaiser Commission on Medicaid and the Uninsured (2010) found that for the states expanding Medicaid, the payment per Medicaid enrollee per year varied from a low of $3,441 in California to a high of $8,029 in Washington, DC.

THE EARLY WINNERS . . . AND LOSERS

Support for the ACA has been variable in the early years (See Exhibit 1.2). At no point did the law enjoy broad support from the electorate. Aside from those whose views of the ACA were shaped by political considerations, the two early beneficiaries of the legislation were young people under the age of 26 and those with preexisting medical conditions. As of January 2011, children, step-children and foster children up to age 26 could be added to their parent's health insurance coverage. The children need not reside with their parents and could be married so long as they met the age requirement. Approximately 3 million young adults are projected to obtain coverage under this provision (Kennedy 2014).

Also in 2011, all employer-based health plans were required to provide coverage for all conditions, including plans offered in the insurance exchanges and Medicaid. The major exception to the requirement was health plans purchased in the individual market. The US Government Accountability Office estimates that 20 to 66 percent of all adults in the United States have preexisting conditions that previously prevented them from obtaining health insurance coverage (Knox 2014).

There are other winners as well, according to one early analysis of firms whose stock value has increased. Advertising agencies retained by federal and state exchanges to promote sign-ups had strong performance in 2013 (Knox 2014).

Information technology (IT) firms were another group of early winners in the run up to implementation of insurance exchanges. Estimates range from $350 million to as high as $634 million spent on IT projects to build the Healthcare.gov site (Kessler 2013, Vlahos 2013). Because of tight timelines, much of this work was contracted outside of normal government procurement processes. The federal exchange was plagued by early IT issues, resulting in contract revisions and terminations.

Exhibit 1.2 Tracking Poll Chart Since 2010

ACA Opinion Still Tilts Negative, But Narrowing Since January

As you may know, a health reform bill was signed into law in 2010. Given what you kow about the health reform law, do you have a generally favorable or generall unfavorable opinion of it?

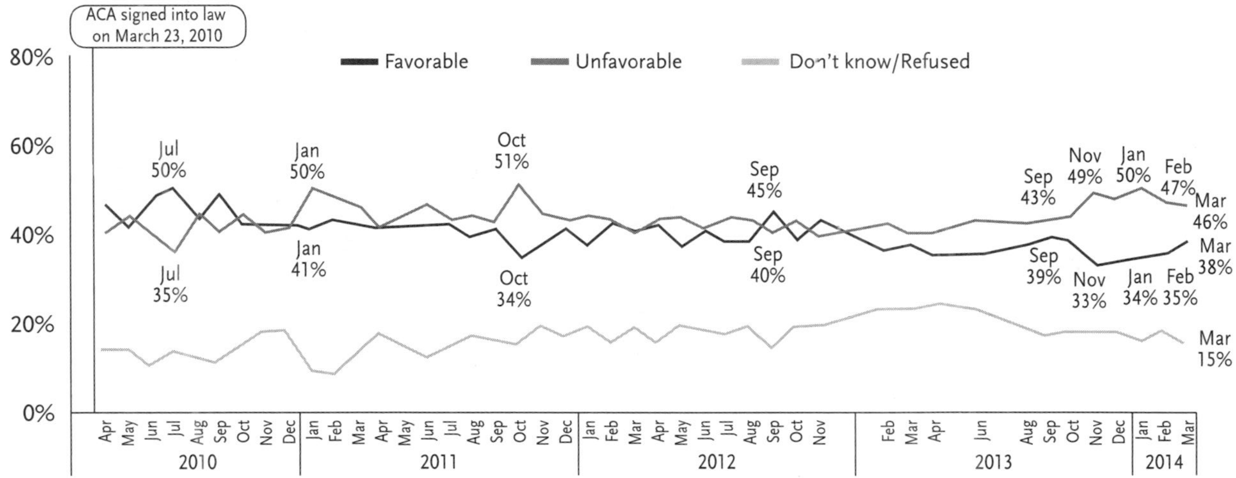

Source: Kaiser Family Foundation (2014).

One of the most glaring expenditures occurred in Oregon, which spent more than $160 million with Oracle, one of the nation's leading technology companies. An additional $100 million was spent on other preparations, including advertising. The website did not function by the time enrollment was closed in early 2014. Oregon then announced that it would give up on a state exchange and join the federal exchange—www.Healthcare.gov.

As of March 31, 2014, the first round of enrollment in the federal exchanges ended. A few losers were emerging as well. The first were employers whose insurance premiums increased to cover the cost of the ACA mandates. United Health Care estimated that premiums would increase 116 percent in the individual market, 25 to 50 percent in the small group market, and 20 to 25 percent in the large group market (Jugan 2012). An independent study commissioned by the State of Oregon concluded that rates for the individual and employer market would climb by at least 35 percent and could increase more than 50 percent by 2015 (Wakely Consulting Group 2012). The American Health Policy Institute, a group representing human resource professionals for larger employers, estimates that the ACA will add from $4,800 to $5,900 per employee to the cost of health insurance for large employers. The total cost of the ACA to all large US employers over the next ten years is estimated to be from $151 billion to $186 billion, or 5.9 percent more than what they would otherwise spend (Troy and Wilson 2014). Regardless of the source, estimates of cost increases to employers that provide insurance for their employees are the norm.

Some employees not qualifying for individual subsidies may also be net losers. Anecdotes abound regarding small employers that have decided to provide a stipend to employees rather than continuing to provide health insurance. In the early roll-out it has been assumed that those who need health insurance coverage due to medical conditions will purchase through the insurance exchanges.

Some employees are also facing changes in the number of hours worked. The ACA defines a full-time worker who must be offered coverage as anyone working for an employer 30 or more hours per week. Anecdotes suggest that some employers are creating positions limited to 25 to 29 hours per week to avoid this requirement. This mirrors pre-ACA enactment when some employers limited employee hours to 35 hours per week to fall below the threshold for providing benefits, including healthcare coverage.

The last group of employees affected by the ACA is unionized workers in the retail sector. Their employers face competition from companies without an organized work force. Unions often maintain healthcare trusts that are employer-funded while nonunion employees may receive insurance through the exchanges. As the union employers encounter stiff price competition from nonunion groups, they will likely be pressured to reduce healthcare costs. This pressure is likely to come in the form of offering higher-deductible plans similar to public-sector healthcare exchanges. Over time, union health trusts will be pressured to reduce the cost of healthcare, even to the point of offering private health exchanges themselves.

THE EARLY NUMBERS

Much has been made of the fact that the administration reached its goal of enrolling more than 7 million people during the opening enrollment period ending March 31, 2014. In some cases the enrollment period was extended, leading to claims that the final number may be closer to 8 million (Kennedy 2014).

This number masks the reality of the enrollment. Remember the original contract—32 million additional insured Americans with approximately one-third enrolled under the Medicaid program and two-thirds enrolled in commercial insurance plans via the exchanges? Most medical provider associations, including the American Hospital Association and the American Medical Association, supported the ACA under these assumptions, despite significant payment cuts also part of the act. The premise was that charity care and bad debt would be substantially reduced to offset payment reductions.

Final numbers from the federal government are not yet available. The early numbers from three states that were aggressive in enrolling individuals under the ACA stand in stark contrast to the original agreement. Current enrollment estimates suggest that 80 to 90 percent of the Medicaid enrollees are Americans who previously had no healthcare insurance. The exchanges are a different story. Current estimates are that only 30 to 40 percent of the exchange enrollees are new.[2] Most are transitioning from other insurance onto the exchange.

Rather than enrolling one new Medicaid recipient for every two commercial/exchange enrollees, current estimates suggest that there are four to five new Medicaid enrollees for each commercially insured exchange enrollee. In the state of Washington with one of the more successful enrollment efforts, as of March 31, 403,852 citizens had been enrolled in Medicaid. The exchange enrolled 146,497 (Healthcare Authority of Washington 2014).

Assuming that nationwide approximately 7 million enrolled in the exchanges and an additional 4.8 million enrolled in the 26 states with Medicaid expansion, it could be estimated based on the Western states' experience that the number of new enrollees would be 7 million—out of the total of 56 million uninsured Americans.[3]

IMPLICATIONS FOR PHYSICIANS AND HEALTHCARE SYSTEMS

Pay for Performance. Pay for performance (P4P) has gotten a lot of attention. Under P4P, hospitals get paid more or less based on performance measures, mostly relating to clinical and patient service quality. Considerable attention has focused on the Institute for Healthcare Improvement's Triple Aim: improving the patient experience of care (including quality and satisfaction), improving population health, and reducing the per-capita cost of care.[4] While the Triple Aim will continue to be the focus of many healthcare systems, a much larger impact on physician and hospital financial health will come from other changes:

- Cuts in Medicare reimbursement beyond what the ACA had envisioned
- New CMS regulations such as the "two-midnight rule" that reduces payments for hospital utilization
- The inability of the ACA to meet the original goals of the program for a robust commercially insured population.

Depending on location reductions in payment from these and other factors could reduce net revenue by 5 percent or more.

Reduced utilization resulting from higher copayments and deductibles will also further reduce net hospital revenue. Combined with other steps to reduce hospital use, admissions will be weak for the foreseeable future. The political calculus in 2010 was that hospital utilization would decline as a result of the industry improving patient quality and safety performance. Whether that calculus was correct is an open and disconcerting question.

Higher Deductibles. High deductibles and more patient participation in the cost of care have had an early and profound impact. While the nation's best hospitals have improved outcomes (Premier, Inc. 2014) there is growing evidence that when faced with a high out-of-pocket payment for care, patients postpone or cancel elective procedures. Physicians and hospitals must now consider themselves in the retail business. When an emergent condition under the terms of Emergency Medical Treatment and Labor Act (EMTALA) does not exist, providers find themselves needing to address the matter of high deductibles. The most progressive organizations are prequalifying patients and making payment arrangements for elective (nonemergent) procedures prior to their scheduling. This single change in practice is causing some patients to reevaluate the urgency of an elective procedure. The risk is that delays could result in conditions becoming more expensive to treat.

Strained Safety Net. States that aggressively expanded the Medicaid enrollment are now finding early access issues, especially to primary care providers. As the Medicaid rolls grow to more than 20 percent of many organizations' revenue, it is now considered likely that some limits on Medicaid service are necessary. As part of the 2013 federal budget agreement, cuts in disproportionate share hospital (DSH) payments to hospitals were postponed until 2016 (CBO 2013). However, as a result of the delay, the cuts will be deeper in future years.

Consolidation. Pressures on utilization and payment make the consolidation of providers inevitable. These pressures include a predicted decline in acute care utilization from 10 percent to 50 percent, increased regulatory requirements, and the push for provider organizations to assume greater risk. Risk-taking by ACOs, Medicare Advantage programs, and Medicaid risk organizations requires sufficient capital reserves to cover financial losses associated with patient care. These factors result in a reduction of net revenue on the same or smaller book of business.

Some futurists predict that the nation will have five to seven large health systems by 2030 with a number of regional niche players. The 2013 merger of Community Health Systems and Health Management Associates created the nation's largest for-profit health system (Brimmer 2013). Similarly the Trinity/Catholic Health East merger created the largest faith-based system in the United States (Selvam 2013). The result of this consolidation is likely to be fewer US hospital beds by 2020 and increased focus on ambulatory settings for care delivery.

This should be no surprise. For most of the post–World War II period, healthcare has operated as a community-based cottage industry focused around the hospital, protected from market forces by cost-based reimbursement. Now market forces have been enhanced by greater consumer participation in covering the cost of medical care. Yet the greatest change, ushered in by the advent of Medicare and Medicaid and enhanced by the ACA, is the role of government as "price fixer" for physician and hospital services. The good old days of cost-based reimbursement are fading, giving way to an era of fixed payments that often do not cover today's cost of delivering care to those who have been given an entitlement to receive that care. In this environment, mergers, acquisitions, and failures are inevitable.

Innovation. Much of the healthcare system was built by and for the post–World War II generation. As social media have become ubiquitous, younger generations seeking healthcare services will hasten innovation in healthcare delivery. High deductibles and the need for convenience make it more advantageous to seek care in easily accessible settings with minimal waiting and easy payment. Retail centers, such as the startup ZoomCare.com, will replace more cumbersome traditional systems of care delivery. Providers in this category focus on the cash-paying patient, typically do not accept Medicaid, and often have advanced technology used to connect to the patient for everything from scheduling to billing.

Many innovations will be technology-based. Eric Topol (2013) describes the "creative destruction of medicine" by detailing the potential of technology to connect patients to providers in real time. While the old notion of house calls by physicians is returning in some communities, a more profound change is likely to take place. Using electronic home monitoring and "telehealth" consults, conditions from congestive heart failure to diabetes can be managed with minimal involvement of traditional clinics. In an extreme example of innovation, the IBM computer Watson is being programmed to assume simple diagnostic tasks that could ultimately replace a number of physicians' diagnostic tasks (Yuan 2011). As physicians and hospitals take more financial risk under ACA, those that survive will be early investors in new technology and innovation.

Information Technology. The American Recovery and Reinvestment Act of 2009 (also known as the stimulus bill) contained a provision that will reverberate for many years—to spend $19.2 billion on healthcare information technology and establish requirements that all physicians and hospitals must meet by 2015 or face fines for noncompliance (HHS 2009). Underlying the act were assumptions that 70 percent of hospitals and 90 percent of physicians would have electronic medical records (EMR) by 2020. Hospital-based providers, those employed in provider-based entities, were not eligible for incentive payments. The penalties for failure to comply, unless granted an exemption due to hardship, were significant—approximately 1 to 2 percent of total Medicare payments to hospitals and 3 percent of the total Medicare fee schedule for physician practices.

Unprecedented expenditures on EMRs began in earnest. While the incentives provided until the penalty period begins in 2015 are usually 10 to 20 percent of the actual cost of an EMR, the penalties persuaded most hospitals and physicians to plan for large investments in IT. Three years prior to the adoption of the stimulus bill, Rand Health estimated that cumulative healthcare IT expenditures would be more than $120 billion by 2020 (Hillestad 2005). Savings resulting from these investments resulting in better care would be five to six times the investment. Today, expenditures in 2020 for mobile healthcare IT alone are expected to be $50 billion (Grand View Research 2014).

Despite these massive investments under way in healthcare, neither the stimulus bill nor the ACA included provisions for interoperability. There is no requirement that systems provided by different vendors and used by various health systems will be able to share common patient information. This requirement will be essential for seamless patient care, one of the goals of the ACA.

SHOW ME THE MONEY

Capital will be critical to transform the American system of healthcare. While capital investment in acute care hospitals' bricks and mortar generally will fade, massive investments in innovation, IT, and ambulatory care will predominate. If the 1990s was the decade of "bricks and mortar" capital, the current decade will be characterized by "clicks and order" capital. Technology investments will predominate, allowing providers to obtain real-time clinical information to manage care and place all orders electronically.

The mainstay of healthcare financing is likely to be tax-exempt bonds for nonprofit community-oriented delivery systems. Organizations that are able to maintain A+ to AA ratings will continue to have access to markets at prevailing market rates. Most access to this form of capital will be secured by a claim on the revenue streams of these organizations.

At the same time, sources of capital are likely to become more diverse. In 2000, approximately 10 percent of all US hospitals were owned by for-profit organizations. By 2010 that number increased significantly and will continue to grow. Investors will play a great role in funding the development of the healthcare delivery system. The 2012 acquisition of HealthCare Partners in California by the dialysis company DaVita for $4.4 billion suggests that public companies see value in healthcare delivery (Tirrell and Kitamura 2012).

Recently, taxable debt has also proven to be a stable source of financing, as an alternative to bond financing. With low interest rates and in a break from traditional tax exempt financing, Catholic Health Initiatives assumed $1.2 billion of new debt in 2012 through a consortium of banking partners (Williamson 2013).

Regardless of the source of financing, the resulting pressures from the ACA and the maturing of the healthcare industry will place greater emphasis on growth, consolidation, and operating success. Successful organizations are likely to have the following characteristics:

- Large organizations with $5 billion or more in revenue with a significant level of integration across the care-delivery spectrum
- Ability to demonstrate annual net revenue growth or compound annual growth rate (CAGR) of 6 to 8 percent

- Strong balance sheet with at least 175 days of cash
- Effective balance of care for public sector patients (Medicare and Medicaid) and commercially insured patients
- Geographic diversity, not dependent upon the policies of any single political jurisdiction for funding and regulation
- Quality, patient safety, and patient engagement scores that are in the top quartile nationally
- Reasonably strong operating performance of at least 9 to 12 percent operating earnings before interest, taxes, depreciation and amortization (EBITDA)
- Substantial market share, often first or second in geographies served
- Ability to manage financial risk in the delivery of care, often having some insurance capabilities

Organizations with at least five to six of these characteristics will have significant advantage under the ACA. In the past rating agencies looked primarily at financial measures. Today, issues related to integration of pre-acute, acute care, and post-acute delivery are given consideration as are measures of quality and patient engagement. While a strong balance sheet and solid annual operating performance are still highly valued by rating agencies, the ACA focus on bundled payment and P4P has placed greater value on attributes beyond simply financial measures.

IT'S STILL EARLY, BUT . . .

Although the most significant elements of the ACA are still early in their development, a number of ideas deserve more scrutiny during implementation. Twenty-six states and the District of Columbia are participating in the Medicaid expansion. Thirteen states will not participate. The remainder are still making determinations regarding participation or are seeking alternate means of participation (see Exhibit 1.3). This factor leads to the first hypothesis that needs further investigation: *States that delayed implementation of Medicaid expansion will have more time to determine how to fund expansion (if at all); providers in those states will be in a stronger financial position.*

In these states virtually all of the new enrollees will be through the exchanges and will have some form of commercial insurance. Since commercial insurance payments to providers are generally higher

Exhibit 1.3 Where the States Stand on Medicaid Expansion

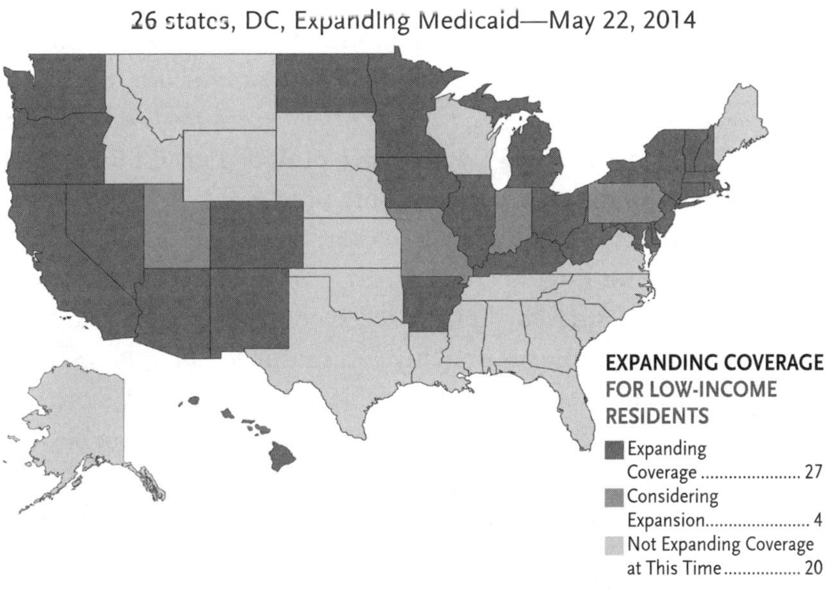

Notes: Based on literature review as of May 22, 2014. All policies subject to change without notice.

HHS has announced that states can obtain a waiver to use federal funds to shift Medicaid-eligible residents into private health plans.

The District of Columbia plans to participate in Medicaid expansion and will operate its own exchange.

Source: The Advisory Board Company (2014).

than Medicaid payments, providers will see a significant benefit with the infusion of new enrollees with payment for health services at higher rates. This will improve the payer mix for these health systems.

Prior to the implementation of the ACA, there were many predictions of an impending shortage of primary care physicians. The ACA attempted to address this matter with higher short-term payments (at Medicare rates) for seeing Medicaid patients. Innovation grants from CMS also provided incentives to create patient-centered medical homes (PCMHs).[5] However, other changes counteract these incentives. Some providers do not serve or have closed their practices to Medicaid recipients. This practice, known as cherry-picking, leaves those practices with patients mostly with commercial insurance or some form of Medicare, including Medicare Advantage.

This leads to the second hypothesis: *For states that expanded Medicaid, the early years will be marked by expanded insurance with limited access to some physician specialties, especially primary care.* Under this scenario, the ACA will have provided insurance to millions of new Medicaid enrollees, some of whom will have limited access to primary care physicians. Where safety net hospitals close due to lack of funding, hospital access also could become an issue.

With the potential for limited access to primary care, one solution that is being explored in many communities is development of federally qualified health centers (FQHCs).[6] Most FQHCs provide primary care services and receive additional federal funding beyond what Medicare or Medicaid generally pays. They also provide services that are similar to those in PCMHs. The additional funding results in FQHCs receiving three to four times the amount of payment that would be provided to non-FQHC health providers. Most private physicians groups and clinics do not qualify for FQHC funding, leading to the third hypotheses: *Specialty mechanisms such as FQHCs will be critical to serving the Medicaid population.* These entities have the effect of transferring additional costs of care under the Medicare and Medicaid programs to the federal government.

Part of the grand bargain of the ACA was 32 million new enrollees and a ratio of two new exchange enrollees for every new

Medicaid enrollee. Early reports suggest that a minority of enrollees through the exchanges are new enrollees, and may be moving from employer-based coverage to individual coverage. While some Medicaid enrollees are moving from other insurance, a far greater percentage of the Medicaid enrollment is from those who are newly insured.

In March 2012 the CBO concluded, "Fewer people are now expected to obtain health insurance coverage from their employer or in insurance exchanges; more are now expected to obtain coverage from Medicaid or CHIP or from non-group or other sources. More are expected to be uninsured" (CBO 2012). By April 2014 the CBO anticipated "that coverage through the exchanges will increase substantially over time as more people respond to subsidies and to penalties for failure to obtain coverage . . . and that coverage through the exchanges is projected to increase to 24 million in 2016" (CBO 2014). Exchange enrollment is then projected to remain approximately the same through 2024.

Accepting at face value the CBO report of 6 million exchange enrollees in 2014, this projection requires a four-fold increase in enrollment by 2016. This large projected gain in exchange enrollment in such a short period of time leads to the fourth hypothesis: *Enrollment in the exchanges will fall short of the estimates envisioned at the time the ACA was passed.*

Other CBO projections in the April 2014 report seem contradictory. For instance, the average annual federal subsidy per exchange enrollee is projected to be $4,830 by 2016. The average annual cost of a silver-level exchange insurance plan is projected to be $4,400 (CBO 2014). During the first year of enrollment more than 80 percent of the enrollees purchased either the silver plan or the less expensive bronze plan. Yet the tax for failing to purchase insurance in 2016 is $695 annually, or 2.5 percent of annual income. This suggests the fifth hypothesis: *Current taxes imposed in lieu of purchasing insurance will prove to be an inadequate incentive to purchase insurance unless the cost of insurance less the federal government subsidy is approximately equal to the $600 annual tax.* If the tax is significantly less than the cost of the insurance to enrollees, most people will make the rational choice of the tax unless they have a medical condition requiring treatment. Since there are no accurate projections for actual market dynamics, only time will yield the answer.

The Commonwealth Health Insurance Connector in Massachusetts provides an instructive lesson for the nation regarding the last issue—the number of health plans offered through the exchanges. When the plan was first implemented in 2007, six major insurance carriers offered health plans in the state. Until implementation of the ACA, two major insurers offered plans and captured a significant share of the market—Harvard Pilgrim and a Blue Cross affiliate. Later Centene Corporation under the name CeltiCare was added, the first new insurance product in the state in 20 years (Corlette et al. 2011). Under the ACA offerings in 2014 a few more, mostly small plans entered the state exchange. Nevertheless the first six years of the Massachusetts Connector suggest the last hypothesis: *The number of insurers and exchanges will consolidate significantly over the next five years, leaving fewer insurance exchange options.* This early Massachusetts experiment did not result in a significant reduction of healthcare costs, which led to implementation of rate controls on insurers in 2013.

BUDGET RECONCILIATION AND GRAND BARGAIN

What we know today as the ACA is actually two pieces of legislation. The first is the Patient Protection and Affordable Care Act, HR 3590. This bill was adopted first by the US Senate, then the House. The second is the Health Care and Education Reconciliation Act of 2010, HR 4872. HR 4872 was adopted by a process known as budget reconciliation, originally designed to make small revisions to federal budget legislation. Over the years creative legislators expanded the use leading to the Byrd Rule, which placed some limits on the process. Most importantly, the legislation cannot increase the federal budget deficit. If a provision increases the deficit, the life of the provision is ten years.

To date the ACA is not subject to the ten-year limitation of the budget reconciliation process because all current projections indicate that its implementation will reduce the budget deficit. The impact of the ACA is being watched carefully with annual projections from the CBO. The most recent calculation is that the ACA will reduce the deficit by less than the original projections: "$152 billion, rather than $206 billion, for that decade" (CBO 2014).

If the budget impact of the ACA threatens to increase the budget deficit, the ten-year limitation on any bill adopted by budget reconciliation will be the subject of significant debate and could automatically trigger review. The Health Care and Education Reconciliation Act of 2010, which contains a number of crucial budgetary matters that support the ACA, could be subject to review in 2020.

While most in Congress now quietly admit that some form of the ACA is here to stay, a potential threat is repeal by the same budget reconciliation process that passed a portion of the ACA. Under this scenario the Republicans would need to hold a majority in the House and Senate and win the presidency. The Supreme Court ruling that the heart of the ACA is the ability of the federal government to assess a tax seems to strengthen the case for repeal by the budget reconciliation process.

All of these scenarios are conjecture. The partisan nature of the ACA's passage, the shift to an individual insurance market with high deductibles, and the unintended consequences inevitable in such a massive overhaul of a large segment of the economy ensure an ongoing debate. Yet the ACA's chance of survival is significantly enhanced by the large-scale entitlement it created, one that will ultimately benefit more than 70 percent of all Americans.

You have to be fast on your feet and adaptive
or else a strategy is useless.

—Charles de Gaulle

Key Takeaways

- The healthcare bill was unfinished when it was passed.
- Reform is not likely to live up to the promise to deliver 32 million newly insured Americans in exchange for the healthcare industry giving up $1 trillion in payments over ten years. The impact it will have remains to be seen.
- The bill is heavily weighted to reducing costs concurrently with increasing coverage—a high-wire act at best to coordinate the timing.
- In order to get the bill passed, Congress used the budget reconciliation process, eliminating improvements that are often made in Conference Committee. The ACA is also at risk for ongoing Supreme Court challenges.
- The bill was imperfectly planned and executed and made more difficult with the Supreme Court decision to eliminate the requirement for Medicaid expansion.
- The focus on IT solutions in the stimulus bill of 2009 and related expenses have created a major impediment to other capital spending.

NOTES

1. The exact number of new pages and details of 2014 IRS 1040 and forms related to ACA are still under development as of June 1, 2014.
2. These estimates are gathered from conversations with various officials who are sampling enrollee's insurance status. McKinsey and Company have completed a sample from across the nation (McKinsey Center for US Health System Reform 2014).

3. The calculation assumes that 80 percent of Medicaid enrollment is new enrollees and that 40 percent of exchange enrollment is new enrollees. As more data become available, this calculation may change.
4. The IHI Triple Aim is a framework developed by the Institute for Healthcare Improvement that describes an approach to optimizing health system performance. It is IHI's belief that new designs must be developed to simultaneously pursue three dimensions: 1) improving the patient experience of care (including quality and satisfaction); 2) improving the health of populations; and 3) reducing the per capita cost of healthcare.
5. The medical home is a concept first introduced by the American Academy of Pediatrics (AAP) in 1967. In its initial version, the AAP defined the medical home as the center of a child's medical records. At the time, the care of children with special healthcare needs was the primary focus of the medical home concept. The definition has evolved to reflect changing needs and perspectives in healthcare. Today's medical home is a cultivated partnership between the patient, family, and primary provider in cooperation with specialists and support from the community. The patient/family is the focal point of this model, and the medical home is built around this center. Another key factor is that the focus of the medical home has shifted to include all children and adults, not just children with special healthcare needs.
6. Federally qualified health centers (FQHCs) include all organizations receiving grants under Section 330 of the Public Health Service Act (PHS). FQHCs qualify for enhanced reimbursement from Medicare and Medicaid, as well as other benefits. FQHCs must serve an underserved area or population, offer a sliding fee scale, provide comprehensive services, have an ongoing quality assurance program, and have a governing board of directors.

REFERENCES

The Advisory Board Company. 2014. "Where the States Stand on Medicaid Expansion." Published September 4. www.advisory.com/Daily-Briefing/Resources/Primers/MedicaidMap.

Brimmer, K. 2013. "CHS and HMA Agree to Merger." *Healthcare Finance News.* Published August 8. www.healthcarefinancenews.com/news/chs-and-hma-agree-merger.

Burwell v. Hobby Lobby Stores, Inc. 2014. 134 S. Ct. 2751.

Centers for Disease Control and Prevention (CDC). 2011. "Deaths: Final Data for 2011, Table 8." Accessed October 27, 2014. www.cdc.gov/nchs/fastats/life-expectancy.htm.

Centers for Medicare & Medicaid Services (CMS). 2014. "2014 Federal Poverty Guidelines." Accessed October 27, 2014. www.medicaid.gov/Medicaid-CHIP-Program-Information/By-Topics/Eligibility/Downloads/2014-Federal-Poverty-level-charts.pdf.

Congressional Budget Office (CBO). 2014. "Updated Estimates of the Effects of the Insurance Coverage Provisions of the Affordable Care Act." Published April 14. www.cbo.gov/publication/45231.

———. 2013. "Summary of the Bipartisan Budget Act of 2013." Published December 10. http://budget.house.gov/uploadedfiles/bba2013summary.pdf.

———. 2012. "Updated Estimates of the Effects of the Insurance Coverage Provisions of the Affordable Care Act." Published March 13. www.cbo.gov/sites/default/files/03-13-Coverage%20Estimates.pdf.

Corlette, S., J. Alker, J. Touschner, and J. Volk. 2011. "The Massachusetts and Utah Health Insurance Exchanges: Lessons Learned." *Robert Wood Johnson Foundation.* Published March 30. www.rwjf.org/content/dam/farm/reports/reports/2011/rwjf69839.

Families USA. 2013. "How Does the Affordable Care Act Affect People Who Buy Health Insurance in the Individual Market?" Published December 20. http://familiesusa.org/product/how-does-affordable-care-act-affect-people-who-buy-health-insurance-individual-market#sthash.oTkieJr2.dpuf.

Grand View Research. 2014. "mHealth Market Analysis and Segment Forecasts to 2020." Accessed September 24. www.grandviewresearch.com/industry-analysis/mhealth-market.

Hancock, J. 2013. "Obamacare Insurance Co-ops at the Starting Gate." Kaiser Health News. Published September 12. www.kaiserhealthnews.org/stories/2013/september/12/co-ops-start-up-health-insurance-aca.aspx.

Healthcare Authority of Washington. 2014. "Apple Health Enrollment Report." Published May 20. www.hca.wa.gov/Releases/Apple%20Health%20enrollment%20report%205-20-14.pdf.

Healthcare.gov. 2014. Accessed October 16. www.healthcare.gov/.

Hillestad, R. 2005. "Can Information Technology Transform Health Care?" RAND Corporation. Published September 16. www.allhealth.org/briefingmaterials/Hillestad_9_16-188.pdf.

Howard, P. 2014. "Private Health Insurance Exchanges Unleash 'Transformational Change.'" Forbes. Published January 24. www.forbes.com/sites/theapothecary/2014/01/24/private-health-insurance-exchanges-unleash-transformational-change/.

Hyde Amendment, Pub.L. 105-119, § 617, Nov. 26, 1997, 111 Stat. 2519, codified as a note following 18 USC § 3006A.

Jost, T. 2014. "Implementing Health Reform: Basic Health Program and More ACA Litigation Results." Accessed September 24. http://healthaffairs.org/blog/2014/03/10/implementing-health-reform-basic-health-program-and-more-aca-litigation-results.

Jugan, B. 2012. "UHC Estimates Premium Increases as High as 116% in 2014 from Health Care Reform (ACA)." *BenefitsCafe.com*. Published December 6. www.benefitscafe.com/blog/2012/12/06/uhc-estimates-premium-increases-as-high-as-116-in-2014-from-health-care-reform-aca.

Kaiser Commission on Medicaid and the Uninsured. 2010. *Medicaid Coverage and Spending in Health Reform: National and State-By-State Results for Adults at or Below 133% FPL*. Accessed September 16, 2014. http://obamacarefacts.com/medicaid-expansion-kkf.pdf.

Kaiser Family Foundation. 2014. "Kaiser Health Tracking Poll: March 2014," Figure 4. http://kff.org/health-reform/poll-finding/kaiser-health-tracking-poll-march-2014/

———. 2009. "Trends in Health Care Costs and Spending." Published March 19. http://kaiserfamilyfoundation.files.wordpress.com/2013/01/7692_02.pdf.

Kennedy, K. 2014. "Obamacare Reports 8M Enrollees." *USA Today Weekend* May 2.

Kessler, G. 2013. "How Much Did Healthcare.gov Cost?" *Wall Street Journal.* Published October 24. www.washingtonpost.com/blogs/fact-checker/wp/2013/10/24/how-much-did-healthcare-gov-cost/.

Knox, N. 2014. "Health Law Already Has Impact on Bottom Lines." *Wall Street Journal.* Published February 24. http://online.wsj.com/news/articles/SB10001424052702304834704579403072411467200.

McKinsey Center for US Health System Reform. 2014. "Intel Brief #6." Published May 8.

National Federation of Independent Businesses v. Sebelius. 2012. 132 S. Ct. 2566.

Premier, Inc. 2014. "Quest Participating Hospital Data."

———. 2011. "Summary of the Affordable Care Act." Presented in September.

Selvam, A. 2013. "Trinity Health, Catholic Health East Complete Merger Deal." *Modern Healthcare.* Published May 1. www.modernhealthcare.com/article/20130501/NEWS/305019969.

Social Security Advisory Board. 2009. *The Unsustainable Cost of Health Care.* Washington, DC: Social Security Advisory Board.

Stevens, R. A. 1996. "Health Care in the Early 1960s." *Health Care Financing Review* 18 (2): 11–22.

Tirrell, M., and M. Kitamura. 2012. "DaVita to Pay $4.42 Billion for HealthCare Partners." *Bloomberg News.* Published May 21. www.bloomberg.com/news/2012-05-21/davita-agrees-to-pay-about-4-42-billion-for-healthcare-partners.html.

Topol, E. 2013. *The Creative Destruction of Medicine: How the Digital Revolution Will Create Better Health Care.* New York: Basic Books.

Troy, T. D., and D. M. Wilson. 2014. "The Cost of the Affordable Care Act to Large Employers." American Health Policy Institute. Accessed September 24. www.americanhealthpolicy.org/Content/documents/resources/2014_ACA_Cost_Study.pdf.

US Department of Health and Human Services (HHS). 2009. "HITECH Act Enforcement Interim Final Rule." Accessed September 24, 2014. www.hhs.gov/ocr/privacy/hipaa/administrative/enforcementrule/hitechenforcementifr.html.

———. 1973. "Church Amendments, 42 USC § 300a-7." www.hhs.gov/ocr/civilrights/understanding/ConscienceProtect/42usc300a7.pdf.

Vlahos, K. B. 2013. "Just How Much Did Healthcare.gov Cost?" *FoxNews.com*. Published October 11. http://www.foxnews.com/tech/2013/10/11/just-how-much-does-healthcaregov-cost/.

Wakely Consulting Group. 2012. "Actuarial Analysis: Impact of the Affordable Care Act on Small Group and Individual Market Premiums in Oregon." Published July 31. www.wakely.com/wp-content/uploads/2012/10/OR_ACA_Market_Premium_Impact_wletter_20120731.pdf.

Williamson, R. 2013. "Catholic Health Deals $1.2B After Downgrades." *The Bond Buyer*. Published October 21. www.bondbuyer.com/issues/122_203/catholic-health-deals-1b-after-downgrades-1056660-1.html.

Yuan, M. J. 2011. "Watson and Health Care: How Natural Language Processing and Semantic Search Could Revolutionize Clinical Decision Support." *IBM DeveloperWorks*. Published April 12. www.ibm.com/developerworks/library/os-ind-watson.

CHAPTER 2

A View from the Trenches

Bradley Taylor

In the overall scheme of things, construction often gets lost. After all, when you look at the pro forma for a hospital, the real estate operation (the mortgage and its related operating costs) usually only represents 6 to 9 percent of the total financial picture of a hospital. As a result, it tends not to get the proper attention from either the C-suite or the board.

There are other negative aspects:

- construction can be disruptive to existing operations;
- projects tend to run over budget;
- projects tend to run over schedule; and
- capital costs for construction usually mean taking on a lot of debt, and compete with other needs.

Taylor shows the value of a thoughtful approach to planning, design, and construction. He makes it clear that although it might be a small portion of the pro forma, it can have a huge impact on both profitability and improved

(continued)

(continued from previous page)

outcomes. He shows that avoiding the "fad du jour" and looking at both sides of an issue play an important and intellectual role.

Someday, therefore, medicine will have to convert itself into a science . . . to provide public health services to the greatest possible number of persons, institute a program of preventive medicine, and orient the public to the performance of hygienic practices. . . . But now old questions reappear: How does one actually carry out a work of social welfare?

—Ernesto "Che" Guevara, MD

OVERALL ACA IMPACT

Along with everyone else in the US healthcare industry, I think it would be really nice to have a crystal ball right about now. In considering the impact the Affordable Care Act (ACA) might have on the capital construction industry, a view into the future would indeed be helpful. That's probably something we shouldn't wait around for, and there is little choice but to plan for what is coming—nothing less than a dramatic change in how healthcare is delivered and paid for across the country. What we can do is methodically consider how the ACA is *intended* to affect the healthcare industry and translate that into the types of project objectives, requirements, and deliverables we can expect to see.

As posted on www.obamacarefacts.com (2014), here is the 100-word explanation of the ACA:

> The Affordable Care Act (Obamacare) increases the quality, accessibility and affordability of health insurance. In exchange most people, who can afford to, must obtain health coverage by 2014 or pay a per month fee. The law eliminates preexisting conditions,

stops insurance companies from dropping you when you are sick, protects against gender discrimination, expands free preventative services and health benefits, expands Medicaid and CHIP, improves Medicare, mandates larger employers insure employees, creates a marketplace for subsidized insurance providing tens of millions of individuals, families and small businesses with free or low-cost health insurance, and decreases healthcare spending and the deficit.

From even this simple explanation, one can make a number of assumptions and expectations. When combined with some expertise about the design and construction industry, it becomes a manageable list of issues most likely to affect capital construction. If the primary intent of the law is to increase the "accessibility and affordability of health insurance," the first and most obvious impact of the ACA is an increase in patient volume and a decrease in reimbursement. Everyone agrees that the cost of healthcare in this country cannot continue to rise. Margins will decrease, and pressure to improve operational efficiency will increase. Given that the act "expands free preventative services and health benefits," another obvious impact is that the increased volume is more likely to occur in primary care rather than specialty care. Tie these intentions in with some preexisting trends, and the plot thickens.

For many years now, a handful of industry trends have shown no signs of changing course. The first is a slow and steady nationwide consolidation of healthcare systems, physicians becoming hospital employees, and ambulatory surgery centers (ASCs) becoming hospital outpatient departments.

A second trend is a significant shift in care, mostly through advanced technology and surgical techniques, from the inpatient facility to the outpatient or ambulatory facility, contributing to an overall excess hospital bed capacity. A third trend is a decrease in the number of people who die in hospital ICUs and an increase of the number who die in hospices, nursing homes, or at home.

Reform is also promoting well-care while preventing sick-care and increasing the number of beneficial health outcomes by shifting reimbursement to pay for the quality rather than quantity of outcomes. In this model, a healthcare system is not paid on a fee-for-service basis but rather a pay-for-performance methodology. The accountable care organization and coordinated care organization models even have the organization accepting the risk of providing all care for a large population for a fixed price per person per year. As these changes begin to take shape, the effect will be profound. Everything the healthcare system provides is now an expense and not revenue—it needs to "flip the pancake." Radiology tests will not increase revenue, only expenses. A higher value will be placed on the effectiveness of care, cost-efficient preventive care, and the ability to accept additional insured lives.

To summarize the changes, many of which have already taken effect:

- Increase in insured patients
- Decrease in overall reimbursement
- Increased operational efficiency
- Increase in primary and preventative care
- Consolidation of healthcare systems
- Shift from inpatient to outpatient care
- Shift from ICU to hospice care
- Shift from sick-care to well-care
- Shift from fee-for-service to payment-for-performance

What kind of picture comes into focus once all of those changes have taken place? Simply put, the industry needs to produce better health outcomes, for more people, for less cost. From a facilities perspective, the next question is how.

Capital projects will be measured in two ways—can they increase operational efficiency, and can they produce better health outcomes? In addition to meeting those two criteria, projects will need to be delivered for the lowest cost possible. So the two primary forces that will change the design and construction industry are:

- the requirement for the most efficient use of space and equipment, and
- the need for the most efficient method of delivering a capital project.

Given that things can be done only so cheaply and care can be delivered only so efficiently—what specifically can change in capital construction to help? Five major objectives come to the fore:

1. Provide facilities that enable more efficient clinical operations.
2. Create facilities that enable optimum care for a growing population.
3. Invest wisely in future flexibility for changes yet to come.
4. Deliver facilities for a lower first cost.
5. Operate and maintain facilities more efficiently.

EFFICIENT CLINICAL OPERATIONS

The pressure is clear to increase operational efficiency across the entire spectrum of healthcare, and facility design is no different. Based on return on investment (ROI) calculations, most healthcare systems are willing, to the extent possible, to make a higher initial capital investment to achieve operational efficiency. How do they evaluate ROI in terms of operating effectiveness and incorporate efficiency gains into the facility? Many planning and architectural firms have brought clinicians in house to lend their expertise to the design process. Similarly, many lean business consultants, promising substantial gains in efficiency, are entering the design and construction industry. Is one concept better than the other? Does one concept lead to better outcomes?

In a typical project delivery process, the architect is hired as part of the project team while the lean consultant is usually part of a separate, ongoing quality improvement initiative. The ideal situation is for the lean consultant, no matter who hires her, to be fully integrated into the same team as the architect, the owner, the contractor, and everyone else—all of whom are working toward a common goal.

NEW SETTINGS FOR MORE CUSTOMERS

The primary aspect of making more efficient use of space is anticipating what types of spaces will be needed. There will be more patients, an increase in preventative care, and an overall shift from inpatient to outpatient care. The first and most obvious thing to expect is an increase in outpatient care facilities, but what type of care will those facilities provide? They will provide care as part of a continuum of care. What will that continuum of care look like?

Many new facilities include spaces for treating comorbidity patients in group settings. So our new center has group education rooms for, as an example, multiple diabetes patients who learn together how to eat well, cope, care for each other, and hold each other accountable. Adjacent to those spaces will be shared offices for the nurse educators, home health nurses, nutritionists, wound care nurses, and social workers. The nearby wing has a primary care suite for family medicine, pediatrics, and/or women's health. Down the hall is the professional services group with a simple diagnostic radiology suite, a lab, and a pharmacy. Another wing has a multispecialty clinic for rotating specialists whose services depend on the particular patient population. The facility will be open six days a week, maybe even seven, including nights and weekends. It will be extremely accessible to the community via all modes of transportation, located near schools, places of work, grocery stores, and housing. The model is no longer physician-centric but team care–focused with the patient in the center.

A separate ambulatory hospital, likely open 24/7, will provide more intense outpatient care with full-time specialty clinics; a shared procedure suite for endoscopy, bronchoscopy, and interventional radiology; a substantial suite of minimally invasive surgery operating rooms (ORs); and postanesthesia recovery and short-stay beds for overnight (less than 24-hour) stays. One or both of the facilities will have urgent care with excellent street presence and even better business hours. Both facilities will be easy to see and find, providing branding and name recognition for the system. Lastly, the inpatient hospital we all know and love will house only the most acute care patients and their essential clinical support: intensive care units (ICUs), emergency department (ED), tertiary care operating rooms and recovery, core lab, inpatient pharmacy, and so on. To attract and support regional patients for specialty care, overnight guest accommodations will be outside the hospital. The driving idea behind all of this is to provide services in the most appropriate setting that will ultimately reduce cost.

In some markets, this model may also evolve into a complete community. For areas with large aging populations, the continuum of care will all be in one "village" that also provides tiered housing for a thriving population as it progresses through independent living, assisted living, skilled nursing facility, and, finally, hospice.

FLEXIBILITY

An idea that has always been popular as a way of maximizing the use of space during times of uncertainty is the idea of flexibility. Flexibility is not specific to healthcare or reform, but it is good to keep in mind its value proposition. Directing a team to make a project "flexible" is easy, but delivering on that objective is much more difficult. It is important is to understand some of the primary forces driving the decision of when to incorporate flexibility and when not to. One aspect is flexibility versus specificity, and a second is first cost versus life-cycle cost. After looking at these two components, it becomes clear that some areas are better candidates for flexible design than others.

Typically, the more flexible something is, the less ideal it is for the specific task at hand. Universal ICU rooms are an easy example. Regardless of how patient care units are organized (by surgical/medical or by neuro/cardiac/trauma), each organization often debates which method is better. So sometimes the decision is that flexibility would be good: if rooms are universal, they can be used for whatever population has the highest census that week, and overall bed census can be higher. The downside of the universal ICU room may be that equipment and layout are not optimal, and nursing support areas are inadequate for staffing and observation ratios. Given that the flexibility choice will have some type of trade-off, an organization has three routes to choose from—commit to the flexible model, commit to the specific model, or (my favorite) negotiate. Going back to the ICU example, this negotiation could result in building a fixed number of specific rooms for each patient population and augmenting the total with a number of flexible rooms in an overflow unit. This approach maximizes the efficiency of both the specific beds and the flexible ones. But each organization should be intentional and transparent about this decision.

The other aspect of flexible design is first cost versus life-cycle cost. In nearly all instances, the initial cost for flexibility is more expensive than that of fixed, but the cost to change a flexible design is far less expensive than remodeling. Furniture versus casework is a perfect example. The building industry is full of studies that demonstrate fixed, plastic-laminated casework can be custom-designed and installed for less cost than modular furniture. But nearly 100 percent of that lower initial cost is incurred again when any changes are made. Modular furniture, on the other hand, has a higher initial cost because of all the parts and pieces that make it so flexible. But with a few hours of labor, it is possible to completely reconfigure an entire team workspace.

To make the furniture versus casework decision, one needs to consider the likelihood and frequency of future changes. Does the culture of the organization change quickly and try many different options? Or does it move slowly only after the entire industry agrees that the model has changed? Too many organizations *think* they change quickly and make the investment. But, really, they only *want* to change quickly and are actually quite slow to adapt. This issue applies to dozens of systems and installations within every facility design.

Another common effort to incorporate longer-term flexibility involves oversizing building foundations for future added stories. This one always sounds appealing and is an affordable first cost. But the actual construction of the future addition is often a horrible thing to live through and is very expensive. A much more expensive first cost option is to shell the future stories to provide space—but one that is far more likely to be built out.

Flexibility of a facility only saves money in the long run if the organization takes advantage of the opportunity to change—otherwise, it is typically just an increase in cost.

PROJECT DELIVERY

Because learning what makes the ideal facility in a reform environment will take years to understand, it is impossible to overestimate the importance of taking the right project management steps to achieve the highest level of success today. There are three essential steps, and without all three, the likelihood of that success is small. First, know what you want. Second, budget for what you want. Third, deliver what you want. Every project has multiple places within each of these steps for things to go wrong. The question is how to make sure they don't.

Right Scope

One system that went to a well-care model first culled its data to find the one patient on whom it spent the most money and asked, "How could we have prevented this?" In this case, the patient was a middle-aged woman with chronic diabetes who was seen once a month in the local ED. What could the system do to prevent this? Working backwards from the most costly idea, they could:

- see the patient daily in the clinic,
- see the patient daily in her home,
- feed her three basic meals a day,
- teach her to take care of herself and monitor her own blood sugar, or
- teach her how to eat better.

So what did they do? They hired a nutritionist who went to the patient's home, threw away all of the unhealthy food, and took the patient grocery shopping. They did this daily for one month, then weekly, and now the nutritionist only checks in once a month. If the organization had cared for more patients this way, health outcomes would be better *and* cost less. Much like the "air conditioner" story that President Obama made so popular, where Medicare reimburses $50,000 to rush a heart attack patient to the ED for care that could have been prevented with a $200 AC unit, healthcare in a reform environment will start much farther upstream. This clearly was not a bricks-and-mortar solution, but it demonstrates precisely the kind of critical thinking that needs to precede major projects.

Project Management 101 spends most of its time preaching the benefits of proper planning and scope identification, yet so many projects go straight to the implementation phase. Important stakeholders are in a hurry to "swing hammers," and project managers are almost forced to give in. (We no longer swing hammers on construction sites and I somehow find that beautifully ironic—administrators insisting that we start doing something sooner that we don't even do at all anymore.) Those same stakeholders think they know what they want, lock themselves into a budget, discover they didn't ever know what they wanted but are now limited by budget only to fail on the ultimate goal of delivering what is wanted. What happened, and how is it best avoided?

What happened is that the owner/client did not take the time and commit the resources to determine what the true success criteria for the project were. Building projects are exciting, and once the momentum gets going, slowing down is difficult. From a leadership perspective, spending adequate time and energy understanding the population that will be served, the services needed for that population, the delivery model for providing those services, and how things will be different when the project is complete are imperative. This understanding is not achieved with a building. This understanding is achieved by asking the difficult questions now, embracing the conflict of disparate points of view, and clearly establishing the expectations of everyone involved. First, know what you want.

Right Budget

Every project starts with big dreams and high expectations. In this environment of doing more with less, the major limiting factor for all of those dreams seems to be the budget, and everyone dreads it. Few things are more deflating than spending months determining what you want only to learn that you can't afford it. Oddly enough, this is actually the result of poor planning. Perhaps the project success criteria should include, "The institution will be in sound financial position with no more than 50 percent of its debt capacity tied to the new facility." Or, "The ten-year ROI for the building will be positive." Or, more likely in a reform environment, "At least ten of the service lines in the new building will target additional covered lives and operate at a loss for the first eight years." Very few organizations have unlimited budget, yet we see budget as the only limiting factor to our dreams. The leader's role is to frame financial goals as part of many that all get balanced and weighed together rather than pit goals against each other with winners and losers.

Budget will always be a critical aspect of new construction. New buildings are expensive and take up a significant portion of the overall capital outlay of any institution. Every chief financial officer I have ever met wants predictability in his extremely uncertain world, and nearly every project charter I have ever read lists meeting the budget as a success criterion. What is the budget and how is it determined? This is different for everyone, but a few common themes are relevant.

First, projects are rarely successful when the budget process is separate from the program process. In other words, don't create a budget in a vacuum independently from all the other needs of a facility—budget for what you want. Tie the needs and wants of all the stakeholders together into one vision that *is* the project—including the budget. A well-planned project with clear success criteria understood and supported by all stakeholders is a joy to execute. The real work of the owner is in the planning.

Right Process

Currently, many local executive suites allow or even encourage individual campuses or departments to develop their own growth strategies. If the business models generate a positive ROI, then those plans get funded. As capital becomes more limited, the importance of local and regional partnerships increases, and overall population health becomes the primary driver, the value of centralizing those planning efforts increases. More systems will create capital planning departments responsible for collecting strategic business initiatives, determining the overall market needs, identifying the facility requirements for implementation, and recommending a limited number of projects to move forward.

Nestled within the healthcare reform agenda is a larger social change prevalent in much of society: collaboration. This new world of collaboration and working together to solve problems contains so many wonderful opportunities to leverage the best minds in the room to find the right solution. The question is no longer who is responsible for a particular decision, but rather who within the stakeholders is best suited to succeed in a particular area, and how is her special talent brought to the forefront.

With healthcare reform driving a focus on building more with less, it is imperative that each action taken moves toward the same goal as efficiently as possible. A critical piece of achieving those success criteria is having the right people on the team at the right time. More and more, successful construction projects are being delivered by teams that don't just understand the scope, schedule, and budget, they helped develop them. For a team to truly be committed to delivering what is best for the project, members need to buy into that vision by helping develop it, not merely be told what that vision is.

Performance expectations have increased, infrastructure systems have become more complex, and the ability of any one individual or firm to understand and maximize those systems has become nearly impossible. Thus, the size of project teams has grown and become more complex. Previously, the design team consisted of an architect and an engineering firm. Now we have design architects, code consultants, Lean consultants, waterproofing engineers, IT network architects, and many more. Similarly, we used to just hire a general contractor after the design was complete. Now we hire a construction manager who hires dozens of specialty contractors, vendors, suppliers, and more. These trusted business partners add even more value when they are brought on early in the design process when their expertise in means and methods can drive good decisions about expensive building systems far better than designers are able to achieve on their own.

How does an owner select and manage such a complex team to best benefit the project?

In the construction industry, all of that rolled up is known as integrated project delivery (IPD). IPD takes many forms, both contractual and ideological, but there are several themes that, regardless of what the contract says, are consistent. The primary concept is that everyone involved in the project is working toward the same goal, and they all share a common definition of success—ideally developed during planning. This vision needs to be prominent, compelling, and well defined. Although previously unheard of, it has become common for architects, engineers, and contractors to contribute their own success criteria for a project. Do they want to get repeat business, make money, and develop the next generation of leadership within the firm? Owners are foolish to believe they are the only ones who need the new facility and that it is just a job for everyone else. These common goals also get every individual rowing in the same direction.

The second concept is that everyone is expected to add value to the team. Individuals and firms must be responsible to lead their portion of the effort and be engaged in and contribute to the effort as a whole. The construction foreman delivering doors to a 13-story building is expected to find the most efficient way to deliver those doors and teach what he learned to the foreman who delivers the cabinets.

Third, every member of the team needs to understand that her individual success is inherently linked to the success of everyone else on the team. One's job is not to be a standout but to bring up everyone else around—all toward the common goals of the project.

Lastly, a well-written contract will link all of these together to build in incentives that reward the team members for the good work they deliver. These rewards could be anything the members of the team find valuable, but they are most often financial incentives. For example, the owner will pay all invoices within seven days of invoice by vendors when the subcontractors hit certain monthly performance targets.

Incentives are typically set by the owner, are the same for everyone, and are committed to by everyone. The goals are then transparently measured across the entire team and prominently displayed to encourage the behavior that will ultimately define the success of the project.

The IPD model is uncomfortable for some owners, particularly those who are risk averse. The iron-clad contract that universally protects only the owner often goes against what is best for the project. Such a contract does not build a relationship to solve problems, proactively address issues, or promote transparency. The owner's contract with the architect or the general contractor sets the stage for the general contractor's contract with the subs, and these same behaviors are passed on down the line. Contracts should be fair and consistent and encourage behavior that generates value for the benefit of the project. The use of IPD ensures the best use of capital and expertise that will only become more critical with healthcare reform.

The idea that contractors no longer "swing hammers" is consistent with the fact that the design and construction industry has become more complicated and sophisticated. Unlike owners and architects, general contractors also became comfortable accepting the inherent risk, allowing their sphere of influence and responsibility to grow faster than others and spur many advances in the industry. The question for the owner is how to bring those gifts to the project team in a way that maximizes their knowledge and contribution to the benefit of the project.

Best value selection (BVS) is a procurement process to deliver just that—the individuals who will add the most value to your project. Historically, the typical contractor procurement process has been to clearly define the exact scope of work needed from a contractor, put that scope on the street in a public request for proposal (RFP), and select the lowest price. Thus, it was the goal of contractors to interpret the defined scope to be as narrowly defensible in order to be selected on the basis of having the lowest price. During the project, the contractors' goal was to add to that scope and make up whatever money was left on the table during procurement. Where in this process is value added for the owner? Are we building new facilities to hone our negotiation skills or to deliver better health outcomes?

BVS assumes that the best group to deliver a scope of work is also the best group to define and determine that scope. Instead of asking for the lowest price, the RFP asks for examples of past projects that have been successful through collaboration. For example, an excavating contractor who works with the geotechnical engineer to determine the most effective shoring method will provide more value than one who simply waits for the construction documents to be delivered.

Many hospital administrators will cringe a little at taking anything other than the lowest (or lowest responsible) price for a general contractor. A quick study of the numbers shows a misplaced concern. In a hypothetical construction project with a total project cost (all inclusive) of $1,000 per square foot, approximately 65 percent, or $650, will be for direct construction. Of that $650, 50 percent goes to mechanical and electrical subcontractors, and 35 percent to other vendors and specialty subcontractors. The conditions that actually hit the books for the general contractor are typically somewhere in the range of 15 percent (with 3 percent as fee, 6 percent to cover overhead, and 6 percent for labor). That 15 percent will never be $0, and generally only a 2 to 4 percent variance exists in a given market. Doing the math, this means that a public RFP to select the lowest-cost general contractor is chasing about 2 percent of the total cost of a building, only to hire the firm most motivated to create change orders. Considering that redoing failed subcontractor work costs four to six times the amount of the original installation, it is easy to realize that investing in a good general contractor can be far more cost effective than investing in a cheap general contractor.

Project delivery methodology has changed quite a bit over the last century, mostly led by the procurement experts at the federal government and then interpreted by state governments, nonprofit entities, and for-profit companies. With computer-controlled manufacturing and fabrication, specialty subcontractors such as plumbers; heating, ventilation, and air conditioning (HVAC) technicians; structural steel fabricators; and glazing contractors have found dramatically increased efficiencies—well beyond those realized anywhere else in the industry. Given that these systems make up the majority of the construction costs, these specialty subcontractors have vaulted from being just another sub on the job to being critical contributors on issues that determine the cost and performance of the building.

Through the use of building integration modeling (BIM), general contractors have led the effort to gather all of the expertise of each trade, assemble the information into one integrated model, and create a three-dimensional electronic version of the entire building with all its systems before any individual piece is fabricated. Over the last five years, with truly amazing results, having nearly all projects designed, fabricated, and constructed using BIM has become common. The especially savvy project teams who are able to truly collaborate have even figured out how to use a single federated model rather than one for the designer and a duplicate for the contractor. Understanding some basics about BIM, how the owner can facilitate (or not) the most benefit from using it, and how it might continue to impact healthcare facilities in the future is important.

One opportunity that can be addressed by the owner is the federated model, a single model centrally managed for the use and benefit of everyone involved. This model is complicated because the construction industry is relatively litigious, and along with ownership of the model comes liability for its content. Today such models are used to convey aesthetic design intent from the designer to the client, equipment performance criteria from the engineer to the HVAC manufacturer, and actual location of sprinkler pipes to the electrician to avoid conflicts in the field. With so many hands making changes and so many decisions being made based on the content, it is easy to see that assuming liability for the model is a common point of contention. The owner is the ultimate benefactor of the project and, I believe, should step up and assume ownership for the model. Both the American Institute of Architects and ConsensusDocs, two common construction contract vendors, have forms that allow this model, and each set articulates clear accountability. Unless the owner takes ownership of the model, various members of the project team will hesitate to share their information, and the full benefit of the technology will not be realized. For this effort to truly be successful, BIM can't just be a good idea or an option to take another step toward enhanced productivity—it needs to be the default, simply the way things are done with 100 percent commitment from everyone. It's not easy, and for many owners it is scary, but it is part of the solution to better collaboration and teamwork.

OPERATIONS AND MAINTENANCE

Accurate and complete building models are key to understanding a good design as well as good implementation of that design. The next frontier for BIM is how it transitions to facilities maintenance and in facilities information modeling (FIM)—often referred to as BIM to FIM. While the construction industry has been relatively slow to change, the facilities maintenance industry remains one step behind in the implementation of new technology. But with astounding results, some facility departments are using a building model to manage work orders, preventative maintenance schedules, energy utilization, and technical equipment specifications. As common as BIM has become in design and construction, it is becoming as common for asset management, and every owner should expect it. The owner can benefit by working with the construction project team to ensure that the information is gathered, and that the *format* of that information is gathered with the final product in mind. While the facility department of today may not be ready to receive gigabytes of building information, it won't be long until it can't operate without FIM—and it will need some help.

Facilities departments will also be driven to reign in expenditures on energy as well as managing more renovation projects. Both of these project types will benefit from FIM, and the owner must play a strong role to achieve it.

Accurate as-built information of an existing facility is critical to the success of any renovation work done within that facility. While the construction industry used to bring raw materials to the jobsite and cut everything to fit, they now rely on the accuracy of the building model or FIM to fabricate everything in a central shop, knowing that it will fit once delivered. Similarly, an accurate building model can bring extraordinary value to the owner in terms of monitoring, managing, and improving energy usage of a facility. Because energy is one of the single largest line items in an operating budget, it is rife with opportunity—especially in the context of recent societal interest, political pressure, and technology improvements. Many ways to improve energy efficiency in facilities exist, but none will be possible without an excellent understanding of the facility and where and why it uses energy. Executive-level involvement and direction will be needed to support implementation of robust FIM components. This support starts during the establishment of BIM in design and construction and continues into postoccupancy.

WHAT COMES NEXT?

Much discussion surrounds what healthcare reform may lead to but not much about what will not change, or about existing trends that might change or even go away. For example, the ACA says nothing about aesthetics. Against the grain of much of the design industry, I doubt any data indicating that using granite and wood paneling leads to better health outcomes will stand up against data that prenatal care leads to better birth outcomes. Patient rooms must be clean, well lit, probably even attractive and soothing, but not at the expense of improved access or safety. There is a question of whether the use of single-patient rooms in the neonatal ICU reduces nosocomial infection rates or is just an argument to justify additional room sizes that are market-driven by parents whose insurance is good enough to cover extended stays. LEED (Leadership in Energy and Environmental Design) certification, while encouraging use of sustainable practices and materials, might really be a marketing effort that doesn't necessarily improve health outcomes. These aren't necessarily bad ideas; the point is that decisions and choices need to be based on improved health outcomes.

Building codes and regulations may be another place to look for potential change. Many of the current requirements are driving up cost in every facet of the facilities arena and may or may not support the overall goal to improve health outcomes for the entire population. Recently, The Joint Commission has embarked on a campaign to reduce fires in operating rooms that, in their opinion, is the next greatest need. This may be a valid issue, but at some point healthcare needs to be declared safe enough. Some data indicate more than 50,000,000 surgeries are performed in the United States each year and 650 fires are documented. The Joint Commission is considering more stringent electrical requirements be installed in new ORs to prevent fires that occur in 0.0013 percent of surgeries. If the country only had one more dollar to invest in healthcare, would this be the next most important thing? Risk assessments will need to be completed for these proposed requirements before they are implemented. Capital construction typically involves large sums of money, and justifying a percent here or a few thousand dollars there to support various initiatives is often easy. These small changes eventually add up to real money. Does everyone look at the bigger picture—improved health outcomes?

Another compliance issue might be the multitude of requirements for inpatient versus short-stay facilities. With the gradual shift of surgeries and procedures from inpatient to outpatient, health systems will continue to push the envelope as to what can and cannot be performed in an ASC environment. The pressure will be to perform more and more complex care in an outpatient environment. As long as that care can be delivered safely and effectively, regulations should adapt to this shift.

Health systems throughout the country are asking their providers to work at the top of their license. In the building industry, we should be asking our buildings to do the same. What does that look like? For years, we have been designing spaces that support the most complex care imaginable for the worst possible scenario because the incremental cost to do so was able to be absorbed in the system. With the drive to reduce cost, this margin will shrink if not disappear altogether. Where OR suites and procedure rooms were previously built to the highest common denominator, they now need to be designed and built to support only the uses that can reasonably be anticipated. Healthcare planners and architects will need to demonstrate a much better understanding of different requirements for these procedures and guide their clients to build the right quantity of the right types of spaces.

At the same time, healthcare systems can anticipate being part of the response to the shortage of primary care providers. As part of the process to increase the number of primary care providers, those providers will need to be trained in medical schools, nursing schools, allied health schools, and so on, and they will need institutions beyond the classic academic medical center for their clinical training. Internships, clerkships, residencies, and fellowships will need to be developed in partnership with nearly every health system across the country, and those programs will need education spaces throughout their facilities.

CONCLUSION

With all times of great change come great opportunities for innovation and success. The systems and facilities that embrace that change and work collaboratively with the experts they choose as partners are the most likely to achieve success in their capital projects.

> ***Key Takeaways***
>
> This discussion on IPD and BVS is especially refreshing, as our industry suffers from a misperception of what is important. Warren Buffett famously said that most investors know the price of everything and the value of nothing. Allowing a low-bid mentality to infiltrate all decisions has led to the low productivity that hinders our industry, so Taylor's enlightened approach is noteworthy.
>
> - Designing and building to the worst-case scenario will be done at the expense of needed programs.
> - IPD provides the correct environment for a successful project.
> - Selection of the team is best done through BVS. The low bidder is not always the best for project.
> - The facilities department deserves a seat at the table when the planning begins.

REFERENCE

Obamacare Facts. 2014. Accessed September 28. www.obamacarefacts.com.

CHAPTER 3

Strategic Planning and Programming

Georgeann B. Burns

For many, the importance of strategic planning and programming lies somewhere in between "a waste of time" and "gotta have it." Those who feel that planning is unnecessary often see the process as chewing up time and money that could be better spent on just designing the building. The participants at the other end of the spectrum sometimes get so caught up in the process that no decisions get made and analysis paralysis ensues. In our opinion, the middle ground is the requisite approach. Without a firm grasp of what bricks and mortar solutions are supposed to accomplish or support, even the most accomplished designer will struggle. This chapter explores some of the history of healthcare planning and how it has and will continue to change.

In order to plan your future wisely, it is necessary that you understand and appreciate your past.

—Jo Coudert

INTRODUCTION

This chapter looks at the impact of the Affordable Care Act (ACA) and reform overall on the planning and programming of healthcare facilities. Multiple forces are reshaping our healthcare delivery system and subsequently the capital project development process:

- Recognition that, as a nation, we pay more and get less than any other developed country
- Expectation of more patients seeking and receiving care while reimbursement is shrinking
- Greater need to retool our facilities to meet new needs
- Decreasing access to capital

As a result, planning—both strategic and facility—as we have come to know it no longer exists. The need to truly match facilities to efficient operational models has never been greater. And the definition of a facility completely aligned with available development resources is even more critical at the beginning of a project—not midway through the design process in schematic design or later.

This chapter examines

- how the planning processes are changing,
- how care delivery is changing,
- how facilities are changing as a result, and
- how the facility development process is changing to provide these new facilities.

THE PLANNING PROCESS—THEN AND NOW

Any change, even a change for the better, is always accompanied by drawbacks and discomforts.

—Arnold Bennett

For many years in the United States, the planning and programming of healthcare facilities consisted of interviewing representatives or owners of the proposed facility (almost always a hospital) to understand their particular ideas of needed spaces and organization of those spaces. This information was then the basis of design and construction documents. Few metrics were involved other than construction cost. With the implementation of the Hospital Survey and Construction Act of 1946 (PL 79-725, also known as the Hill-Burton Act), efforts began to systematize facility planning. The facility focus was on construction standards for life safety and building performance as contained in the 1947 *General Standards* that appeared in the Federal Register as part of Hill-Burton implementation regulations. (The current guidelines can be found at www.fgiguidelines.org.)

In 1974, with the passage of the National Health Planning and Public Resources Development Act (PL 93-641), a significant attempt to provide a rational structure for health facility planning was begun (Mott et al. 1976). The law consolidated the Hill-Burton program, the Regional Medical Program, and the Comprehensive Planning Act. The resulting program created federal, state, and local resources and agencies whose mandate was to review and approve or deny applications for healthcare services and related construction. Local health system agencies, state health planning and development agencies, and certificate of need (CON) processes were hallmarks of this legislation. In 37 states, CON regulations are still in place to control the ostensible proliferation of healthcare services and facilities.

Strategic Planning

The kind of planning required to develop a strategy to meet CON requirements is often referred to as health planning or strategic planning—as opposed to facility programming or planning. Strategic planning is a "set of organizational processes for identifying the desired future of the organization and developing decision guidelines" (Ginter, Swayne, and Duncan 2002) and provides a map for how an organization will achieve its objectives and goals.

As the healthcare systems delivering care became larger and more sophisticated, so did the processes and studies for determining what services would be provided and where they would be provided. Strategic health planning became an industry with specialized consultants largely focused on acute care facilities and how to maximize market share and revenue.

Population Health

Now the perspective has broadened to population-based strategic planning. Examining true clinical need and coupling it with effective facilities to meet those needs makes this form of planning even more important. According to an article by The Advisory Board (2013), the forces of reform "are pushing providers past the point of incremental change toward a new business model centered on delivery of comprehensive care and management of total cost risk." The article lists three foundational elements an organization must develop:

1. Information-powered clinical decision making
2. Primary care–led clinical workforce
3. Patient engagement and community integration

The time for big data is now. It is already used by many institutions to understand physician practice patterns and to coach outlier providers on better surgical procedures, antibiotic use, patient follow-up, and so on. It is also used at the broadest scale to analyze the health needs of a given population.

With the growing use of patient-centered medical homes (PCMHs), the need for primary care providers (PCPs) is clearly a national focus. However, according to The Advisory Board (2013), these PCPs now need to be at the helm of population health management efforts. With new responsibilities for managing other providers and support personnel, the PCPs will also need to be able to lead in providing integrated care. While many members of the PCMH are clinicians, the PCMH will also include community health workers, trained copatient mentors, language translators and interpreters, and many others.

The last requirement, to engage patients and community, means looking beyond the patients who come through an institution's doors today. It means working with other providers and systems to provide healthcare and wellness support to those throughout the community.

ACOs

Accountable care organizations (ACOs) are in some ways the ultimate expression of population health management. They initially were included in the ACA as a means of reaching the Institute for Healthcare Improvement's (2014) Triple Aim goals for Medicare patients. According to Gamble and Punke (2013), the term *accountable care organization* was coined in 2006 by Elliott Fisher, MD, director of the Dartmouth Institute for Health Policy and Clinical Practice in Hanover, New Hampshire.

An ACO is a group of payers, physicians, hospitals, and other healthcare providers voluntarily collaborating to provide coordinated care to an assigned population of patients (Gamble and Punke 2013). If providers reduce costs and/or improve specified quality metrics in a certain timeframe, they are able to receive financial rewards from or share in the savings with Medicare or a commercial payer. ACO arrangements can also involve risk, in which the provider pays back a portion or all of the costs that exceed the payer's established benchmark.

The same planning concepts that underpin population health management apply to ACOs. However, now there can be specific risks and rewards tied to formalized contractual arrangements. The need for gathering and using big data becomes even more important to understand the needs of the population being served. And an equal imperative exists to provide the right services in the right place at the right time. In other words, planning is critical.

Master Planning

With the focus on macrostrategic healthcare planning, the participation of third parties who may be new to healthcare development, and the desire to lower first capital costs, sometimes the longer-range view of a facility gets lost in the mix. While many in the healthcare planning field believe the inpatient bed is an endangered species, none of us may anticipate circumstances that will require some sort of inpatient facility in the future to serve a particular population. Even though it may be highly unlikely that inpatient beds would be required on a new or redeveloped site, the question should be asked. And, even if the answer is "no beds will be needed," land acquisition and site planning should allow for some form of growth over time. Vehicular and pedestrian access onto and around the site, parking, building entries, vertical circulation cores, and several other site and building aspects should be evaluated for both the initial project and also in a master plan.

Some capital planning and design teams, in their rush to construct a facility to meet current needs, eschew master planning. In their view, such planning for incorporation of growth concepts is unnecessary and too expensive in both time and money to the development process. This view is limiting and can cause significant obstacles to logical growth and change in the future.

Especially given the need for lower capital cost facilities, the idea of a throwaway building is not reasonable. As a result, some developers are requiring planning of ambulatory care buildings for future use as nonhealthcare structures. Intrinsically, this kind of flexibility has value, but not if it comes at the expense of current operational efficiency or patient access.

Facility Planning and Programming

Advances in construction codes and regulations have ultimately led to the *2014 Guidelines for Design and Construction of Hospital and Outpatient Facilities,* published by the Facility Guidelines Institute (2014). Going beyond building construction and building system operation, this consensus-based document reaffirms the need for each complying project to have a "functional program" completed as part of the project planning to serve as the basis for design. In addition to summaries of space by department or function, individual room-by-room space lists, and indications of proposed circulation patterns, the planner must also include "projected operational use and demand loading for affected departments and/or project components." Until the advent of the more advanced versions of the *Guidelines*, space programs were not always produced as part of the planning and design process. Thus it was possible for an inexperienced architect to unintentionally omit key rooms or functions. Successive editions of *Guidelines* and other governing agencies began to promulgate minimum standards listing required rooms and even critical dimensions and sizes for selected rooms. Now, virtually every healthcare project has at least a space list if not also some depiction of critical functional adjacencies.

A major proponent of such programming was the American Institute of Architects' (AIA) Committee on Architecture for Health (CAH). This subset of the AIA represented those firms and AIA members specializing in the fledgling healthcare architecture field. The committee's successor group, the Academy of Architecture for Health (AAH), continues to be a major source of knowledge in the planning, design, and construction of healthcare facilities of all types. As one of the major sources of expertise on healthcare facilities, this group supplied the volunteer effort to compile the initial *Guidelines* documents. The group also promoted the use of space and functional programmatic documents, presented educational programs on key functional components of hospitals, and supported efforts to create standards that responded to operational and technological change. The related group, the American Society of Healthcare Engineers (ASHE), a subset of the American Hospital Association (AHA), has also contributed significantly to the *Guidelines* documents.

The kinds of data and analysis required for "demand loading" are typically also needed to substantiate the need for specific services and their capacity in CON applications. Thus, an institution wishing to establish, for example, a new obstetrics program including a birthing center would need to demonstrate compliance with the respective state health plan by:

- documenting the total anticipated number of births in the service area—current and projected;
- identifying any other local birthing centers or hospital labor and delivery services with their individual capacities;
- demonstrating the need for additional birthing resources at the applicant institution;
- quantifying that need, including numbers of birthing rooms, operating rooms for cesarean sections, recovery spaces or rooms, and postpartum capability;
- listing all the other supporting resources needed and available within the applying institution; and

- compiling a comprehensive project cost, construction cost, and schedule.

States have different degrees of complexity in their respective health plans and/or the supporting analyses they require from CON applicants. However, the general idea of the guidelines was to eliminate unneeded duplication of clinical services, thereby eliminating unnecessary construction expense and operational cost. The states that have eliminated their CON programs did so largely on the grounds that the processes did not really affect the duplication and/or had become too expensive and overly burdensome to applicants—obstacles to free enterprise. The CON programs were also seen by many as clubs used to stop or drastically slow down healthcare facility construction.

But these programs did begin to establish a platform of project planning that begins with understanding the clinical needs of the service area of a given institution and then matching resources to those needs. So, now, even in those states without CON programs but who have adopted the *2014 Guidelines*, the need for this strategic project analysis remains. Such analysis is going to be even more critical as we move toward population health and capitation.

Importance of Strategic Planning

If past history was all there was to the game, the richest people would be librarians.

—Warren Buffett

Until the CON programs were implemented, detailed strategic planning didn't have much perceived value if an institution had or could raise funds needed for construction. And after CONs became the norm, for many institutions the CON process became one to garner as much market share, and therefore revenue, as possible. The concept of understanding and meeting community need was often a secondary concern.

As we know, these programs and legislation were all based on an existing free market system that included commercial and federal insurers. Even the ACA is predicated on continuing with these financial bases. However, the major difference with the ACA comes in the change to value over volume. This is a sea change in how healthcare facility operational success is measured. Success in the hospital is no longer evaluated by the number of total patient days and related revenue but by the overall health of a given individual, maintaining or improving his physical well-being in the most cost-effective way. Services that traditionally were or are revenue streams are now becoming cost centers. And the hunt is on for more effective methods of delivering care and more effective environments in which to deliver it.

CARE DELIVERY CHANGES

The only thing we know about the future is that it will be different.

—Peter Drucker

The hospital, once the epicenter of care delivery, has become just one point in a continuum of care locations. The concept of hub and spokes, with the hospital as hub and virtually every other facility as spokes, has given way to an array of sites where patients are monitored, diagnosed, and treated—starting with where they live. As outlined in other chapters, technology advances now allow constant monitoring of a vast array of physiologic data that no longer requires a visit to a physician office, let alone the hospital. And procedures—both diagnostic and therapeutic—are increasingly done on an outpatient basis. Again, the hospital—the operationally expensive, technology-intensive behemoth—is becoming a place to be avoided unless it is the only appropriate location for critical care and extremely advanced interventional procedures.

So, what do some of these other locations look like? Now often referred to as "hospitals without beds," these facilities can range from the traditional provider office or suite to comprehensive ambulatory care centers, federally qualified health centers, or medically oriented hotels.

Newer facilities are beginning to share a common orientation: the patient as the focal point as opposed to the technology or the clinician. The resulting patient-centered care is a consequence of an increase in consumerism throughout our culture and the work of organizations like Planetree.

Planetree (2014), founded in 1978, promotes the organization of care around the needs of the patient. Now, in addition to working with hospitals and healthcare systems around the world, Planetree is also part of the National Quality Forum, a group established under the ACA to develop a national quality strategy through the National Priorities Partnership. This 51-organization effort is a key component in defining, tracking, and implementing healthcare quality strategies.

One of these tracking methods is the Hospital Consumer Assessment of Healthcare Providers and Systems (HCAHPS) survey. The survey measures the patient's perception of care quality through a series of questions given after a patient is discharged from the hospital (HCAHPS n.d.). Per requirements of the ACA, the Center for Medicare & Medicaid Services (CMS) uses scores on HCAHPS to calculate CMS reimbursement. While HCAHPS is all about hospital care, it is only a matter of time until this same type of assessment is extended to outpatient facilities.

Integrative medicine is also a major force in care delivery. As PCPs go beyond the role of gatekeeper, either facilitating or limiting access to specialists, they are the focal point for treatment of chronic conditions. The Agency for Healthcare Research and

Quality identified the following major healthcare cost factors (Stanton and Rutherford 2005):

- The five most expensive conditions
    1. Heart disease
    2. Cancer
    3. Trauma
    4. Mental disorders
    5. Pulmonary disorders
- The five major chronic conditions
    1. Mood disorders
    2. Diabetes
    3. Heart disease
    4. Asthma
    5. Hypertension

As the need for effective and efficient treatment of patients with these conditions increases, the role of integrative medicine is also increasing. *Integrative medicine* is defined as "a healing environment, a passion for prevention and wellness and not just diagnosis and treatment; working with the patient and the patient's family as partners; understanding the deeper causes of illness and symptoms; providing approaches for self-care and taking enough time to address all of the patient's concerns" (Schimpff 2014). And it often means including "proven complementary practices such as acupuncture, yoga, massage, nutrition and health coaching and personal fitness training" (Schimpff 2014).

The PCMH model of care delivery includes an ongoing relationship between provider and patient and a comprehensive approach to coordination of care. The American College of Physicians and the American Academy of Family Physicians have endorsed the medical home as an approach to improve care delivery. Defined by the Patient-Centered Primary Care Collaborative (2014), the medical home is a "model or philosophy of primary care that is patient-centered, comprehensive, team-based, coordinated, accessible, and focused on quality and safety." A PCMH incorporates the following features:

- **Patient-centered:** A partnership among practitioners, patients, and their families ensures that decisions respect patients' wants, needs, and preferences, and that patients have the education and support they need to make decisions and participate in their own care.
- **Comprehensive:** A team of care providers is wholly accountable for a patient's physical and mental healthcare needs, including prevention and wellness, acute care, and chronic care.
- **Coordinated:** Care is organized across all elements of the broader healthcare system, including specialty care, hospitals, home healthcare, community services and supports.
- **Accessible:** Patients are able to access services with shorter waiting times, "after hours" care, 24/7 electronic or telephone access, and strong communication through health IT innovations.
- **Committed to quality and safety:** Clinicians and staff enhance quality improvement to ensure that patients and families make informed decisions about their health.

CHANGING FACILITIES

The job of buildings is to improve human relations: architecture must ease them, not make them worse.

—Ralph Erskine

Subacute Facilities

While not new facility types, these facilities are receiving increasing attention and development. According to the California Hospital Association (2014), "Subacute-care units provide a specialized level of care to medically fragile patients. Subacute patients are individuals who do not need acute care, but who are too ill to be cared for by most skilled-nursing facilities. Frequently, these individuals are ventilator-dependent or require frequent respiratory treatments. While subacute beds are licensed as skilled-nursing beds, they are reimbursed differently and are subject to additional staffing and patient criteria requirements." These subacute beds may also be reserved for specific rehabilitation needs, such as postsurgical rehabilitation.

Free-Standing Emergency Departments and Urgent Care Centers

Several types of facilities are springing up as systems try to move care closer to patients and decongest hospital campuses. Texas, often the location for innovation unencumbered by major regulation, is a leader in the number of urgent care centers (UCCs) and free-standing emergency departments (FSEDs).

In Texas, these facilities can be owned by anyone but must, in the case of an FSED, be operated by licensed emergency physicians and abide by the Emergency Medical Treatment and Active Labor Act (EMTALA) (Texas Administrative Code 2014); a UCC can be staffed by a nurse practitioner. If the FSED is not a hospital-based facility, it cannot charge for the facility fee reimbursed by CMS. These facilities are springing up in better payer markets as a means of meeting consumer demand for access and convenience. They are generally not located in lower socioeconomic areas where the reimbursement is either lower or nonexistent. But they do extend the reach of a system wanting to put care closer to its patients in urban or suburban areas.

The UCC or FSED can be a standalone facility or an anchor tenant in a larger ambulatory healthcare campus. When part of a larger facility or campus, companion services often include diagnostic imaging, women's imaging, an ambulatory surgery center, retail pharmacy, provider suites, and medically based wellness or fitness centers. These fitness centers often incorporate physical therapy, cardiopulmonary rehab, and/or occupational health services, sharing equipment and perhaps staff. They may also include therapeutic and recreational pools.

Such facilities are replacing traditional medical office buildings (MOBs) by expanding the scope of programs beyond what was conventionally provided in a physician office. Because of increased at-grade entry points to allow more direct access to key services, these buildings are taking a larger footprint, which often dictates a larger site in order to accommodate the building footprint and overall surface parking needs if a parking structure is not an option.

Retail and Hospitality Focus

Internally and externally, these outpatient centers at every scale are looking more like retail establishments than their institutional or commercial office building predecessors. Concourses with open waiting areas, small cafes, retail areas, and children's play areas are all borrowing from the hospitality and retail industries. The goal is to make these buildings and campuses more accessible, inviting, and comfortable. Some developers consider these campuses as the initial or key component in new town development. Examples abound in the US Southeast and Southwest.

Intergenerational Facilities

Healthcare system involvement in facilities for seniors has varied over the years. In the past, systems and hospitals affiliated with skilled nursing facilities (SNFs) or included them as part of their campuses. Then, as these centers became part of a continuing care retirement community (CCRC) with different types of housing as well as an SNF, they were often developed separately and by completely separate operators. Now, as our population is aging so dramatically, many CCRCs are looking at ways to integrate with health systems to minimize duplication of clinical services and enhance community and social support. Again, the focus is shifting from sick care to maintaining and supporting health for all ages.

FACILITY DEVELOPMENT PROCESS

Design is not just what it looks like. Design is how it works.

—Steve Jobs

Design and Documentation Processes

The processes to create these buildings are also changing. The advent of building information modeling is a huge advance in compiling and accessing all the information about a building's components through computer-aided drafting and related documents. Now, once a building is complete, virtually all the information about every component is available electronically to help with maintenance, repair, or renovation.

Evidence-Based Design

Another major change is the use of evidence-based design (EBD). EBD uses rigorous research to understand the impact of environments on users and to identify beneficial environments that promote and support efficient and effective care. The country's leading proponent of EBD is the Center for Health Design (CHD). Established in 1993, the center's "mission is to transform healthcare environments for a healthier, safer world through design research, education, and advocacy" (CHD 2014) Again, the focus of healthcare environments research started in the acute care setting but is rapidly expanding to include outpatient facilities. And many of the acute care principles also apply to ambulatory care. Previously, an administrator, a key board member, or a respective spouse could drive the architecture and/or interior design of a healthcare facility; now an extensive and growing body of knowledge exists that can positively inform design decisions. CHD's Pebble Project and its evidence-based design accreditation and certification program have developed much of this research. Once seen as the overly introspective analysis of design choices, EBD is now a legitimate tool for making design decisions in the face of anecdotal evidence or personal taste.

User Involvement and Other Tools

The use of focus groups is increasing. Their use allows participation and buy-in from the community and end users, including patients and family members. Also the use of mockups, both full-scale and virtual, has increased dramatically. Their use is seen as a critical tool to avoid space or equipment placement errors, especially to verify operational and functional assumptions about repetitive rooms, such as exam rooms, or technologically intense and expensive rooms, such as operating rooms. For institutions that do not have several other successful outpatient centers from which to draw, the use of site visits is also increasing. Touring other institutions' facilities is often an invaluable tool for learning what to emulate and what to avoid.

As part of the extensive involvement of end users, the participation of caregivers has increased at every level. Groups such as the

Nursing Institute of Healthcare Design are becoming advocates for clinician involvement throughout the planning and design process.

While no substitute exists for personnel based in existing facilities and/or those who will operate the new or renovated facility being part of the planning and design process, many others are available and willing to participate. Many vendors, such as Herman Miller, employ consultants with clinical backgrounds to assist institutional clients and their planning and design teams as they grapple with reinventing care delivery processes and the impact of change on facilities. Herman Miller has also partnered with The Joint Commission to conduct educational programs for healthcare senior leadership members to understand and participate more effectively in the design process (Joint Commission Resources 2011).

The use of multidisciplinary user group teams has also become standard. Their participation can minimize the lack of comprehensive information that is needed to understand and support the complex activities occurring in today's healthcare facilities. Interviewing the department manager, respective administrator, or medical director is no longer enough to understand the scope of activity in a given area.

Even with a broad cross-departmental team, asking about what works and what does not work in existing facilities is no longer adequate. The impact of operational decisions on the long term cost of operating a facility and in providing optimum healthcare outcomes is now understood to be profound. The use of Six Sigma and Lean methodologies prior to or during programming has become essential. Understanding the ideal patient pathway, removing facility-imposed patient hand-offs, and being able to incorporate more effective processes in the planning (but not necessarily currently in use) are all becoming essential skills for today's planner.

Despite greater knowledge about how to make environments more effective in supporting care delivery, we know that such knowledge has a relatively short shelf life because of rapid advances in diagnostic and treatment methods. So the building that works perfectly today may well not be configured to provide optimum care in ten or even five years. The need to create flexible space and building systems has increased dramatically. Making use of optimum structural bay sizes and floor-to-floor dimensions allows different kinds of uses over time. Understanding potential long-term mechanical and electrical requirements—not just the lowest first cost systems—is important to avoid unintended premature building obsolescence.

Impact of Developers

This issue is becoming increasingly common as third-party developers enter the scene. Often concerned primarily with the market lease rate, developers sometimes push institutions into selecting less flexible building configurations, systems, and materials. Still perceived by the less experienced and sophisticated developers as merely being bigger MOBs, these new buildings are often just as complex as their acute care counterparts. Yet many developers persist in treating their development as simply bigger real estate and investment efforts geared solely to returning a profit to their investors. These decisions can have lasting effects on the operational efficiency of the building as well as its flexibility to adapt to changing delivery and technology needs.

CONCLUSION

More than ever, the planning, design, and construction of all healthcare capital projects requires those same levels of expertise and attention that we have come to expect in successfully creating acute care hospitals:

- The need to understand and plan in the context of the facility's or system's service areas is greater.

- The shift to population health management demands a broader perspective than mere increased utilization and market share.
- The tendency to treat ambulatory care facilities as either just bigger retail centers or MOBs can lead to major missteps in facility design and operation.

In short, every well-spent dollar used for integrated planning and programming as part of an integrated project delivery process is worth many times that in helping to produce effective healthcare environments.

Key Takeaways

- Functional and strategic planning has not always been part of our culture. Today it must serve as the basis of design.
- As a result of the ACA, with the need to be operationally efficient and still respond to limited reimbursement's impact on available capital, properly defining the project at the earliest possible time is more important than ever.
- Every party to the capital project process must understand the impacts of changed care delivery and support the goals of flexibility, sustainability, and innovation.

REFERENCES

Advisory Board Company. 2013. "Research Briefing: Three Key Elements for Successful Population Health Management." Accessed October 20, 2014. www.advisory.com/~/media/Advisory-com/Research/HCAB/Research-Study/2013/Three-Elements-for-Successful-Population-Health-Management/Three-Key-Elements-for-Successful-Population-Health-Management.pdf.

California Hospital Association. 2014. "Subacute Care." Accessed October 17. www.calhospital.org/subacute-care.

Center for Health Design (CHD). 2014. "About." Accessed October 17. www.healthdesign.org/chd/about.

Center for Healthcare Research and Transformation. 2008. "Demonstration Project: Patient Centered Medical Home Project Summary." www.bcbsm.com/pdf/PCMH_Project_Descripton.pdf.

Facility Guidelines Institute. 2014. *2014 Guidelines for Design and Construction of Hospital and Outpatient Facilities.* Accessed October 17. www.fgiguidelines.org/guidelines2014_HOP.php.

Gamble, M., and H. Punke. 2013. "ACO Manifesto: 50 Things to Know About Accountable Care Organizations." *Becker's Hospital Review.* Published September 3. www.beckershospitalreview.com/accountable-care-organizations/aco-manifesto-50-things-to-know-about-accountable-care-organizations.html.

Ginter, P. M., L. E. Swayne, and W. J. Duncan. 2002. *Strategic Management of Health Care Organizations.* Oxford, UK: Blackwell Publishing.

Hospital Consumer Assessment and Healthcare Providers and Systems (HCAHPS). n.d. "Home." Accessed October 20, 2014. www.hcahpsonline.org/home.aspx.

Institute for Healthcare Improvement. 2014. "IHI Triple Aim Initiative." Accessed October 17. www.ihi.org/Engage/Initiatives/TripleAim/pages/default.aspx.

Joint Commission Resources. 2011. "Special Report: Safe Health Design Learning Academy Pilot Program." *Environment of Care* 14 (8): 4–7.

Mott, P. D., A. T. Mott, J. M. Rudolph, E. R. Lane, and R. L. Berg. 1976. "Difficult Issues in Health Planning, Development, and Review." *American Journal of Public Health* 66 (8): 743–46.

Patient-Centered Primary Care Collaborative. 2014. "Defining the Medical Home." Accessed October 17. www.pcpcc.org/about/medical-home.

Planetree. 2014. "About Us." Accessed October 17. http://planetree.org/about-planetree/.

Schimpff, S. C. 2014. "The Role of Integrative Medicine in Primary Care." *KevinMD.com.* Published April 16. www.kevinmd.com/blog/2014/04/role-integrative-medicine-primary-care.html.

Stanton, M. W., and M. K. Rutherford. 2005. "The High Concentration of U.S. Healthcare Expenditures." Agency for Healthcare Research and Quality. *Research in Action*, Issue 19. http://archive.ahrq.gov/research/findings/factsheets/costs/expriach/expendria.pdf.

Texas Administrative Code, Title 25 Health Services, Part 1 Department of State Health Services, Chapter 131 Freestanding Emergency Medical Care Facilities.

CHAPTER 4

Portfolio and Project Management: Strategies for Accelerating the Vision of the Triple Aim and Affordable Care Act

Dawn M. Naney and Clay W. Goser

What do the pyramids built more than 4,000 years ago and a hospital built in 2014 have in common? They both were built by laying one block at a time. Why is it that productivity trends for all nonfarm industry have improved at the average rate of 3 percent per year over the past 50 years, but productivity in building construction has actually decreased 0.32 percent annually during the same period? The actual tools and technology used for building structures can't be getting worse, obviously, so other forces must be at work to retard progress in the construction sector.

Some possibilities include:

- unique work products built by varying teams, under varying site, regulatory, and weather conditions;
- a procurement system based on competitive rather than collaborative teams;

(continued)

(continued from previous page)

- poor use of data based largely on paper documents produced by a highly fragmented team; and
- an industry characterized by many small firms performing a significant percent of the work and work that is often remodeling and renovation of existing facilities as opposed to new work.

So considering all of the above, it becomes more important than ever to change the way we think about delivering building programs and projects for healthcare as well as making good use of the buildings we have. That is at the heart of this chapter, as Naney and Goser show that productivity is not limited to the physical attributes of construction, but can be achieved with the right intellectual approach to healthcare delivery and project delivery.

INTRODUCTION

We can't solve problems by using the same kind of thinking we used when we created them.

—Albert Einstein

Healthcare delivery in the United States is not plagued with a lack of talent, inadequate technology, and insufficient funding. On the contrary, the industry is one of the most advanced and lucrative in our economic system. Poor quality, waste, and skyrocketing costs are not a result of individual care givers, hospital administration, or payer organizations, nor are they a result of care practices, the built environment, or technology. Rather they are a result of a poorly coordinated system of systems, whose failures can be attributed to all of these relationships.

The Institute for Healthcare Improvement (IHI) created the Triple Aim framework for a more holistic, integrated approach to improving healthcare while reducing cost and improving the patient experience—quality and satisfaction (IHI 2014). This initiative spawned legislative action leading to the passage of the Affordable Care Act (ACA) with a similar mission of increasing access to care, maintaining or improving quality, and reducing the total cost of care. While the vision and mission have been defined, the steps to get there are not, leaving organizations and the industry to their own devices to design new strategies for delivering better care for less cost to more people.

In order to deliver on these changes, efforts to build the infrastructure to support accountable care must also be integrated to optimize the solutions. The buildings we design must be flexible and adaptable to a volatile and ever-changing healthcare landscape that will birth new developments in how care is delivered and how technology is utilized to support that care. Our medical technology must remain responsive to the ever-changing care platform that is evolving from traditional environments like hospital and outpatient care to the physician office, home, and communities in which we live. Finally, the methods by which we manifest this change, in portfolio and project management, must exhibit these same integrated and collaborative concepts.

THE HISTORY

In the 1920s, healthcare was less complicated given limited clinical and medical knowledge, with comparatively few technological advancements. As providers learned more and knowledge became specialized, care became decentralized and costs began to increase. As technology advanced, the care platform—previously the home—changed to hospitals, physician offices, and care centers, driving costs higher.

Healthcare today is a complex system of interaction between patients, providers, payers, government, and leadership. This complexity exists in different care levels and in different settings: provider office, ambulatory center, hospital, assisted living center, long-term acute hospital, even the local drug store. Each setting has a distinct reimbursement process, making the payment process complex and burdensome. Providers face unprecedented pressures while dealing with systems bureaucratically layered with government regulations and accreditation organizations, often with a variety of different motivations, legislation, and/or litigation that continually redefines the rules of engagement.

THE PROBLEM

This vague and constantly changing environment represents significant uncertainty that leads to poor coordination across the continuum of stakeholders. Since 2001, organizations have enacted many strategies to provide quality care while improving the bottom line, as evidenced by Lean and Six Sigma implementations in health systems nationwide. Organizations rushed to train front-line staff, hoping incremental improvement would result in widespread organizational success. Unfortunately, many of these efforts failed for a variety of reasons. Most lacked sustainable adoption and the ability to deliver immediate results. Organizations with incremental success stories are often perplexed by the lack of movement in key performance areas, not recognizing that the inefficiencies of some of these "improvements" in one area create new waste in others.

This fragmented and incremental approach to the improvement of healthcare, focusing on examining individual processes without understanding the interdependencies and risks to other processes, is our greatest risk to realizing truly sustainable, affordable, and accountable care. Take for example the early adopters who engaged as pioneer accountable care organizations (ACOs) to support the move from "fee for service" to "fee for value." The

ACOs learned to deliver care more efficiently, as evidenced by the Centers for Medicare and Medicaid Services (CMS) report on improvements in quality. But only a third actually lowered the cost of care (Advisory Board Company 2013). For many health systems, the greatest risk is that early efforts to reduce costs prior to effective payment reform will actually result in a significant drop in operating margins, threatening the solvency of the system (Miller 2012).

As healthcare systems mobilize to respond to this movement from volume to value and population health, we need efficient transformation methodologies that will provide sustainable changes without collapsing the economic infrastructure of healthcare. The level of collaboration needed to reengineer something as complex as healthcare requires a new approach that optimizes a system of mutually dependent parts if the challenge is to provide a quality experience for less.

THE APPLICATION OF AN OLD APPROACH: SYSTEMS THINKING

Interdependence is a fact; it's not an opinion.

—Peter Coyote

The approach to aligning and optimizing a system of systems for the provision of a nation's health requires us to think differently. Instead of focusing on how to fix individual parts, we require an informed strategy that shifts focus to how those parts interact, their cause-and-effect relationships, and the desired outcomes.

Systems thinking is a methodology designed to improve social systems, shifting the focus of analysis from each individual component to the more holistic view, while understanding the components as they relate to the entire system. The core principle behind systems thinking ensures that the component parts are transparent so that internal and external interdependencies can be explicitly understood, especially as related to behavioral shifts. This comprehensive understanding and coordinated improvement approach lays the foundation for sustainable change (Aronson 2006).

WHY SYSTEMS THINKING IS HARD

The challenge with the ACA is that it defines the vision—affordable quality care for everyone—and it defines the initial measures of success—improved quality metrics and lower cost per capita—but it doesn't come with a how-to manual. The law forces stakeholders to share accountability, forcing regions to collaborate and forcing health organizations to think of new approaches to solve this complicated puzzle.

Systems thinking is focused on alignment, transparency, and mutual benefit for all parties. This shared culture needs to exist internally in organizations as well as externally in the regional markets. Healthcare reform redefines the relationships between organizations where vague, little, or no controlling authority exists. However, the traits of systems thinking or culture are not traditionally part of the healthcare industry. Improvement in the following areas is needed to empower systems thinking:

- *Collaboration:* Currently, stakeholders are incented internally, focusing on outcomes immediately favorable to them. Future solutions will require deeper collaboration between key constituents and respect for what each stakeholder needs to ensure long-term success and viability.
- *Holistic solutions:* Recent strategies center on incremental improvements in departments, facilities, and so on. Instead, a concerted effort is required to focus on the "big rocks in the jar" first, to get the greatest rate of return and

set a solid foundation upon which smaller improvements can build.

- *Transparency:* The industry intrinsically holds data and information close to the vest for a variety of reasons, both good (HIPAA regulations) and bad (competition). Transparency is paramount in creating a safe environment that allows others to participate respectfully in designing optimal solutions and strategies.
- *Behavior:* Legacy behaviors have included tactics to avoid the risk of uncertainty. A culture that incentivizes good collaboration, holistic solutions, and transparency is imperative to alter these behaviors.

Traditionally, organizations have used varying project management techniques to produce strategic projects. However, given the interdependent changes that organizations are trying to achieve, traditional project delivery may not be an effective vehicle to achieve the sustainable solutions needed. Current project delivery methodologies fall short of producing the right projects for the limited capital organizations have to invest.

CHANGING HOW WE INTERACT IN THE SANDBOX

As the ACA is implemented, and organizations begin to learn more about what does and doesn't work, health systems will be challenged with making improvements internally and externally. Internally, value chain improvement is needed for operational sustainability. Externally, they will need regional or broader partnerships with other health systems, private health plans, and physician organizations outside their own clinically integrated networks to improve the nature of US healthcare in the larger sense. From a systems thinking approach, the most effective and efficient way to optimize the health delivery system both internally and regionally is to collectively define the most advantageous opportunities and devise the optimum solutions to meet the Triple Aim.

Many high-return ideas for improvement are likely to affect several organizational entities and/or key regional partners, requiring early input and support of likely solutions. Strategic plans for capital investments in construction, equipment, and information systems will likely be affected by the redesign of care and administrative processes. These strategic plans should inform any solutions in those investments so they in turn empower and multiply the effectiveness of alterations to care delivery.

REMOVING CONSTRAINTS TO CARE INNOVATION

Everything you see exists together in a delicate balance.

—Mufasa, *The Lion King*

Systems thinking helps consolidate the constituent parts of a system, integrating the interdependent relationships of key components. Four mutually dependent variables affect the experience, quality, and cost of care:

- Care delivery and administrative process
- Medical equipment
- Physical environment
- Information technology

How these four systems operate within the larger system of healthcare delivery becomes the cornerstone for true transformation.

The greatest opportunity for cost reduction lies in streamlining the direct provision of services (manpower and logistics). Capital investments in support structures innovatively designed and adaptable will enable quicker improvements to care practices. The ability to deliver on the Triple Aim will be a direct result of organizations' ability to design care that is delivered in the most effective and efficient environments available. Care platforms, traditionally defined as hospitals and physician offices, are already morphing into our homes, offices, schools, and even local retail.

A think tank called LongWave Group was assembled in 2010 with a mission to remove the constraints and reimagine healthcare. The LongWave concept included the notion of a "dumb room" with a "smart" bed that is self-contained with all the interoperable care components needed to provide care to a patient (LongWave Group 2010).

The resulting patient room is flexible, accommodating low acuity to ICU patients with power, oxygen, nitrogen, and suction as portable parts of the bed. Standardized connections (consider the USB port as an example) for medical equipment and modular components allow change in support components when moving or transporting patients. Current technology can already gather biometric, charting, and other critical data and wirelessly feed that information to a central repository to provide in the moment predictive and prescriptive metrics. Imagine the difference such capability would have made in Joplin, Missouri, in 2011 to the five ICU patients killed after they were disconnected from their life support following the seventh deadliest tornado in recorded history.

Moving regionally from volume to value in partially and fully capitated reimbursement models will drive shared accountability and collaboration. Care providers will need to find commonality among their routine and nonstrategic management practices, taking advantage of economies of scale and economic buying power. For example, standardizing how organizations collect and share cost data for design and construction projects could support better business case development. Such decisions would be informed by more accurate conceptual estimates and economic buying power, similar to the concept of group purchasing organizations.

Applying systems thinking to healthcare delivery requires deep collaboration, a holistic approach to improvement, transparency, and changes in legacy behavior. This involves new facilitation and management methodologies. Applying the same concepts of systems thinking to strategic portfolio and project management, we create a different environment that picks the right projects at the right time, designs effective solutions, and implements those solutions as efficiently as possible.

The alignment of the business models, creation of the systems and structures needed to empower accountable care, and the cultural shift from volume to value will all succeed or fail on tactical project deployment. The way we use portfolio and project management to implement strategy will set the foundation for a successful transformation during a time of cultural change and operational uncertainty.

TRADITIONAL PORTFOLIO AND PROJECT MANAGEMENT

Management by objectives works if you first think through your objectives. Ninety percent of the time you haven't.

—Peter Drucker

Project management is "the application of knowledge, skills and techniques to meet the project requirements" (PMI 2013). Much like healthcare reform, the Project Management Institute's (PMI) *Project Management Book of Knowledge* (PMBOK) doesn't come with a how-to manual but a set of management methodologies proven to deliver projects successfully, with success being defined as on time and on budget.

Portfolio management is the adaptation of project management methodologies to the aggregate delivery of a portfolio of work.

Good portfolio management structures build outcome and performance metrics, informing future process improvements and project design and implementation. The same project management concepts of managing scope, schedule, cost, resources, quality, and risk can be applied to portfolios of work to ensure efficient and effective aggregate project delivery (PMI 2013)

While the definitions sound inviting, the reality is that the implementation of good project and portfolio management varies widely within and across organizations. Organizations often manage portfolios of projects as independent efforts with separate capital buckets of construction, information technology, equipment procurement, and operational excellence.

CHALLENGES

Some of the same challenges encountered in healthcare delivery plague project and portfolio management as well. For instance, in current practice, architects have approached the design of new and renovated space based on current department business practices or popular trends in healthcare. Given the time it takes to complete construction, these spaces are often obsolete before the space is occupied.

With the introduction of accountable care, the rate at which care processes will change in response to new population health management techniques will grow exponentially. This shift requires future designs to be more adaptive to change to avoid constraining innovation. As patient census shifts from the hospital to other care platforms (physician offices, in-home care, specialty centers), we must consider organic flexibility to allow future repurposing.

According to a study commissioned by the National Academy of Sciences in 2008, several variables are responsible for the decline in national construction productivity, rendering current practices unsustainable and a threat to our future national infrastructure investment. Cited are segmented processes from project conception through life-cycle operation, adversarial relationships between project stakeholders, lack of coordinated industry efforts to improve construction efficiency, and lack of effective performance metrics as key reasons productivity continues to suffer in construction projects (National Research Council 2008).

The maturity of portfolio and project management skills vary from organization to organization, as does the value. Organizations often feel project management is too bureaucratic, slowing down activity and creating busy work. In healthcare this mentality is most prevalent. Planning doesn't always feel good to those who are not used to planning. Instead they are masters of triaging, providing care in the moment and applying course corrections as they learn more information.

STRATEGIC PORTFOLIO MANAGEMENT

Management is doing things right, leadership is doing the right things.

—Peter Drucker

Given that 44 percent of strategic initiatives fail (Economist Intelligence Unit 2013), change is needed in the management of portfolios to ensure strategy realization. These changes should follow the same principles of systems thinking: address the need for deep collaboration, empower holistic solutions, create transparency, and reward the right behaviors.

Gartner, Inc. (2014), one of the world's leading information technology research and advisory companies, predicts that the largest global organizations will rely on enterprise project management office (EPMO) leaders to cut across silos and connect strategy to program execution. This concept has started to take root. PMI's *Pulse of the Profession* reported losses of $120 million per every $1 billion spent on programs and projects and a $135 million loss in 2013. The analysis provided by PMI indicates that the decrease in 2014 to $100 million is due to a refocus of the role of the project management office (PMO) to better align the services provided to the strategic goals for the organization (PMI 2014).

The role of an EPMO focuses on three key concepts. The first is creating a solid organizational structure and governance with the right stakeholders present at the table, ensuring a solid connection to the organizational strategy.

The second is the planning and management of the people who are needed to implement the strategy. This includes balancing the portfolio to ensure a respectful use of resources positioned to deliver with a predictable velocity. Often healthcare organizations have a large appetite for change. They start concurrent initiatives involving their most valuable staff, whose duties are now divided among patient care, administration, and an unsustainable project workload. This situation often results in project delays and failures. It is better to focus teams on a few top priority initiatives, ensuring increased speed of quality improvements instead of unmanageable workloads and marginal outcomes.

The final focus should be on establishing process and outcome metrics in portfolio and project management.

COLLABORATIVE PROJECT MANAGEMENT

Using a solid portfolio management strategy positions projects to succeed, ensuring that we are building the right project at the right time with the right resources. Continuing the application of systems theory—ensuring that *how* we deliver is as effective as *what* we deliver—is the next evolution in project management.

A key failure in current project management practices is the lack of time spent on understanding not just the "what" of the projects we implement, but the more important "why and when." The why and when questions shape all conversations going forward. Aligning the team around the project objectives helps generate the right discussions during project development. Context and systems thinking are key. Teams aligned around why and when are better positioned to make the best choices during the design and implementation.

Once aligned around the project goals and objectives, collaborative project management then focuses on ensuring everybody wins. Teams are often mobilized quickly and expected to perform immediately without the benefit of understanding the commitment to the team and the group norms. Skipping this step often results in the degradation of team performance when challenges arise that put the key stakeholders at odds. Hidden agendas, past experiences, and preconceptions can pit team members against each other, especially as issues expand outside their own internal organizations.

For example, in capital construction, teams are often formed and reformed throughout different stages of the project. During conceptual development, the architect is hired and develops a relationship with the owner to determine what the owner wants. Together they begin to design the project and establish the game rules of how they will interact and govern project decisions. In schematic design, the construction manager is often introduced. A new dynamic is created, redefining channels of communication and where scopes of service start and end. At bid time, myriad additional trade contractors—each with their own interpretations of scope, processes, and procedures for implementing work—are introduced. Throughout the process, the rules of engagement are continually evolving as each participant frames how he or she will interact with others and what is needed to win as an individual. Often projects start at odds with the owner wanting to pay the least amount possible while the architect, construction manager, and trades are trying to maximize their bottom lines.

Organizing the project team to succeed is a critical first step. This new organizational structure must focus on the information needed to deliver both on the project success and team satisfaction and includes understanding and incentivizing the right behaviors to get people to participate differently. The structure must ensure that participants are provided opportunity for mutual benefit, with each member identifying activities that threaten to harm the others as the project progresses and ensuring they keep that from happening. As Robert Fulghum (1989) wrote in his book, *All I Really Need to Know I Learned in Kindergarten*, sometimes the team needs to remember, "When you go out into the world, watch out for traffic, hold hands and stick together."

This ideology doesn't change based on the type of project being implemented. A variety of stakeholders are being asked to come together to share risk and reward. They are being asked to design the operating agreements that govern how they will interact and participate.

The second most important condition that defines collaborative project management is applying methodologies that align project solutions with the capital available to spend.

The adoption of techniques designed to reduce waste, improve quality, and accelerate velocity are part of the collaborative project manager's strategy and toolkit to identify root causes. Lean methodologies to reduce waste, the adoption of Six Sigma to find opportunities for improving quality, and agile methodologies to ensure phased delivery of value, when applied appropriately, not only allow teams to deliver on-time and on-budget but often to deliver the best value for the right program.

The third imperative for delivering collaborative project management is using transparency to empower teams and inspire improvements through active learning. According to the old adage, "That which is measured is done." A collaborative project manager focuses on increasing performance by making team members accountable for their commitments. Using predictive project metrics throughout the management lifecycle can focus the team on processes to build trust, identify waste, and recognize potential opportunities and risk early in the management lifecycle.

Take for instance the Last Planner System, developed by Gregory Howell and Glenn Ballard of the Lean Construction Institute (n.d.). A key component of their system is to ensure predictability in the schedule by monitoring the critical commitments kept by the team. This simple adaptation of tracking plan completion demonstrates the variance, thus the predictability, of the plan. This metric can be an effective team motivator and accountability tool, providing transparency into the bottlenecks encountered during implementation. If implemented properly and not punitively, it becomes a positive motivation for others to see that partners can be trusted to deliver what they promised.

The final key component to collaborative project delivery is using change leadership theory. Studies of organizational change have shown that the extent of interdependent relationships existing in systems dictates the level of difficulty of implementing and adopting change (e.g., Kotter 1996).

Leaders must develop clear, coordinated, and sustainable strategies for change leadership. Acceptance of new models requires influential leaders to champion the development of clear and well-aligned visions that both internal and external stakeholders support. It requires a transition roadmap that is respectful of the speed at which new social groups are prepared to change and thoughtful consideration of how the portfolios are organized to deliver on the strategy. Aligned coalitions designed to breed and reward the right behaviors are needed to ensure continued growth of sustainable systems and structures (Kotter 1996).

Deliberate change leadership is the single most important characteristic to empowering the adoption of systems thinking approaches to a new healthcare vision both within organizations and within the regions in which they collaborate. It is a key responsibility of strategic portfolio management and collaborative project management. This long-term endeavor must be constant and orchestrated, teaching organizations to crawl and walk before running. It must move at a pace that stakeholders can accept, increasing the speed as they achieve success.

CONCLUSION

> *Successful reform is not an event. It is a sustainable process that will build on its own successes—a virtuous cycle of change.*
>
> —Abdullah II of Jordan

The vision of the IHI Triple Aim and the ACA to deliver affordable, effective, and responsive healthcare is achieved by applying a systems thinking perspective. This approach applies to how we treat performance improvement in both the solutions we design and how we deliver them. Applying a more strategic and comprehensive approach to how we manage portfolios and projects promotes collaboration, holistic solutions, transparency, and the behaviors needed to support this new business model. The results will enhance our ability to deliver on the strategies designed to support a migration from volume to value.

Organizations will be able to select the right projects, implement them as efficiently and effectively as possible while conserving valuable resources. These techniques should be applied at all levels of healthcare delivery, from hospitals to provider organizations to regional collaboratives, challenged with working together to enhance the experience and outcomes of every patient. This is true healthcare reform, not just focused on payment reform but also on the optimization of the entire system, which eventually improves the entire industry and achieves the vision and spirit of the Triple Aim and ACA.

Key Takeaways

- The Triple Aim initiative (better care for individuals, better health for populations, and lower healthcare cost) led to the ACA.
- An integrated approach (collaboration) is required to address the complexity of delivery of both implementing the Triple Aim and capital portfolios and projects.
- Systems thinking (a methodology of understanding components as they relate to the entire system) is needed to change the dynamics of delivery of capital portfolio and project delivery.
- The design team has an obligation to design to the future (skate to where the puck is going to be, not where it is) and this requires the deliberate design of nimble strategies.
- Portfolio management is the adaptation of project management methodologies to the aggregate delivery of a portfolio of projects.
- To create projects truly in the spirit of the IHI and the ACA, systems thinking must be applied to the technology and clinical activity of care delivery as well as to the delivery of projects.

REFERENCES

Advisory Board Company. 2013. "Nine ACOs Are Leaving the Pioneer Program." *The Daily Briefing*. Published July 16. www.advisory.com/Daily-Briefing/2013/07/16/Nine-ACOs-are-leaving-the-Pioneer-program.

Aronson, D. 2006. "Overview of Systems Thinking." *The Thinking Page*. Accessed October 21, 2014. www.thinking.net/Systems_Thinking/OverviewSTarticle.pdf.

Economist Intelligence Unit. 2013. "Why Good Strategies Fail: Lessons for the C-Suite." Accessed October 21, 2014. www.pmi.org/~/media/PDF/Publications/WhyGoodStrategiesFail_Report_EIU_PMI.ashx.

Fulghum, R. 1989. *All I Really Need to Know I Learned in Kindergarten.* New York: Ivy Books.

Gartner. 2014. "Gartner Says PPM Leaders Must Prepare for Extreme Transformation or Prepare New Resumes." Published April 15. www.gartner.com/newsroom/id/2709317.

Institute for Healthcare Improvement (IHI). 2014. "Triple Aim for Populations." Accessed October 21. www.ihi.org/Topics/TripleAim/Pages/default.aspx.

Kotter, J. P. 1996. *Leading Change.* Boston: Harvard Business Review Press.

Lean Construction Institute. n.d. "The Last Planner." Accessed October 23, 2014. www.leanconstruction.org/training/the-last-planner/.

LongWave Group. 2010. "The Search for Effective Healthcare—Care Studio Exhibit." Healthcare Facilities Symposium and Expo. Chicago, September 14–16.

Miller, H. D. 2012. "Ten Barriers to Healthcare Payment Reform and How to Overcome Them." Center for Healthcare Quality and Payment Reform. Accessed October 21, 2014. www.chqpr.org/downloads/OvercomingBarrierstoPaymentReform.pdf.

National Research Council. 2008. *Advancing the Competitiveness and Efficiency of the U.S. Construction Industry.* Washington, DC: National Academies Press.

Project Management Institute (PMI). 2014. *Pulse of the Profession In-Depth Report: The High Cost of Low Performance.* Newtown Square, PA: PMI.

———. 2013. *A Guide to the Project Management Body of Knowledge (PMBOK).* Newtown Square, PA: PMI.

CHAPTER 5

Finance: At the Center of Everything

Robert D. Levine

In any business, financing is at the center of everything. We're told that 90 percent of new businesses fail within their first year. That's not because they don't know what they're doing; it's because of inadequate cash flow. Healthcare has two major headwinds that are unique. One is that its normal margins are low, averaging only 2 to 3 percent net profit each year. The second is that because of heavy regulation, its ability to increase that profit margin is capped, leaving little room for mistakes or downturns.

Each time major healthcare legislation has passed, profits have plunged. Hospital profits peaked at 6 percent prior to Medicare, then dropped to 2 percent five years later. Profits recovered back to 6 percent by the 1980s, and then dropped to 2 percent after diagnosis-related groups were enacted in 1985. Profits once again recovered to the 6 percent area, and are now heading back down after enactment of the Affordable Care Act (ACA).

(continued)

(continued from previous page)

So the combination of the critical need for positive cash flow and heavy regulation have forced constant change in the way we address the financial challenges in the healthcare industry. This chapter looks at current thinking and lays out a good road map for where the industry is going regarding the need for consolidation and privatization of funding.

We at Chrysler borrow money the old-fashioned way. We pay it back.

—Lee Iacocca

NOT THAT LONG ago—starting in the late 1990s and lasting about ten years—healthcare capital development experienced one of its strongest periods in modern history. According to McGraw Hill (2007), new construction for hospitals was $22 billion per year in 1998, and it topped out at $28 billion per year in 2008. New hospitals were going up in the suburbs to meet the demands of the suburban sprawl started during the 1980s and 1990s, and existing hospitals were replacing themselves with new facilities, rather than trying to renovate a 40-year-old hospital in place while still delivering healthcare. In 2007 McGraw Hill was projecting that healthcare capital development would top $35 billion per year by 2012.

Just as we experienced in the housing market during that time, many hospitals were financing their projects with short-term variable rate bonds, some as short as turning over weekly, to take advantage of the lower rates. All of that changed, of course, with the financial crisis in 2008: the variable rate market froze, and those bonds didn't roll over as anticipated. Additionally, the banks providing letters of credit to support those bonds dropped out of the market. Hospitals that could refinance were forced into fixed-rate, longer-term, 30-year bonds. The resulting debt service for the new, higher interest rate bonds became a financial hardship for those hospitals.

That was the backdrop when in 2010, the Affordable Care Act (ACA) became law. The ACA, along with the stress in the economy caused by the financial crisis, created strong underlying trends affecting healthcare finance. As a result, pressures on profitability and demand for capital are driving health systems to explore other strategies, such as monetization (for existing) and developer selection (for new) nonhospital healthcare real estate assets. These trends are leading hospitals and healthcare systems, both large and small, rated and unrated, to explore alternative ways to access capital and fund new projects.

WHERE ARE WE TODAY?

The financing landscape had already begun to change by the time the ACA was enacted. With the law and the economic backdrop that existed, several key trends developed:

- The ACA is creating uncertainty as the law is unfinished and is a moving target.
- Major margin compression is occurring due to economic shifts, primarily unemployment levels.
- Philanthropy is decreasing due to donor investment losses (and lower returns on investment because of lower interest rates).
- Hospitals and health systems have an ongoing need to fund deferred capital improvements.
- Investment portfolios have changed due to market fluctuations and abnormally low interest rate returns.

- Reimbursements have declined because of recent (and probably ongoing) federal budget cuts.
- Ongoing and unprecedented industry consolidation has focused on operating efficiencies.
- Investors are making more conservative investment decisions.
- Ongoing exploration of physician alignment and integration is leading to more practice acquisitions.
- Challenges to nonprofit tax-exempt status and credit rating downgrades are invariably increasing costs and decreasing the availability of capital.

This scene is quite different from that of ten years ago and requires new delivery models for financing.

NEW DELIVERY MODELS

Economic changes as a result of the financial crises and the dramatic impact of the ACA are forcing providers to move to new delivery models that can help create new revenue streams. It's now necessary for all providers to determine the appropriate strategy. Preventive care (keeping people out of the hospital) is a major component of reform. That's driving new ventures between for-profits and not-for-profits as well as with developers. And it's creating new funding sources that specialize in nonhospital buildings, such as ambulatory care centers, medical office buildings, and specialty clinics.

The landscape for financing capital development projects has clearly changed. Health systems are moving as much as possible out of the expensive environment of a hospital campus into less capital- and code-intensive nonhospital buildings. As a result, although looking at financing traditional hospital capital projects is important, it's even more important to look at the nonhospital buildings, as their needs and solutions are dramatically different.

HOSPITAL BUILDINGS

Normally, the financing of not-for-profit (NFP) hospital work has been achieved either through capital generated from operational cash flow or from the capital markets through the issuance of tax-exempt revenue bonds (Dohrmann 2013b). Notwithstanding the pressures mentioned above, since the financial crises began, hospitals are generally starting to improve their financial status. Some hospitals have been upgraded by Standard and Poor's, fewer hospitals are being downgraded, and the majority of hospitals are being affirmed (i.e., no change in rating). There are fewer negative outlooks: hospitals have stabilized their cash, have improved their liquidity, and have less debt. So the capital markets are starting to become available for their hospital building development work.

Most hospitals have undergone cost-cutting programs with more conservative policies, and they've worked hard at improving quality. Commercial paper, long a staple for short-term funding for hospital operations, is once again becoming available without the need for credit enhancement (letters of credit). Bank direct loans that are nonamortizing (both fixed and adjustable) are also now becoming available again. And with cash flows increasing, self-funding is once again becoming available for larger systems.

Larger is the operative word; since 2010 hospitals and health systems have dramatically increased their merger, acquisition, and expansion strategies, both to expand their delivery platforms and to combine and build new facilities. The creation of bigger platforms has, in some cases, been slowed by fear of credit downgrades because of impacts on the balance sheet of the combined and obligated group. To avoid an impact on credit, a wide variety of alternatives have been used to finance both the acquisitions and construction of satellite hospital facilities. For example, NFP consolidations are most often structured either as a joint venture, a noncash merger, or a transfer of sponsorship, all so as not to affect credit. As an alternative to a sale or complete change of control, joint ventures between NFP and for-profit (FP) organizations have also been utilized.

Traditionally, tax-exempt bonds have been issued through taxing authorities, which vary by state. Many hospitals use the federal programs (such as the Federal Housing Authority, or FHA) to guarantee and enhance their credit ratings.

FEDERAL HOUSING AUTHORITY PROGRAMS

A February 4, 2013, announcement from the Department of Housing and Urban Development (HUD) formalized new rules for acquisition, construction, and refinancing as an alternative source of funding (Dohrmann 2013a). Effective March 7, 2013, acquisition or refinancing of an existing hospital, not already insured by FHA, is now allowed. Limited construction or renovation is also permitted, providing the costs are less than 20 percent of the loan amount. This new program was streamlined to improve access to capital on a nonrecourse basis for both acquisitions and refinancing.

A wide variety of projects qualify, but capital can only be used for a licensed acute care hospital under the program. Ownership of the project can be an NFP, an FP, or a governmental entity (public). There's no maximum loan amount, but no cash-out (100 percent refinancing) is permitted. Also, refinancing transactions can't exceed the cost to refinance existing indebtedness (loan payoff amount plus transaction costs).

Under this program, acquisition transactions can't exceed the cost to acquire the hospital (purchase price including land and improvements). The term is for a 25-year, self-amortizing permanent loan, nonrecourse and assumable, but with FHA approval.

Several FHA programs can be used, but the two most prevalent are the FHA Section 223f and the FHA 242 programs.

FHA 223f

This program is generally used for refinancing. After a preliminary review and preapplication meeting, the lender prepares and submits the application, HUD reviews it and underwrites the application, and then HUD issues the mortgage insurance commitment, followed by the closing and funding. Depending on the credit strength and complexity of the transaction, this funding can be completed in six months. Today, most FHA-insured hospital projects are funded with the Government National Mortgage Association (GNMA) mortgage-backed securities, in order to achieve low interest rates (currently in the mid-3 percent range) with a 25-year amortization.

Since the effective date of March 7, 2013, loans to finance new construction, expansion, modernization, equipment, as well as refinancing of existing debt, are included in the FHA 242 mortgage insurance program.

FHA 242

To be in this program, the facility must be an acute care hospital with no construction already in process. There's no maximum loan amount, but there is a maximum of 90 percent loan-to-value (90 percent of estimated replacement cost of the hospital project); the required 10 percent equity can be in the form of land. An existing organization must have an aggregate debt service coverage ratio greater than 1.25 × operations and an aggregate operating margin greater than zero (meaning showing a profit) for each of the past three fiscal years. So qualifying is far from a slam dunk. Ownership of the project can be an NFP, an FP, or a governmental entity (public). The term is a 25-year, self-amortizing permanent loan, nonrecourse and assumable with FHA approval.

As with all FHA programs, a certificate of need must be issued or pending for the hospital project if it is required by the state. Davis-Bacon prevailing wage requirements apply to all construction contracts. Upon commencement of amortization, a mortgage reserve fund is created and funded over a ten-year period in an amount equal to two years' annual payment on the loan. Because of the nature of new construction, the process time from application to closing and funding is approximately nine months in today's markets. Today, most FHA 242–insured hospital projects are also funded with the GNMA mortgage-backed securities to achieve low interest rates (currently in the mid-3 percent range, as stated earlier) with the 25-year amortization.

NONHOSPITAL BUILDINGS

As mentioned previously, because of the lower reimbursements caused by the ACA, hospitals are moving lower-acuity services out of the hospital setting and into the noncore buildings (Beebe 2012). These noncore buildings (specialty clinics, ambulatory care centers, and medical office buildings) are conducive to both monetization as well as third party financing.

Importance of Cash

In the current market environment, rating agencies pay particular attention to liquidity (such as days cash on hand) when underwriting hospital or healthcare system credit. As such, cash should be viewed as the "option of last resort" when funding large investments: don't spend it if you don't have to.

Internal Financing

Before even thinking of using internal financing, consider these three things:

1. *Return on investment.* This is dependent on investment market conditions, it's an important source of cash flow in lean years, and it's typically considered supplemental funding.
2. *Operating cash flow.* This normally results in an uncertain annual amount, it's insufficient for large projects, and it has significant government influence (reimbursement rates, mandates, and so on).
3. *Cash and investments.* Both are important for bond ratings, they are insufficient for large projects, they are typically considered supplemental funding, and they have a high imputed cost (return on cash, impact on debt capacity and rating, and future flexibility).

So internal financing, except for smaller projects, is never suggested as the way to go. Internal financing might make sense for small, ongoing capital projects, but it is never appropriate for larger projects, and it rarely makes sense for anything over just a few million dollars.

Third-Party Financing

Before considering third-party financing, examine these three important factors:

1. *Philanthropy.* This source of funding is high profile and the least expensive, but it requires a long lead time.

2. *Tax-exempt bond financing.* Obviously, tax-exempt status is required. It's very much liquidity driven by market demand, which can vary; it is normally inexpensive; it has a longer lead time; and it requires economies of scale. This type of financing is mostly used to refinance existing debt or for capital projects.
3. *Real estate capital markets.* This method can be used for taxable and tax-exempt projects; there are both debt and monetization options; and there can be various structures to meet specific goals: to gain liquidity (cash), to maintain (and enhance) debt capacity, and to minimize capital commitments.

COST OF CAPITAL

Hospital and health systems have access to various options to finance both operating and capital needs (Beebe 2012). Each has distinct actual and imputed cost of capital. While specific options may be the least expensive, they may be limited in availability or inappropriate for certain uses.

With more than $2 billion expected in sales in 2014, healthcare real estate monetization has clearly become a factor (Beebe 2012). Today, health systems can choose from the many favorable ownership structures that have evolved over the past ten years. Current structures allow a system to sell assets to third parties and still maintain significant control as well as protect and strengthen relationships with physicians and patients.

Monetization

For the purpose of this discussion, we define monetization of real estate assets as the conversion of that real estate to money. It could either be done as an outright sale, with no further intent to use that property, or a sale/leaseback, with the intent to continue use, but as a lessee and not an owner. (In pure economic terms, monetization means conversion of debt to equity, but we're not concerned with that here.)

Not all real estate assets are appropriate for monetization. While medical office buildings (MOBs) have been the primary focus of monetization activities, volume is also relatively strong in the monetization of other outpatient and clinically related buildings. Other assets that should be considered for monetization include ambulatory surgical centers (ASCs) and specialty centers. These asset types have attracted significant interest in the real estate investment community over the last few years. Properties types such as parking garages, dormitories, commercial buildings, and excess land also represent monetization opportunities.

1. *Medical office buildings.* Of the three assets, MOBs are the largest in square footage and overall value in the transactions completed annually. The strongest demand used to be for on-campus buildings with some space, typically around 20 percent, leased back to the system. Off-campus buildings tended to attract interest from more entrepreneurial investors. That's changed, however. As a result of the ACA, with more physicians integrating into the hospital systems, the potential for retaining tax-exempt status for the entire building is growing. The average income capitalization rate (cap rate) spread for a comparable building on-campus versus off-campus is between 80 and 150 basis points, meaning that, in comparable situations, an on-campus asset will have a lower cap rate and a higher value.

   For both on- and off-campus buildings, investors are focused on both existing and new development projects. In fact, many owner-operators of MOBs have development subsidiaries that source potential acquisitions. On-campus transactions are typically structured with a ground lease providing the system with certain ongoing control provisions, while off-campus transactions are typically fee simple transactions (land is sold along with the building).

2. *Ambulatory surgical centers.* The last ten years have seen a shift toward less invasive surgery and improvements in anesthesia and technology. As a result, procedures performed in surgical centers, as opposed to hospitals, have dramatically increased. At community hospitals, total outpatient visits have also increased, from approximately 400 million in 1996 to approximately 760 million visits in 2014 (HHS National Center for Health Statistics 2013, 1996). While less than 4 percent of health systems currently have freestanding centers on their campuses, we anticipate that the substantial increase in outpatient procedures will lead to more ASC development on hospital campuses around the country. Using a third-party developer–owner structure can be an effective tool to monetize existing facilities and finance the development of new facilities.
3. *Clinics.* Health systems and physician groups typically use clinics to build or strengthen relationships with providers and to increase market share in a community. Clinics are typically 95 to 100 percent leased to a single user and are located in highly desirable retail or office areas on main corridors or in prominent medical office parks. Similar to ASCs, a developer–owner structure can be an effective tool to monetize existing facilities and finance the development of new facilities. It's important to note that current monetization structures, which will be discussed in further detail, enable health systems to monetize the cash value of

the noncore real estate assets—such as MOBs, ASCs, and clinics—and still maintain ownership-like controls over the properties.

Sean Moghavem (2014), president of the Archway Company of Los Angeles, specializes in the repurposing of existing buildings. According to him, "Buying distressed properties and then creating contiguous space, in a building that is three to four miles away from the hospital allows for a newer version of the hub and spoke concept."

Issues

When reviewing potential assets for monetization or third-party development-ownership, identifying issues that can both unfavorably and favorably affect value is important. Condo provisions, bond covenants, deferred maintenance, insufficient parking, environmental services, shared services, and tenant and occupancy issues can add complexities to a transaction. These complexities don't rule out a transaction, but they will often require creative structuring. Identifying potential issues up front will provide for a smoother transaction.

Financial

A review of the potential financial benefits of monetization focuses on four concepts: capital allocation, average cost of capital, debt capacity, and future required capital expenditures for real estate assets (Shattuck Hammond Partners 2005).

1. *Capital allocation.* Through ownership of nonhospital real estate, a health system has allocated cash, always a scarce

resource, to the real estate business and away from the healthcare business. By owning MOBs, ASCs, and clinics, many systems miss economic opportunities to allocate cash to projects that will:

- increase income,
- build physician loyalty,
- increase market share,
- ensure a first-rate reputation, and
- enhance patient satisfaction.

2. *Cost of capital.* Do the returns of the nonhospital real estate assets exceed the system's weighted average cost of capital (WACC)? The average cost of capital for the publicly traded FP hospital management companies, in many cases the competitors of nonprofit providers, is around 2.2 percent. The average return for most nonhospital real estate is around 8 percent. However, since many health systems tend to overimprove their MOBs and other real estate, the average return can be 50 to 100 basis points lower. Given this disparity between real estate returns and the WACC of most health systems, monetization of these assets or allowing a third party to develop and own new projects generally makes financial sense.
3. *Debt capacity.* Nonhospital real estate can carry a fair amount of debt, typically between 50 and 75 percent of the building's value. This debt can have a meaningful impact on a system's balance sheet. Through monetization or by using a private developer to fund new projects, a system can reduce its overall debt, potentially resulting in an enhanced credit rating and with a subsequent ability to borrow at more attractive rates.

   In addition, monetization and third-party development will result in additional debt capacity, which will allow a system to fund its core healthcare mission and strengthen its market position.

4. *Future capital requirements.* MOBs, ASCs, and clinics all require capital expenditures as the buildings age for items such as new roofs, common areas, and mechanical systems. In addition, when a given tenant's lease expires, the improvements necessary to make the space rentable for a new physician practice or service can cost between $30 and $50 per square foot. Along with general maintenance items, the capital requirements of real estate ownership create a sizeable ongoing liability for many systems. Monetization or third-party development–ownership of the nonhospital real estate will dramatically reduce this deferred or future liability.

Health systems that have successfully monetized or used third parties to develop or own part or all of their real estate portfolio have typically been successful systems with

- Investment-grade credit ratings (BBB or higher),
- strong market share,
- nationally and regionally recognized departments, and
- desirable demographics.

From the perspective of a third-party investor, acquiring a system's real estate or developing a new project for a system, even if completely occupied by third-party tenants, is effectively "going long" on that system's credit. As a result, investors focus heavily on the system's balance sheet, credit and historical performance, market share, and growth potential.

While some strong systems have analyzed their portfolios and capitalized on their saleable assets, others have opted to hold on to their portfolios because no capital pressures exist. The cash dilemma is an important issue to consider. Health systems can receive maximum value for their portfolios when they are financially stable because real estate investors are willing to pay a high price to establish a relationship with a financially strong partner.

When liquidity pressures exist, they will, at best, receive suboptimal prices, and at worst, they will be unable to monetize their properties. As a result, high levels of solvency should not be considered as a reason to be fixed. While there are concerns, issues, and long-term goals that need to be addressed prior to any real estate transaction, having a specific designation for the capital that would be derived from a monetization is not necessary.

The two general monetization and development options—joint ventures and third-party ownership—need to be coupled with various control mechanisms and system space leases for a health system to achieve its ongoing control and occupancy goals. In either case, the system will be able to monetize the asset while maintaining the asset's strategic value.

WHEN TO MONETIZE

An analysis of when an asset should be monetized must consider both macro and micro factors (Shattuck Hammond Partners 2005). Macro factors include general market conditions and investor appetite. Micro factors include both asset-specific issues and health system issues. It is important to identify and analyze both, striking a balance between them to achieve optimum pricing.

Macro Factors

The two primary macro factors to be considered are market conditions and investor appetite. Macro market conditions for real estate are driven by cost and availability of capital. Specifically, interest rates and required equity yields determine the strength of the real estate market.

Interest rates. Since 2010, the interest rate environment has been favorable. In addition, lending sources have gained comfort with lending to healthcare real estate, resulting in loan-to-value (LTV) rates as high as 85 percent. The combination of low interest rates and high LTVs, along with a high demand by investors and a limited supply, has contributed to the superior pricing achieved in the market place. While increases in federal fund rates in the past have resulted in a corresponding increase in short-term interest rates, intermediary and long-term rates have remained stable or decreased slightly.

Required equity yields. Pension funds, high-net-worth individuals, and endowments are typically the groups that determine required equity yields for real estate, in conjunction with expected returns across other asset classes. Given expected returns in the equity market hovering around 8 percent and the declining enthusiasm for hedge funds, we expect target internal rates of return for healthcare real estate to remain in the low teens.

Investor appetite. Institutional money allocated to real estate has grown dramatically over the last few years. This growth can be attributed to volatile equity markets and strong real estate fundamentals. Healthcare real estate has benefited from this increase resulting in new entrants and existing investors with substantially deeper pockets.

While pension funds, high-net-worth individuals, and endowments continually modify their asset allocations, it appears that real estate and healthcare real estate allocations will remain high. Coupling low interest rates and lower required equity yields should result in continued favorable macro conditions for the foreseeable future.

Micro Factors

Building-Specific Issues

Typically, an asset with strong net operating income (NOI) is a good candidate for monetization. However, in-place NOI is only a small part of the analysis. The following building specific issues must also be considered to determine appropriate timing for monetization:

1. *Occupancy.* To achieve optimum pricing, any vacancies should be positioned as an upside opportunity for a potential investor. To do that, demand for space must be demonstrated. Buildings do not need to be 100 percent occupied to qualify for monetization. However, the potential for lease up must exist when the system is willing to take responsibility for vacancies.
2. *Lease rollover.* If the asset has a sizeable lease expiring in the short term, it may be best to determine the tenant's plans prior to monetization. If the tenant can commit to renewing, added security will be provided to the cash flow. If the tenant vacates the space, significant upside opportunity exists. Each scenario appeals to a different investor type and would require a different monetization strategy.
3. *Capital needs.* If the asset has deferred maintenance issues, it is best to quantify the dollar amount prior to monetization. Disclosing these issues prior to buyer due diligence will help ensure a smooth closing, avoiding any potential retrading.

Health System–Specific Issues

Potential balance sheet and bond covenant issues must be considered when evaluating an asset's potential monetization. Specifically, a system should evaluate any bond covenants that may encumber the asset. In addition, net book value and the resulting gain or loss on the sale should be calculated. These internal issues need to be identified and quantified to ensure board support for monetization. Conversely, the positive impact real estate monetization can have on a system's balance sheet should also be quantified. Real estate monetization could positively impact:

- days cash on hand;
- long-term debt to capitalization ratio;
- earnings before interest, taxes, depreciation, and amortization; and
- total revenue and debt service coverage ratios.

Quantifying the positive impact on these ratios is also crucial to ensuring board support.

Another perspective of development came from Clayton Corwin, managing principal of Stonecreek Company, Rancho Santa Margarita, California. Corwin (2014) said, "We are now seeing a disruptive retail model, meaning we must build for the consumer of healthcare, and, like retail, they want convenience and quality. We must drive customer loyalty. Medical systems are trying to build a brand, just like retail. It used to be that a patient went to the hospital that their doctor sent them to. Yes, a patient needs to go where their doctor sends them, but with the advent of ACA, and the lessening of healthcare through employment (that's going away), the patient (and their satisfaction) will have more of a say where they go. They can choose doctors that are in the systems they want, that use the hospitals that they want." A major change in thinking. Per Corwin, "Navigating the conflict between an unsustainable cost curve and growing demand, while changing delivery methods to meet that demand and its changing needs is a huge challenge."

CONCLUSION

As we've discussed, healthcare systems can greatly benefit from monetizing nonhospital real estate assets through a variety of transaction structures that are specifically designed to maintain needed controls, while at the same time allowing the trapped cash to be extracted for investment in the system's hospital operations or to improve its financial position.

While conditions are favorable for systems considering a monetization of existing buildings, or third-party development, ownership of new buildings, how these transactions are structured, and with which group they are executed, are of paramount importance. Bad deals are still being done. There is no substitute for careful planning, especially on the goals and objectives in the early phase of the process, so that transaction structures are designed in a way that's consistent with the system's overall objectives.

The options available are great, and even smaller projects can attract the attention of national investors throughout the country. Systems can benefit from the work done to date by other leading healthcare providers and be educated consumers of these monetization and development services.

Working with an independent advisor—one that does not invest or develop real estate itself but is in business strictly to serve its clients' needs through unbiased advice—is usually a good way to ensure the alignment of interests and guard against potential conflicts. Further, broad exposure to a large number of investors or developers for a particular project will ensure that a system is getting the best deal for its particular project. Finally, not every building or new development opportunity is suitable for monetization or third-party development. The fact is, it depends. There is no one-size-fits-all transaction structure or investor.

Now is an ideal time for health systems to execute real estate transactions—values are at reasonable levels, the demand outweighs supply, maximum controls can be retained, and a plethora of qualified healthcare investors and developers are available to work with you. Properly planned and executed, a health system will benefit for many years to come from a real estate transaction designed to meet its specific needs.

Clearly a tug of war exists between the dramatic headwinds to reimbursement that the ACA is causing and the equally dramatic demographic trends (aging population) that are already in motion. Add to that the equally important changes to the country's economic growth caused by globalization and technology, and we have moving targets everywhere.

But the outcomes are clearly aligned. If hospitals are now cost centers and not profit centers, the move to less expensive building environments can clearly be met with new nonhospital buildings. If financing with internal cash flows is no longer feasible, or if capital markets are no longer available to all credits, then private equity is abundant.

Key Takeaways

- Healthcare is not immune to the economic cycle.
- Consolidation is creating large systems that can access credit markets.
- Lower-acuity activities are moving to noncore buildings.
- Because of reimbursement pressure, cash is precious, driving third-party development and financing.
- Monetization of assets can free up cash for operational and growth programs.

REFERENCES

Beebe, H. 2012. "Trends in Healthcare." Marketing brochure. Healthcare Real Estate Capital.

Corwin, C. 2014. Phone interview, May 7.

Dohrmann, A. 2013a. "FHA Unveils 242/223(f) Acquisition and Refinancing Guidelines." Presentation to BJC Healthcare, St. Louis, MO, February 4.

———. 2013b. Presentation to Turner Construction, April 17.

Shattuck Hammond Partners. 2005. "Strategies in Healthcare: Real Estate Monetization and Development." Marketing brochure.

McGraw-Hill. 2007. *Construction Outlook 2008 Report.* New York: McGraw-Hill.

Moghavem, S. 2014. Phone interview, May 15.

US Department of Health and Human Services (HHS), National Center for Health Statistics. 2013. *National Hospital Ambulatory Medical Care Survey, 2013*. Hyattsville, MD: US Department of Health and Human Services, National Center for Health Statistics.

———. 1996. *National Hospital Ambulatory Medical Care Survey, 1996*. Hyattsville, MD: US Department of Health and Human Services, National Center for Health Statistics.

CHAPTER 6

Real Estate Development: Solutions for a Changing Environment

Robert D. Levine

Healthcare reform has clearly changed the way healthcare providers do business—from service delivered in an inpatient setting to outpatient centers, from independent physicians to employed clinicians for all specialties, and from hospitals as revenue generators to hospitals as cost centers. Given the dynamics of reduced reimbursement and increased demand, resources are becoming more and more constrained.

So today, asset allocation and the return on those assets are even more critical drivers of both profitability and successful business strategies. Since real estate represents more than 50 percent of all assets of most hospitals, it becomes obvious that healthcare property and plant must be managed more effectively to drive returns.

At the same time, healthcare reform, federal and state budgets, and economic forces are all affecting the availability

(continued)

(continued from previous page)

of debt and the types of debt that the healthcare sector can access. Consolidation is leaving fewer stand-alone community hospitals, and the surviving large organizations are seeking capital in a highly competitive market.

This book devotes several chapters to this subject of real estate. We discuss it in Chapter 5, as it relates to both core and noncore buildings, and in Chapter 10, on privatization as an alternative to ownership. But as this chapter will show, there are many new approaches and opportunities to address these issues, and we can't emphasize the importance of this subject enough.

In my experience in the real estate business, past success stories are generally not applicable to new situations. We must continually reinvent ourselves, responding to changing times with innovative new business models.

—Akira Mori, CEO, Mori Real Estate Trust

Note: This chapter is adapted from Strategies in Healthcare, Real Estate Monetization and Development (2005), *a white paper by E. Hunter Beebe, managing principal, Healthcare Real Estate Capital.*

WHILE MOST ANALYSES of health systems focus on the delivery of quality care to patients, the development of the next generation of surgical procedures, and the improvement of patient satisfaction, little attention has been given to a health system's real estate holdings. On average, a health system's real estate can comprise of 30 to 50 percent of its total assets. Historically, most chief financial officers feel a health system needs to own real estate. As a result, few formal cost–benefit analyses have been done on a system's real estate portfolios. This chapter concentrates on the noncore aspects of real estate holdings—medical office buildings (MOBs), ambulatory care centers (ACCs), and specialty clinics.

A BRIEF HISTORY

Since 2005, the healthcare industry has witnessed the evolution of everything from third-party real estate transactions with fee developers to highly structured joint ventures with publicly traded real estate investment trusts (REITs).

More specifically, since the passage of the Affordable Care Act (ACA), we've seen a dramatic increase in monetization of noncore real estate, particularly the sale of MOBs and third-party development and ownership. Demand for MOBs by institutional capital has outpaced the increase in the supply of MOBs available for sale, resulting in an increase in pricing. MOB sales volume has increased from $622 million in 2000 to over $3 billion in 2014 and average income capitalization rates (cap rates), which are defined as the net operating income divided by the sales price, have declined from approximately 10 percent to 6 percent or lower in that same period.

As returns from equities declined since 2007, institutional investors turned their attention to the real estate sector. In addition, positive trends caused by the ACA, such as physician integration, have fueled the increase in demand for medical-related real estate.

More than ten publicly traded REITs focus on healthcare, with a combined market capitalization well in excess of $12.5 billion. While healthcare REIT performance lagged both the Standard & Poor's and general REIT indices during the 1990s, by 2002 healthcare REITs began to more closely mirror overall REIT performance. As healthcare industry trends began improving, and healthcare real estate became a more mainstream product, the investment community began viewing healthcare REITs more like traditional office and retail REITs.

In addition, an ever-increasing number of private owners/developers and domestic and foreign pension funds focus on this sector. As a result, we anticipate the appetite for healthcare real estate will remain strong moving forward, despite what is expected to be an increasing interest rate environment.

Much has changed over the past several years. Previously, the only way for a health system to monetize a building or to develop a new building with a third party was for the system to provide full credit support to the investor/developer. This was done either through a master lease or through a support and control agreement, in which the system retained virtually all of the lease-up risk. Times have changed. As a result of the attractiveness of real estate yields, low interest rates, and a dearth of investment alternatives—combined with the enhanced liquidity in the capital markets for healthcare properties—an influx of new investors and developers have emerged. The supply and demand balance has shifted in the favor of the health system. Not only does a system not give up value by retaining controls over the property, investors realize that controls designed to benefit the adjacent hospital will only serve to strengthen physician loyalty and the stability of the tenant base in their properties—as goes the hospital, so goes the noncore real estate.

BENEFITS OF MONETIZATION AND DEVELOPMENT

Evaluating the benefits of both noncore real estate monetization and third-party development and ownership is best done in a framework that considers strategic, financial (discussed in prior chapter), operational, and regulatory issues. This framework will help articulate both potential benefits and risks of monetization. As long as they're identified early in the process, many potential risks can be mitigated through the transaction structure, which will be discussed later.

Strategic. A health system's primary goal is to deliver first-rate care to its patients while retaining and recruiting top-flight physicians. Some of the strategies currently used to achieve this goal include building physician loyalty to the system and addressing patient preferences for a well-coordinated hospital–physician experience. Clearly, offering physicians and patients modern and convenient MOBs, ASCs, and clinics is an important element to these strategies, but is system ownership required?

Through the sale of these noncore assets to, or development of these assets with, a qualified third party, and the retention of necessary controls, a system can still build physician loyalty and address patient needs, while using its cash for other things, such as to enhance credit ratings, improve liquidity, and invest in core operations. Strengthening the core hospital services will only further enhance physician loyalty and increase market share.

Operational goals. Real estate ownership requires not only an allocation of capital but also an allocation of human resources. Running an MOB and other noncore real estate requires managing leases and tenant relationships, controlling expenses, and maintaining the buildings to a level consistent with competitive buildings in the area as well as with tenant expectations. Similar to capital, which could be allocated away from noncore real estate to core businesses, the time and talent dedicated to real estate operations can be reallocated to more critical areas.

The same issue is relevant for the time and resources dedicated to a "self-developed" new project. Many systems are under the misconception that serving as the physicians' landlord is a crucial part of executing the system's strategy of building physician loyalty. A primary concern regarding monetization or third-party development or ownership is that a third party will jeopardize the hospital–physician relationship. However, the reality most systems experience is that their role as landlord results in unsatisfied physicians and frustrated staff. By providing professional, high-quality management, a third party can actually strengthen hospital–physician relationships.

Regulatory considerations. Ownership of noncore third-party physician-occupied real estate can result in potential exposure to fraud and abuse laws, particularly the federal Ethics in Patient Referrals Act of 1989 (Section 1877 of the Social Security Act), also known as Stark laws. In addition to federal Stark laws, many states have instituted additional regulatory provisions. As a result, systems that continue to own MOBs, ASCs, and clinics need to monitor these provisions closely to ensure compliance. While third-party ownership of these assets won't eliminate exposure to Stark laws and similar provisions, it will reduce the potential exposure.

Summary of Stark laws. The federal physician self-referral law prohibits a physician from referring a patient to an entity for the provision of designated health services (DHS) for Medicare and Medicaid patients from entities with which the physician has a "financial relationship." A financial relationship is defined in the Stark laws to include both compensation arrangements and investment and ownership interests. Under the Stark laws, the term *referral* is defined more broadly than merely recommending a vendor of designated health services to a patient. Instead, referral means for Medicare Part B services "the request by a physician for the item or service" and, for all other services, "the request or establishment of a plan of care by a physician which includes the provision of the designated health service."

Although the Stark laws originally only applied to the provision of clinical laboratory services, effective January 1, 1995, the laws were amended and currently apply to a host of DHS including the following:

- Clinical laboratory services
- Physical, occupational, and speech-language pathology therapy services
- Radiology and certain other imaging services
- Radiation therapy services and supplies
- Durable medical equipment and supplies

- Prosthetics, orthotics, and prosthetic devices and supplies
- Home health services
- Outpatient prescription drugs
- Inpatient and outpatient hospital services

In an attempt to establish a test for identifying DHS more specifically, the Centers for Medicare & Medicaid Services (CMS) have defined certain DHS by publishing specific lists of the current procedural terminology and CMS Healthcare Common Procedure Coding System (HCPCS) codes that physicians and providers most commonly associate with a given service.

Violations of the Stark laws can result in various penalties:

- Denial of payment for the designated health services provided
- Refund of monies received by physicians and facilities for amounts collected
- Payment of civil penalties of up to $15,000 for each service a person "knows or should know" was provided in violation of the Stark law
- Exclusion from the Medicare program and/or state healthcare programs, including Medicaid
- Payment of civil monetary penalties for attempting to circumvent the Stark law of up to $100,000 for each circumvention scheme

Statutory/regulatory exceptions. An exception to the prohibition must be satisfied in order for a physician to refer Medicare and Medicaid patients for the provision of DHS to an entity with which he or she has a financial relationship. While some exceptions apply to compensation arrangements and some apply to ownership and investments interests, several exceptions also apply to referrals for health systems that have successfully monetized or used third parties to develop or own.

WHO ARE THE BUYERS OF THESE NONCORE BUILDINGS?

REITs. REITs are companies that own and manage pools of income-generating properties, mortgages, and other real estate assets. As long as REITs distribute 90 percent of their income, their distributions to shareholders are not subject to income taxes at the corporate level. REITs must derive at least 75 percent of their gross income from either rents or interest from mortgages on real property. It should be emphasized that REITs principally generate revenue from their properties' rents, as opposed to management or development fees. REITs tend to keep their properties in excellent condition, resulting in high occupancy levels and steady income growth.

Numerous public and private healthcare REITs focus on a wide range of assets, including MOBs, ASCs, clinics, senior housing properties, and acute care hospitals. These companies have significant experience owning and operating healthcare properties. They're well capitalized, use low levels of leverage, and are long-term holders. Public REITs actively pursue sizeable acquisition opportunities as they attempt to grow and achieve economies of scale. The market capitalization for publicly traded healthcare REITs has more than tripled since 2010 from $3.5 to $12.6 billion.

Private developers. Developers are typically private companies that assemble the parties necessary for the construction of new buildings. The relevant parties include the landowner, architect, engineers, contractors, and debt and equity sources. Developers may build speculative or preleased buildings or acquire existing buildings to renovate and/or reposition. However, developers sometimes have limited capital to fund projects. As a result, they will seek out equity venture partners looking for the appropriate risk-adjusted returns associated with development.

While many equity sources expect returns in the short-term, an increasing number of institutional equity sources are available to developers. Those institutional equity types of investors have also devised structures in which physician tenants can act as equity investors in the buildings they occupy. Physician interest in real estate has been on the rise and is projected to continue.

In addition, developers often leverage the cost of development, resulting in debt levels ranging from 70 to 80 percent of cost (on average debt levels are around 75 percent of cost). Lately, developers have been acquiring properties to further bulk up their portfolios or as a means of forming an alliance with healthcare companies for future, more profitable, development projects.

Local and regional investors. In many markets, there are local or regional players that have emerged with sizeable real estate portfolios. In addition, they are knowledgeable about local markets and politics and can move quickly to execute a transaction. However, most are not focused specifically on medical assets, typically use higher debt levels, and may have limited access to capital.

Pension funds, insurance companies, and foreign investors. Pension funds, insurance companies, foreign investors, and other investment funds have shown interest in this product type. Their interest has resulted in more competitive pricing and other terms. These groups typically do not have any healthcare real estate management experience and will typically try to partner with an experienced group as the operator.

Private investors (domestic and foreign). Wealthy individuals have expressed interest in healthcare real estate that typically requires little to no management and stable cash flow. Their interest has also resulted in more competitive pricing and other terms. These groups tend to focus heavily on less management intensive assets, such as sale and leaseback transactions, or have partnered with experienced MOB operators.

Physician groups. In certain instances, physician tenants in MOBs express a desire to have an ownership position in the asset they currently occupy or, in the case of a new development project, will occupy. Generally, the physician ownership options are joint venture, condominium, or direct physician ownership. These options may be coupled with ground leases, mortgage debt, and other elements to achieve all parties' goals and objectives.

HOW TO STRUCTURE THE TRANSACTION FOR PHYSICIAN OWNERSHIP

Joint venture (JV) structure. This structure allows the asset to be contributed to, or developed by, an entity in which the hospital would retain, and physician tenants could take, an ownership position. This could be done with or without a professional healthcare real estate investment partner (e.g., REIT, private healthcare developer). Under this structure, an appropriate amount of mortgage debt might be used to leverage the property to the optimal capital structure. This structure could take many forms, but the most common would include limited liability partnerships, trust structures, preferred equity, and/or mezzanine debt structures and others.

The advantages of a JV are that it achieves the real estate investment desires of the physicians, and it preserves asset value. It allows for professional management, and it aligns the physicians with the hospital. The disadvantages are that consensus is needed for decision making, and joint ventures provide relatively illiquid investment.

Condominium structure. This structure allows for direct ownership by the tenant in a specific portion of the real estate. Under this scenario, the hospital would set up a legal condominium structure that allows physician tenants to own the suites they occupy. Existing assets can be converted into condominiums. In the case of new development projects, the condominium structure can be implemented at the outset. A condo board is established to oversee the building's management and capital improvement program. In addition, the hospital uses a ground lease to maintain the appropriate amount of control for on-campus and strategic off-campus assets.

The advantages of the condominium structure are that it achieves the real estate desires of the physicians, a third-party manager can be used, and it provides tangible asset ownership. The disadvantages are:

- it dilutes asset value;
- the condo board can cause friction in decision making;
- a commercial condo is typically a highly illiquid investment, complex, and costly to set up;
- values used for condo sales have to be considered in terms of fraud and abuse laws; and
- external financing is difficult and does not allow for third-party professional oversight for management, capital improvements, leasing, or financing.

Direct physician ownership. Another option to consider is the direct sale of an asset to physician tenants or having the physicians develop and own new projects.

This option, which might be better suited for smaller, single-occupant assets, is one in which the physician tenants buy the building they occupy from the hospital or develop a new building on hospital land, using a ground lease. This can be done with a single tenant or a group of tenants acting as partners. As with all options, the hospital should use a competitive process to ensure the sale is completed at arm's length to avoid any fraud and abuse law concerns.

The advantages of direct physician ownership are that it achieves the real estate investment desires of the physicians, and it provides tangible asset ownership for physicians. The disadvantages are that fluctuating real estate values could cause friction with physicians that take a loss, negotiation of terms and ground leases could strain physician relationships, fraud and abuse laws must be considered, and, lastly, if the physician and hospital relationship changes, asset ownership could become a problem.

WHO WILL OWN THE BUILDING?

Numerous ownership options are available to healthcare systems with regard to owned and to-be-developed noncore real estate assets. These structures can be broken into three main categories: hospital owned, JVs, and third-party owned. These strategies can also be combined with other options, such as ground leases, support and control agreements, master leases, condominium structures, sale of air rights, purchase options, and others, to allow a healthcare system to maintain the appropriate control of assets (from minimal to ownership-like controls). The following is a summary of the different structures and when they might be considered.

Hospital owned. Under this structure, the health system has ownership of the title of the building and has absolute control and responsibility for the building. The development or acquisition of the asset is funded with the health system's own capital or debt, and the system has responsibility for operating and capital expenses and the management associated with the building.

In addition, the health system shoulders the real estate investment risk associated with the building, generally defined as the fluctuation in real estate values. This structure is most often used when a healthcare system occupies the majority of a facility for core uses. This structure should also be considered for properties the system views as strategic that will be needed for future expansion and/or redevelopment.

JV with hospital and third party. For either the monetization of an existing asset or the development of a new asset with this structure, the health system enters an arrangement with a third-party investor or developer for the joint ownership of a building. JV structures can be used for existing buildings, which would be sold into the new venture, or to-be-developed buildings, which the health system and third party would codevelop as partners.

While the exact structure of joint ventures can vary, typically the third party will bring private capital, development, leasing, and management expertise. JVs can also be structured to provide the opportunity for physician-tenants to buy into the partnership alongside the health system and/or the third-party investor or developer.

To ensure the appropriate level of control, health systems can use a ground lease or other structures to provide certain protections against any future disagreements over the operations of the property. This structure may be appropriate for systems that believe their properties have an upside in value due to undermarket rents, lower occupancy, or mismanagement—difficulties that can be addressed by professional managers or investor JV partners. In this way, the system will benefit from improving real estate values as a result of their JV partners.

Third-party ownership. In this setup, a third party enters an arrangement with the health system either to purchase an existing building or develop a new one. Depending on the location and occupancy of the building, the health system may want to have a certain level of ongoing control of the asset. Typically, a health system has a desire for additional control when a building that is being monetized or developed is on a system's campus, or the building has some other strategic value to the health system. If this is the case, the appropriate level of control can be achieved by using a ground lease or other control mechanism.

Depending on the health system's occupancy of the building and the types of rights built into the transaction, the sale of the asset to a third party can be structured so the asset and associated debt are not on the health system's financial statements. In addition, a sale provides for distribution of 100 percent of the property's value to the health system up front with the monetization of the asset and can be structured so the health system is not required to contribute any capital on a new development project. It also eliminates the system's role as developer or landlord and manager of the property and the potential associated conflicts.

The advantages to the health system of a third-party ownership include the following:

- The system receives 100 percent of the value that is achieved in the sale.
- The system can maintain appropriate control through a ground lease.
- The ownership can be structured to be off financial statements.
- The ownership can be structured to be off credit.
- No upfront capital is required for development projects.
- There is no future capital expenditure requirement.
- The ownership avoids exposure to fraud and abuse and violation of Stark laws.
- The ownership avoids real estate risk.

CONTROL MECHANISMS AND OTHER TRANSACTION CONSIDERATIONS

Several options exist to protect a health system's operational and financial goals. These include the following:

Ground leases. Typically on-campus assets and strategic assets are sold or developed with a ground lease. By using a ground lease, a health system retains ownership of its valuable campus land, derives a return in the form of a lease payment for the land, acquires ownership of the building at the termination of the ground lease at no cost, and, most important, has created a legal document with control provisions to protect the system's relationship with the physicians.

A ground lease is a structure under which the improvements, or building, are sold or constructed and the underlying land is leased from the health system to the owner or developer of the improvements. Ground leases are typically long-term, usually 65 years or more, and are structured in such a way that the buyer can finance the building as if it owned it outright (fee simple).

The ground lease payment is typically set to give the health system some return on the land. This return can vary depending on the health system's goals: if the goal is to maximize proceeds, the health system may consider reducing this expense to the seller and opt for more money from the seller in the form of a higher purchase price and a lower annual return from leasing the land.

In the past, many health systems wishing to execute third-party monetization or development projects used *support and control agreements*. These agreements were often required by the investor and were structured so that the health system would guarantee, or support, a certain minimum return on the investor's capital. In return, the health system would gain the control it wanted on the monetized or to-be-developed asset. However, as this industry has evolved and more investors and developers have entered the market, competition has greatly increased, making the support component of these agreements unnecessary. As long as sufficient demand exists to lease space, a health system will not need to provide any financial support to a project beyond making lease payments for any space it wishes to occupy in an asset. As such, support arrangements have been largely abandoned with health systems benefiting from the real estate market supply/demand inequality.

When monetizing an asset, or developing an asset with a third party, the ground lease is used so a health system can maintain virtually all the rights of ownership, including but not limited to the following:

- Requiring that tenants be noncompeting, on-staff physicians
- Right of first refusal to lease space as it becomes available
- Right of first refusal to repurchase properties
- Reversion of the improvements at conclusion of ground lease, or other agreement

- Compliance with system directives
- Right to cure in the event of a default or mortgage debt
- Requirement of buyer to maintain satisfactory management
- Minimum holding period
- Requiring tenants' work to be consistent with the mission of the healthcare system.

Sale and leaseback. This transaction structure falls under the third-party ownership umbrella. The structure is typically used when a health system has a desire to occupy 100 percent of a building for the long term but wishes to extract the cash value trapped in the asset while eliminating real estate investment risk. With a sale and leaseback, the health system enters an agreement with a third party to buy a building and lease it back to the health system under a long-term master lease, typically a minimum of 12 to 15 years. This lease would be triple-net, which means that the health system, in addition to the rent it would be paying, would have full responsibility for operating expenses, maintenance, insurance, and property taxes.

This transaction structure allows the health system to have full control over the operations of the building. With careful consideration, this type of transaction can be structured as an off–balance sheet transaction for accounting purposes.

A sale and leaseback is best suited for buildings owned by health systems that are primarily occupied by the system. This allows the system to extract any capital locked up in this asset and redirect that capital to other uses. In addition, some for-profit healthcare providers have executed sale and leaseback on their core acute care facilities.

Variations on the sale and leaseback model include:

- sale and master leaseback, in which the system takes a lease on the entire building and then subleases portions of it to third parties;

- sale and partial leaseback, in which a system leases back only the space it occupies with third parties having a lease directly with the new owner; and
- sale with a fall-away master lease in which the system leases space it does not occupy and over a short period these leases expire.

Other Considerations

Other elements may need to be considered in all of these models.

Shared services. In certain cases, the assets to be monetized receive services such as utilities, security systems, heating and air conditioning, and other building systems from the acute care facility or the on-campus central plant, which the system will continue to own. These situations can complicate transactions greatly and should be handled on a case-by-case basis. Typically the health system charges the new owner for its pro rata portion of the shared service, or the services are separated with an additional meter either before or just after the property is monetized.

Parking. Health systems typically have a large amount of parking associated with their operations. This parking is either surface or structured, serving either core or noncore facilities or both.

When the parking associated with a building is strictly serving that asset, then the ownership of the parking is typically transferred with the building, subject to a ground lease if applicable. In the case of parking shared with facilities that are not being sold, the health system must provide the buyer with an easement to the parking, giving the new owner of the asset the right to use the appropriate amount of parking to service that building.

If the parking associated with an MOB generates income, the parking income should be presented with the income of the asset being monetized so the health system achieves full value for that asset. In addition, the health system may consider a transaction with a third party specializing in parking garage ownership management and/or development.

However, when selling parking or working with a developer to build and own income-generating parking, a healthcare system should consider requiring that the rates charged at the parking facilities be consistent with those charged elsewhere on-campus and elsewhere in the market. Because hospitals usually discount parking, changing parking rates and ongoing controls must be given special consideration because they affect physicians, patients, and visitors. This can be done through a ground lease, if there is one, or through a separate parking agreement.

Sky bridges and tunnels. In many cases, assets considered for monetization on a health system's campus are attached to other facilities via above-ground enclosed passageways, known as sky bridges, or underground tunnels. If this is the case, consideration should be given to who will own those structures and who will be responsible for maintaining them. Usually, the health system owns these connectors.

FINANCIAL ACCOUNTING STANDARDS BOARD—ACCOUNTING AND CREDIT IMPLICATIONS

Because accounting rules often change, any healthcare system contemplating a real estate monetization or third-party development project should consult with its accountants, legal counsel, and investment bankers beforehand. Transactions will likely be viewed from both accounting and credit rating perspectives, and generally three Financial Accounting Standards Board (FASB) rules dictate the treatment of the sale of real estate assets:

- FASB 66 (sale of real estate)
- FASB 98 (sale and leasebacks)
- FASB 13 (leases)

Rating agencies will generally view these real estate transactions similarly to the accounting firms. The exception is a sale and leaseback transaction. For this type of transaction, rating agencies will typically use a multiple of the annual lease payment to derive what would be the equivalent amount of debt for the healthcare system. That number will be included in the rating agencies' analysis of the system's long-term debt capacity. If off–balance sheet treatment is a critical goal for the health system, special consideration should be given to these issues.

HOW TO EXECUTE A TRANSACTION

Any healthcare system contemplating a real estate monetization or new third-party development project should begin with the end goal in mind. The transaction that's chosen should be driven by the health system's overall long-term organizational goals and the long-term goals with regard to the specific building.

Establish goals. The first step should be to gain a clear understanding of the healthcare system's goals regarding a monetization or new development project. These goals will include many of the following:

- Maximize cash (for monetization) or limit cash contribution (for development project).
- Remove debt from balance sheet and/or prohibit additional debt.
- Maintain control of occupants and uses.
- Retain right to lease any space.
- Replace management.
- Retain a positive community image with regard to the buildings.
- Use the expertise (not necessarily available in-house) of experienced healthcare real estate manager and/or developers.

Compile and review property data. When analyzing assets for potential monetization, the health system or hospital must compile:

- gross and rentable square footage,
- occupancy (both health system and third party),
- current and market income and expenses,
- the physical condition of the properties, and
- future development project(s) or needed improvements.

Estimate asset value(s). After gathering this information, a value estimate of the properties should be prepared. This estimate of value should take into consideration the current income and expenses of the asset and any future changes to the cash flow associated with the property. These changes could be due to new or expiring leases or extraordinary future capital expenditures.

After determining the specific operating income derived from the asset, that income should be used to determine what an investor might be willing to pay for the asset. A valuation of a real estate asset is traditionally achieved by generating a present value of the cash flow produced by the asset over a five- to ten-year period. The discount rates used for a present value calculation for these types of investments typically range from 9 percent for stabilized assets to 2 percent for nonstabilized assets or development projects.

Alternatively, stabilized properties can be valued using an income capitalization rate, or cap rate. The cap rate, historically between 7 percent and 0 percent, is similar to the discount rate in that it represents the expected rate of return from an asset to an investor. The cap rate is divided by the first year net operating income (income less operating expenses) to generate a value. For example, if a real estate asset has a net operating income of $1,000,000 and an investor requires a 9 percent return, using a 9 percent cap rate the value of the asset would be $1,000,000/0.09 = $11,111,111.

Determine optimal transaction. The health system should compare the available transaction structures with its goals for the transactions and for the specific assets. By doing this, the health system will be able to determine which transactions make the most sense for each asset individually. The transactions should then be analyzed from a credit and accounting standpoint. This final step should include creating post-transaction financial statements and financial ratios to determine the potential financial benefits of the transaction to the system.

Obtain constituency buy-in. If certain transactions make quantitative and qualitative sense for the health system, the next step is to ensure constituency buy-in. This step is vital and may include the finance committee of the board, the full board of trustees, administrators, physician tenants, community officials, and others. They must be made aware of the transaction and indicate support if necessary.

Completing the Transaction

Once the transaction structure is identified,

- rents or purchase prices should be calculated;
- potential investors, partners, or purchases should be identified;
- marketing materials, if needed, should be prepared;
- the offering memorandum should be developed;
- due diligence materials should be assembled;
- negotiations should be conducted; and
- closing should be completed.

CONCLUSION

Nonhospital buildings are going to be at the heart of healthcare delivery going forward. Fortunately, however, we don't have to invent the process for managing them as healthcare real estate, since this form of development work has been going on for decades. The best practices for this work are clearly in place.

Although many hospitals and systems have in-house real estate staff or departments, many well-qualified real estate consulting firms have no conflict of interest with the development work, do have a much broader knowledge of major potential partners, and do have years of experience in managing the multiple issues surrounding these transactions. Their participation can bring more opportunities and can mitigate and manage the attendant risks.

Key Takeaways

- The conventional wisdom of hospitals owning their own real estate no longer applies.
- There is a big market for development: REITs, pension funds, and private developers are all competing for properties.
- Hospitals can still retain control of assets even under third-party ownership.
- There are options as to how to structure the deal, and those options will vary with specific hospital or system needs.
- A thoughtful competitive approach will benefit from the use of a real estate consultant who does not have a conflict of interest.

REFERENCES

Beebe, E. H. 2005. *Strategies in Healthcare: Real Estate Monetization and Development.* New York: Shattuck Hammond Partners, LLC.

Ethics in Patient Referrals Act of 1989, HR 939, 101st Congress (1989).

CHAPTER 7

Healthcare Design Evolution

Paul J. Whitson

The built environment is an essential component in an integrated bundle of solutions to both improve care and maximize reimbursements. Success depends on the early engagement of the design team to discuss the impact of design decisions on healthcare outcomes, using a life-cycle rather than a first-cost investment approach. Implementation of the Affordable Care Act (ACA) provides the design community with a singular opportunity to provide evidence-informed solutions to reshape the healthcare experience.

We expect to see a rise in collaboration between the health sector and the construction and design industries and between academia and industry. These partnerships will create a robust and actionable knowledge base to inform cutting-edge design practice, as Whitson so aptly discusses in this chapter.

Partes ipsius architecturae sunt tres, aedificatio, gnomonice, machination . . . Haec autem ita fieri debent, ut habeatur ratio firmitatis, utilitatis, venustatis . . .

—Vitruvius, "De Architecturae"

Well building hath three conditions: firmness, commodity, and delight.

—Sir Henry Wotton's translation

WHAT IS DESIGN?

Almost all design students receive the Vitruvian definition of *architecture* as part of their introduction to the study of design as a profession. Subsequently their heads are filled not only with the complexities of theory but also with all the technical realities necessary to complete their education. For those of us who engage in the design of healthcare facilities, further criteria come into play, such as throughput, optimal work flow, and evidence-based design. But at its core, one can find no more succinct measure to evaluate architectural success than those three words.

Design innovation supports the delivery of healthcare by fulfilling the fundamental qualities outlined by Vitruvius in the first century BCE. Our role as designers translates the complex processes and specific requirements of healthcare delivery into a meaningful environment for care to be delivered and received.

For *firmness* we must provide solid enclosures that optimize resources, keep out the rain, and resist the forces of nature in order to create basic shelter for the execution of the healthcare mission. For *commodity* we have to create efficient flows at macro and micro scales that support the needs of providers, patients, and public who interact in specific ways. Finally, the notion of *delight* informs the overall experience of the built environment and is the basis of the therapeutic role that architecture can play in healthcare delivery.

CONTEXT

"Healthcare costs are killing us. Examples: Insurance premiums have increased 97 percent since 2002. The price of a Tylenol at a hospital is upwards of $13. Staggeringly, 22.8 percent of Medicare enrollees make up 81.9 percent of the program's payments" (Phillips 2013).

Across the country, healthcare facilities are beset with aging infrastructure that limits the effectiveness of the providers giving care and restricts the potential benefits of implementing the ACA. Many facilities have grown by accretion, adding one pavilion after another to an obsolete core primarily to accommodate new care models, building systems, or technology. The result is facilities that inhibit rather than enhance the patient experience: patients struggle to find their destinations and often end up in noisy rooms that lack privacy and space for family. Furthermore, the stress of working in inadequate facilities adversely affects the ability of providers to do their jobs, decreases staff satisfaction, and contributes to errors in patient care.

"A good place to start is to talk about the role of hospitals. Over the past 25 years, hospital usage has dropped. More than 200,000 hospital beds have been closed in the United States. Not coincidentally, outpatient visits have risen by 200 percent over the same period. It's not to say people no longer need hospitals; rather, the purpose of these structures is changing. The one-size-fits-all hospital is morphing into an integrated healthcare system combining high-volume specialty centers with widely accessible primary care services" (Cosgrove 2013).

According to Chip Kahn, president of the Federation of American Hospitals, "When we're looking at this trend toward consolidation, we have to look at the changing environment. Only the larger institutions with integrated services can meet the tremendous accountability that's required by hospitals today by Medicare, Medicaid, and private payers. We're moving into a period where electronic medical records will not only be necessary, they'll be mandated. That takes capital and concentration, and it takes larger institutions. The freestanding hospital is just going to have a hard time sustaining itself in that environment" (Weisman 2014).

A study by the Center for Healthcare Economics and Policy and FTI Consulting (Guerin-Calvert and Maki 2014) suggests the hospitals that join forces will be in a stronger position to improve their healthcare delivery and "realize operating efficiencies" by closing facilities that offer overlapping services, eliminating unneeded beds, and making other cost reductions.

"Consolidation may lead to realignment of services and a reduction in excess capacity as well as slower cost growth and increases in economies of scale," the report says (Weisman 2014).

Clearly, we have our work cut out for us. Changing needs, constrained resources, and uncertainty—just the right challenge for design innovation and excellence.

SOLID BUILDINGS (FIRMNESS)

For the purposes of this discussion, we are taking as a given that all healthcare buildings built today meet basic life safety requirements and will withstand the majority of the forces of nature. Buildings from the last century—especially those few hanging on from the 1800s—do not necessarily meet those criteria. But assuming that structural and enclosure soundness can be achieved in comparatively straightforward ways, we will focus on the other two Vitruvian qualities.

EFFICIENCY (COMMODITY)

Sustainability

The ACA does not include requirements that buildings meet particular performance goals, but as designers, we can anticipate consequences for not designing high-performing buildings. We know that healthcare buildings contribute to the therapy of patients and that they should also "do no harm" to the world in which we and they live. Thus, we have a significant role to play in maintaining a healthy, sustainable environment for those around us. Sustainable building begins at the earliest stages of planning and design.

We all understand the value of thinking green, both in our private lives as well as in industry. When you decide whether to recycle, use solar panels on your house for hot water, use water-restrictive shower heads, or drive a hybrid car, you are making a statement. But when you are responsible for the pro forma of a new building, or whether the lower operating costs will justify the additional initial capital investment, then more is on the line than just doing the right thing.

Is sustainability worth the cost? The ACA demands that we lower fixed costs, but what can we really do to lower fixed costs without damaging the budget on the facilities side? On the surface, justifying a major investment in green building while also staying competitive is difficult. Most developers say they can't make the numbers work and still deliver a competitive lease rate. But when you take a step back, there are thoughtful avenues for sustainability that do work.

According to Moler (2007), the link between smoking and lung disease was common knowledge long before the surgeon general's warnings were added to cigarette packages. Decades later, smoking is restricted in US hospitals, transportation, public buildings, and hotels. Today, design and construction industry professionals are working to improve healthcare buildings with physical changes that push the envelope despite limited peer-reviewed supporting research. Nevertheless, we know that health is aided by good nutrition, a benign environment, adequate rest, sunlight, fresh air, enjoyable physical activity, beauty, compatible relationships, and a sense of adventure. Disease—actually a physical state of dis-ease—often accompanies imbalance in those factors.

When a hospital design is conceived, project teams give a lot of attention to the building and healthcare delivery system—that combination of technology and human activity has proven safe and effective by experience and scientific analysis. Yet there are environmental factors associated with healthcare delivery that can defeat the best medicine available. What if the building subverts health in subtle ways that actually stimulate human dis-ease (Moler 2007)?

There are places—buildings—we enjoy visiting. We leave feeling revived and enlivened because of an instinctive response to environments that work in harmony with the qualities that lead to good health. The first place that springs to mind should be the local hospital or ambulatory care center (Moler 2007).

The US Green Building Council's LEED for New Construction version 2.2 Building Rating System has 69 possible credits for incorporating qualifying measures. While some institutions have opted to pass up obtaining any level of LEED certification, many have still chosen to build facilities that are LEED principled. This approach is driven by two major goals: to be good stewards of the environment and to reduce operating costs. Preliminary assessment shows that most projects can incorporate these measures at no cost, reduced cost, or nominal construction cost (Moler 2007).

Irrespective of the motivation, common sense should drive our culture and thinking to consider the following (Moler 2007):

- *Site selection.* Every project has a site. Choose one that has little environmental baggage—not a flood plain, prime farmland, wetland or watershed, parkland, or endangered species habitat, or a site that is contaminated.

- *Development density.* Avoid sprawl. Build in areas with nearby community services, transportation, shopping, housing, and so on. For a rural facility, increase density on an existing site rather than move onto undisturbed land.
- *Transportation.* Eliminate car trips and parking issues by locating near public transportation. Encourage bicycle use by offering secure storage and showers. Provide preferential parking for carpools and alternative-fuel vehicles.
- *Footprint.* Require contractors to limit site disturbance on undeveloped portions and design to exceed the open space zoning requirements by 25 percent.
- *Stormwater management.* Create naturalized stormwater control elements and add visual impact to the site.
- *Night lighting.* Confine night lighting to emergency access and parking areas, and carefully select interior and building exterior illumination.
- *Water-efficient landscaping.* Reduce water use for irrigation or eliminate it completely, and use native or adapted plantings.
- *Refrigerant management.* Avoid the use of CFC refrigerants, and use equipment using industry standard refrigerants that reduce global warming.
- *Green power.* Consider wind, hydro, solar, geothermal, or biomass options to reduce pollutants in the air and water—and to save operating costs.
- *Existing building rehabilitation.* Reuse existing building stock rather than demolishing it and/or recycle to less acute functions.
- *Construction waste management.* Separate and process the waste stream to reduce hauling and tipping expense and/or generate revenue.
- *Recycled content.* Use construction materials (steel, aluminum drywall, carpet, and ceiling tile) with recycled content.

- *Local/regional materials.* Use materials sourced within 500 miles of the project site.
- *Construction indoor air quality plan.* Use air testing or operation of ventilation systems with sufficient outdoor air to dilute and remove vapors from finishes and furnishings prior to occupancy.
- *Low-emission materials.* Use low-emission sealants, adhesives, paints, coatings, and floor coverings (carpet).

It will not serve the healthcare industry well to let decades pass before embracing the benefits of a healthy, high-performance building. While the research continues, follow intuition to good health. It's better, and it's affordable.

Operational Effectiveness

Parallel to the growth of evidence-based design as an important design tool, institutions recognized that designers contribute to the success of healthcare facilities in another way: maximizing return on capital investment. It is not unusual for owners to evaluate the relative success of a project not just by its aesthetic and programmatic achievements, but by how closely the actual cost adheres to the budget and how quickly the facility becomes operational. A beautiful facility does no good if the hospital doesn't get heads in beds and increase throughput in the diagnostic and treatment modalities. In today's healthcare economy, the average operating margin for large not-for-profit hospitals is 2.5 percent (Dunn and Becker 2013). To maintain viability in the market, healthcare institutions must rely on the efficacy of capital expenditures to ensure overall corporate health.

Acute Care

The principal metric for institutional success under the ACA requires reduction in hospital readmissions of patients. Patients need to leave the hospital healthier and closer to "well" than they ever have before. Our role as designers and our ability to create environments where patients can heal are critical.

Hospitals are required to keep readmission rates below thresholds for myocardial infarction, congestive heart failure, and pneumonia (Exhibit 7.1). If they don't, up to 3 percent of Medicare reimbursement is at risk. Needless to say, a hospital needs to be a place for patients to rest and recover so they can leave and not come back. As designers, we can create such a place. An adequately sized, single-bed room represents the fundamental building block of the inpatient enterprise. Defining how the patient experiences her environment demands a designer's complete attention and forms one of the biggest impacts that a designer can have over healthcare outcomes. Almost equally important, integrating the needs of providers into facilities completes the therapeutic framework in which patients can heal.

The fundamental nature of who is a provider has changed in recent years. No longer is the physician the sole touch-point for understanding the diagnosis and prognosis of a patient. Nurses, physician assistants, nutritionists, discharge planners, physical therapists, and a host of others—and increasingly the patient's own family—all play a role in the care and recovery of patients. Family members contribute to the care of patients through palliative and active intervention. Therefore, designers have had to expand their understanding of the inner workings of a patient room and develop layouts that provide space for all providers to inhabit and work together.

Patient rooms have continued to grow, with the median size for a single patient room more than 300 square feet. To accommodate all modalities of care, as well as to provide optimal work environments for the providers, room sizes have reached a point where "right-sizing" is now part of the design process. Overly large rooms mandate more capital expenditure, draw larger environmental resources, and lengthen travel distances for providers, perhaps

Exhibit 7.1 Hospital Penalties, Year Two

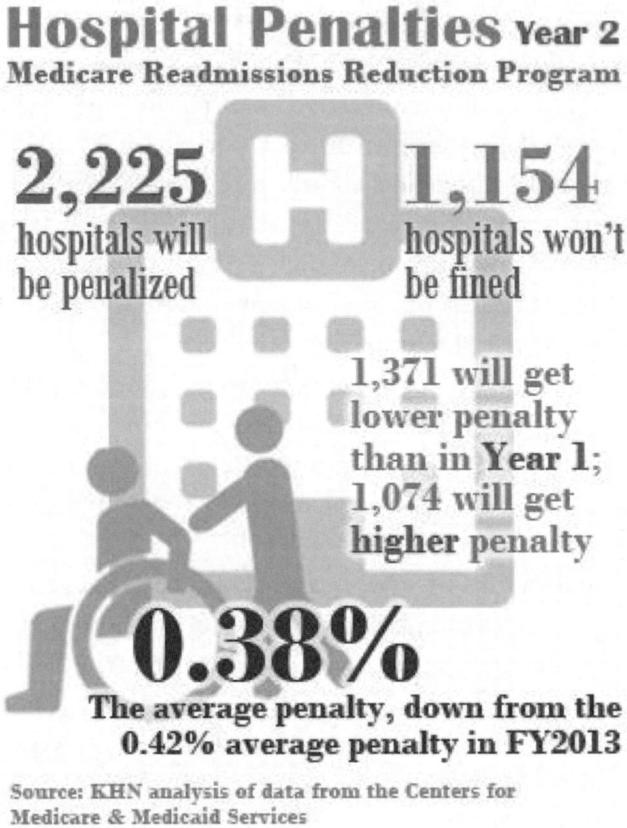

unnecessarily. Exhibit 7.2 shows essentially the same program rendered in mirrored and same-handed configurations. While the back-to-back plumbing wall in the mirrored version provides economies in first-cost construction, those economies may come at the expense of additional staff errors due to the need to adjust to a different layout.

Exhibit 7.2 Mirrored and Same-Handed Patient Rooms

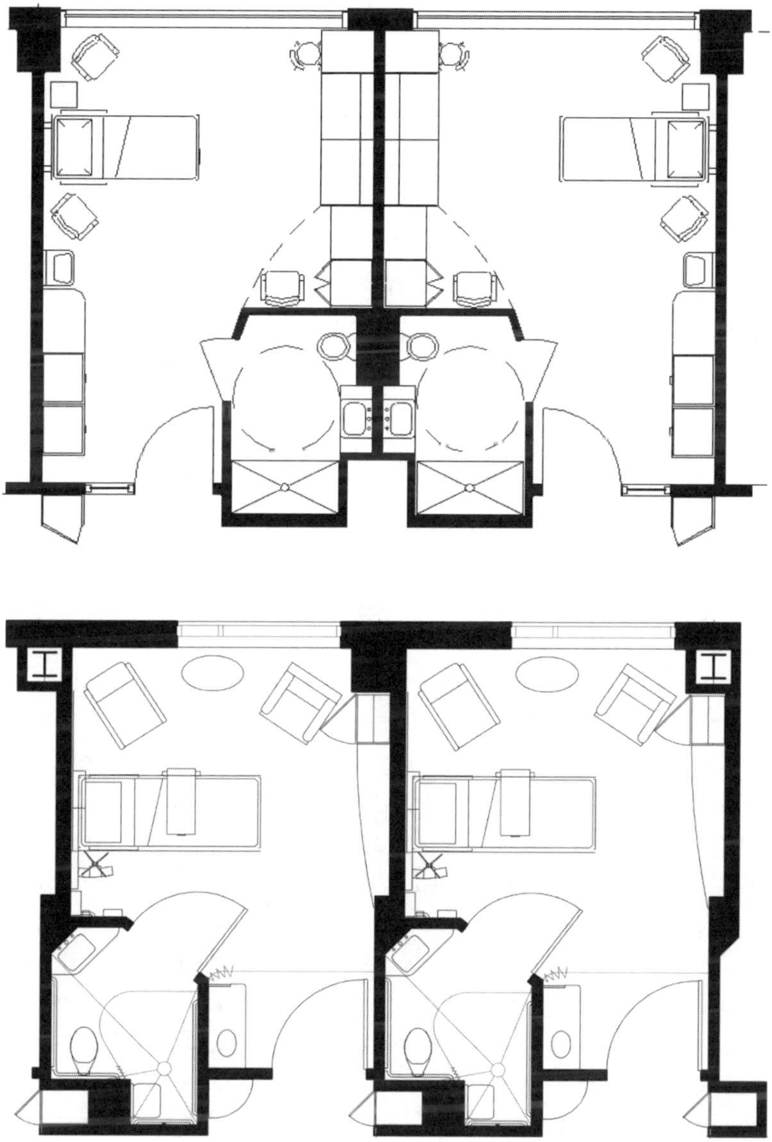

Source: HOK (2014).

The same-handed room, especially with the canted geometry (Exhibit 7.3), can provide:

- better views to nature,
- larger work areas for staff,
- closer spacing between rooms, and, significantly,
- a larger family area.

Just as patients are more informed about their care process and are encouraged to make informed decisions about healthcare, their families have become significant players in the healthcare delivery team. Family members can act as an extra layer of quality control and risk avoidance just by being with the patient for longer periods. All patient room layouts should enable family to stay in the room and participate in the care of their loved ones.

But how do we as designers demonstrate the value and utility of a properly sized patient room? Mock-ups are becoming a mandatory part of any inpatient design process and in other repetitive or technology-intensive rooms. Beginning with digital representations and moving to actual construction of specific rooms on site validates planning and design decisions far in advance of actual construction (Exhibits 7.4 and 7.5).

Institutions are closely examining how facilities affect efficiency. At a tertiary care hospital with a fragmented cardiovascular unit, the patient volume data indicated that there was adequate program space to meet the needs of the service through the foreseeable future. However, the clinical leadership had other concerns. Because of incremental development of the program over time and resulting distances that providers had to travel between program components, at least 14 hours of senior clinical staff time were being lost *each day*—equal to 1.5 full-time equivalents per year. Many more staff were inefficient due to the limitations of their physical environment. While capital improvements can be expensive, the accumulated labor savings over time could more than pay

Exhibit 7.3 Same-Handed Patient Room with Canted Geometry

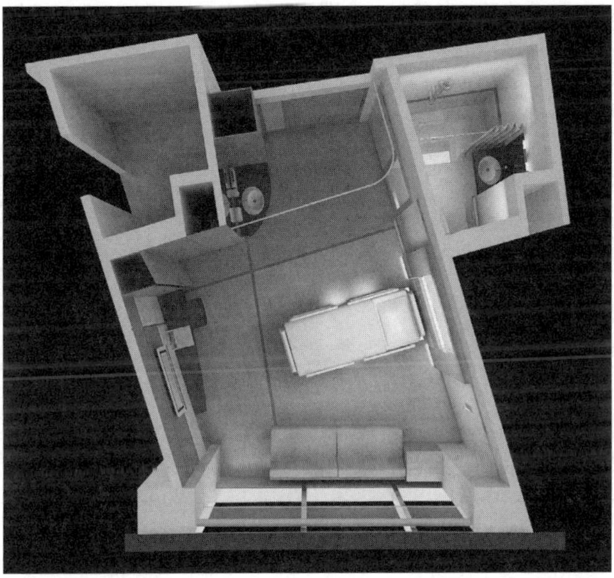

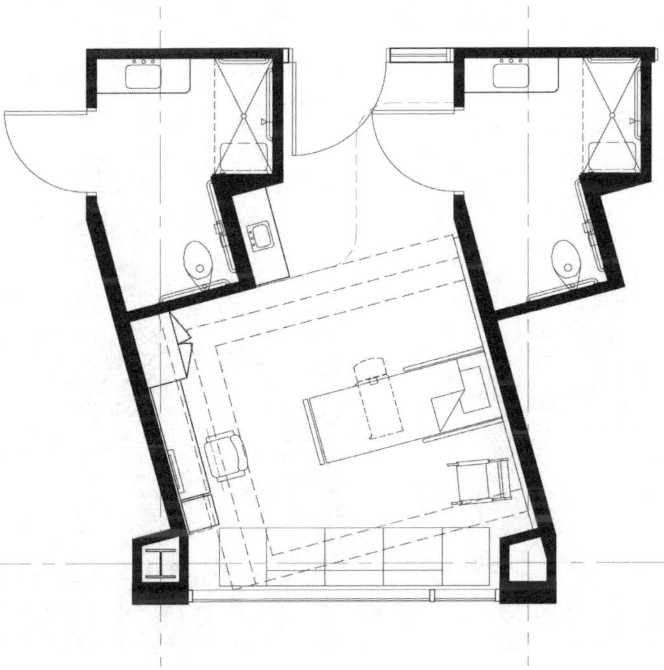

Source: HOK (2014).

Exhibit 7.4 Digital Image of Operating Room

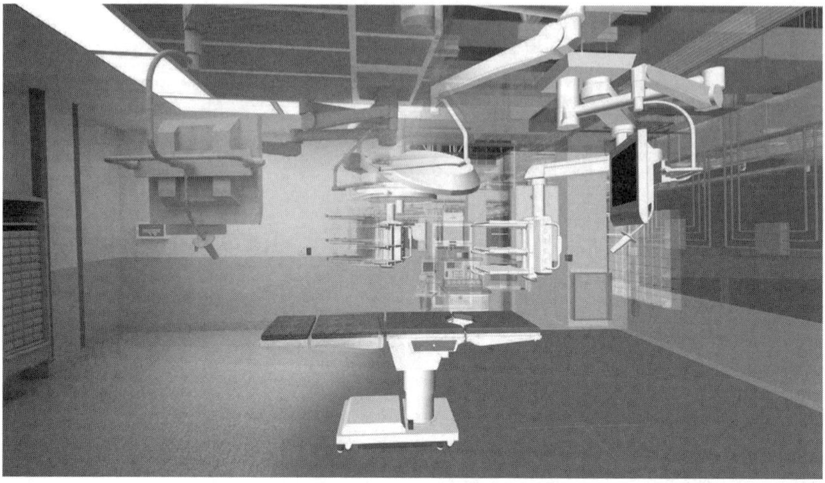

Source: HOK (2014).

Exhibit 7.5 Physical Mock-up of Room

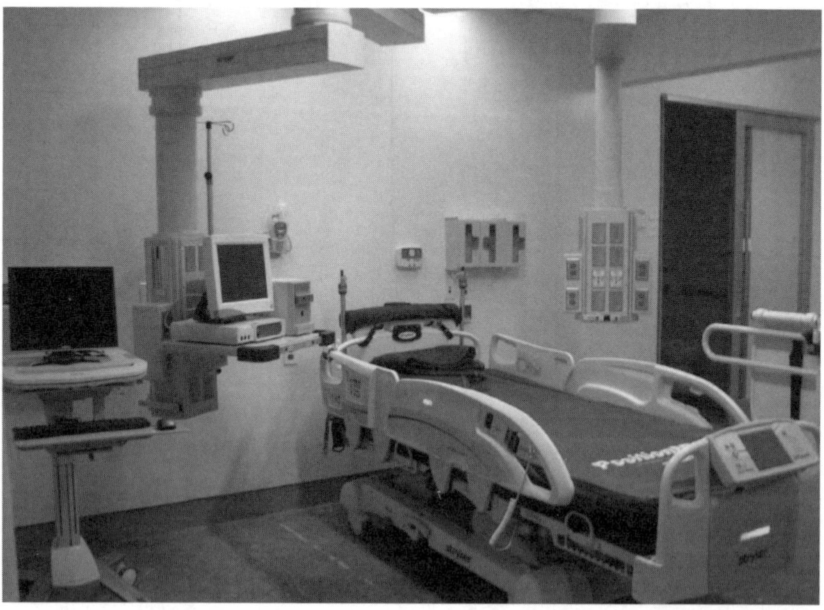

Source: HOK (2014).

for reconfiguring spaces. In addition, the physical fragmentation of the program leads to large amounts of non–value added waiting time for patients. This hidden cost reduces patient satisfaction and drives Hospital Consumer Assessment of Healthcare Providers and Systems scores down with negative consequences under the ACA. Exhibit 7.6 shows potential areas of waste.

Avoiding Errors

Another key metric for success under the ACA is the reduction in medical errors and hospital-acquired infections (HAIs).

"According to a 2007 study by the CDC that examined hospital data from 2002, approximately 1.7 million HAIs occur annually. The number of estimated deaths associated with HAIs in US

Exhibit 7.6 Potential Areas of Waste

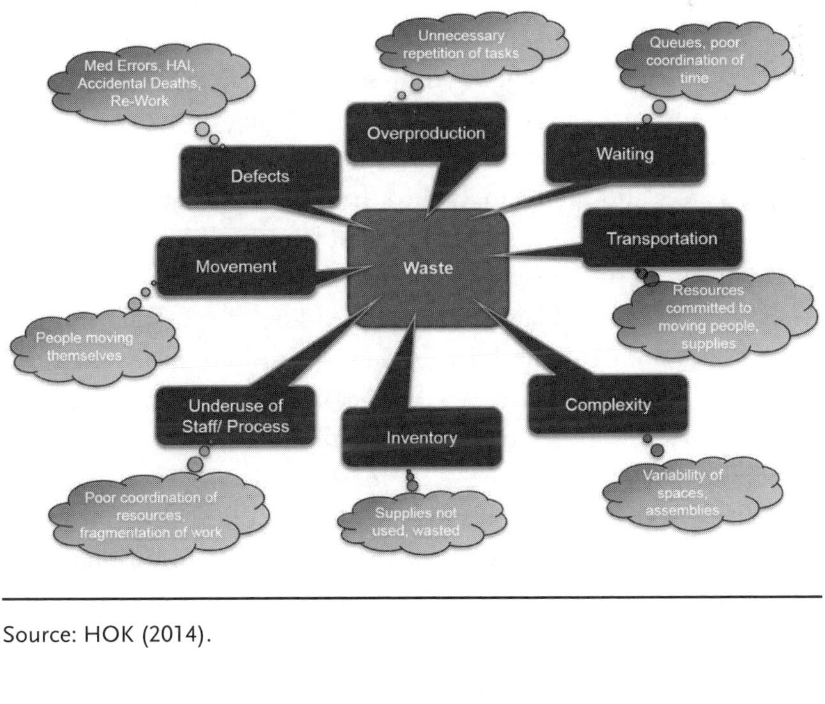

Source: HOK (2014).

hospitals was 98,987. Of these, 35,967 were for pneumonia, 30,665 for bloodstream infections, 13,088 for urinary tract infections, 8,205 for surgical site infections and 11,062 for infections of other sites. According to the CDC's analysis of the study, HAIs in hospitals are a significant cause of morbidity and mortality in the United States" (Dunn and Becker 2013).

Beginning as early as 1947, a set of federal guidelines established baseline design requirements for healthcare facilities. These guidelines aimed to create safe, consistent physical infrastructure to aid in the care and recovery of patients. Fast forward to now, and we see that the current version of the Facility Guidelines Institute's (FGI 2014) *Guidelines for Design and Construction of Hospitals and Outpatient Facilities* specifically defines the areas, utilities, arrangements, and overall organization of the care delivery environment accompanied with detailed architectural and engineering requirements. Not every state has adopted the *Guidelines,* but it remains the standard and a national baseline for life safety and architectural requirements.

Even with all this guidance, designers need to go further and collaborate with institutions to create spaces where providers can work well and efficiently and, most importantly, safely. My own firm has a policy of designing only same-handed patient rooms in order to minimize the potential for errors arising from provider disorientation. We carry that policy as far as possible to include procedure spaces and increasingly into the outpatient setting as well.

These design concepts coincide with an overall trend in healthcare delivery to provide uniform standards of care. In *The Checklist Manifesto*, Dr. Atul Gawande (2011) outlines the adaptation and adoption of preflight checklists into guides for physicians performing surgery. He elaborates on the ideas of uniform, systematized care delivery. In "Big Med," his *New Yorker* article, he posits success in care delivery can be achieved by following the model of the Cheesecake Factory. Gawande begins by contrasting the operation of the Cheesecake Factory with that of his own hospital: "I'd come from the hospital that day. In medicine, too, we are trying to deliver a range of services to millions of people at a reasonable cost and with a consistent level of quality. Unlike the Cheesecake Factory, we haven't figured out how. Our costs are soaring, the service is typically mediocre, and the quality is unreliable. Every clinician has his or her own way of doing things, and the rates of failure and complication (not to mention the costs) for a given service routinely vary by a factor of two or three, even within the same hospital" (Gawande 2012).

By acknowledging that systemization of delivery is a key to success, Gawande concludes: "Those of us who work in the health-care chains will have to contend with new protocols and technology rollouts every six months, supervisors and project managers, and detailed metrics on our performance. Patients won't just look for the best specialist anymore; they'll look for the best system. Nurses and doctors will have to get used to delivering care in which our own convenience counts for less and the patients' experience counts for more. We'll also have to figure out how to reward people for taking the time and expense to teach the next generations of clinicians. All this will be an enormous upheaval, but it's long overdue, and many people recognize that."

While both starting points seem far outside the realm of medicine, the message is consistent: healthcare improves under a paradigm that reduces potential mistakes through the application of consistent methodologies. Again, designers sit at a unique point within that paradigm; we must acknowledge that our solutions must both adopt and anticipate new healthcare delivery models.

Technology

Robust electronic health records are at the heart of the new healthcare delivery environment. These records provide critical links between providers and patients as well as among all the providers who form the patient care delivery structure. Our designs used to include huge medical records storage rooms and tiny data closets, if any information technology (IT) infrastructure was included at all. Now, not only have data closets grown to main distribution frame and intermediate distribution frame program elements, the location of these elements throughout patient care spaces creates a new physical reality that must be fully integrated into the built environment while maintaining data security. Understanding the programs and physical demands for data storage and transmission figure greatly in the future of healthcare design. Accordingly, we must work closely with institutional IT departments as well as with expert consultants to shape healthcare environments.

Ambulatory Care

"When you go for your medical appointment, you'll be seen by a team of caregivers that might include a nurse practitioner, physician assistant or other highly trained caregivers. If appropriate, you'll be able to get shared medical appointments with others who have similar conditions. Shared appointments are popular in diabetes and women's health. You get private time with caregivers plus a chance to hear from and compare your experience with other patients" (Cosgrove 2013).

The focus that the ACA places on wellness emphasizes engaging with potential patients as early as possible at the lowest degree of acuity to ensure that they remain outside the high-cost diagnostic, treatment, and inpatient environments for as long as possible. Exhibits 7.7 and 7.8 show the huge shifts from inpatient to outpatient, ambulatory care models. Consequently many providers, even large systems or academic medical centers, are spending capital to create effective outpatient facilities. These facilities can reside on the medical center campus or out in the community. Lean design and other flow improvement strategies figure greatly in the development of these facilities.

In addition to similar complements of providers found in inpatient settings, these ambulatory facilities often incorporate virtual healthcare interfaces, which are particularly useful in reaching patients in remote locations.

The rise of retail-based urgent care centers, particularly based in existing pharmacy chains, provide another outlet where patients

Exhibit 7.7 Changing Focus in Care Delivery

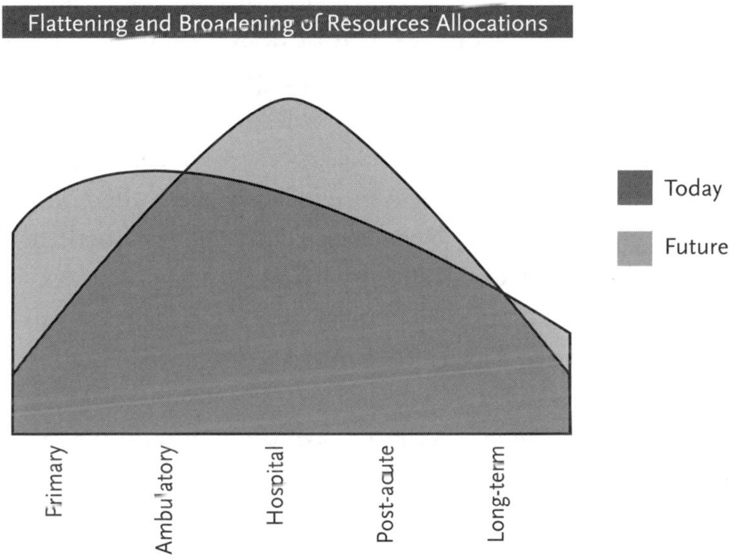

Source: HOK (2014).

Exhibit 7.8 Changing from Inpatient to Outpatient Models

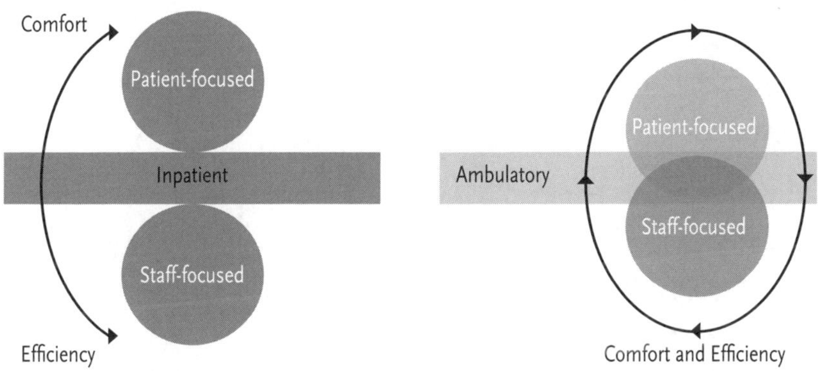

Source: HOK (2014).

can directly access care before their conditions become acute. Coincidently, The Advisory Board (2014) published the results of a study about the attributes patients most desire in an outpatient setting. Not surprisingly, convenience and speed of service rated high on the scale (Exhibit 7.9).

In St. Louis, Missouri, the Schnucks grocery store chain has created Schnucks Infusion Solutions to provide outpatient chemotherapy (Liss 2013). Shocking, no? Not really. Schnucks has long held a ubiquitous presence in five states in the Midwest and, in almost all locations, offered outpatient dispensaries. Taking advantage of its pharmaceutical expertise and its proximity to residential neighborhoods, it is expanding its reach to patients who don't really need to or want to travel to larger medical institutions simply to receive ongoing treatments. Those urgent care settings that are linked with an established health system or provider can be even more effective.

Exhibit 7.9 Top Ten Preferred Primary Clinic Attributes

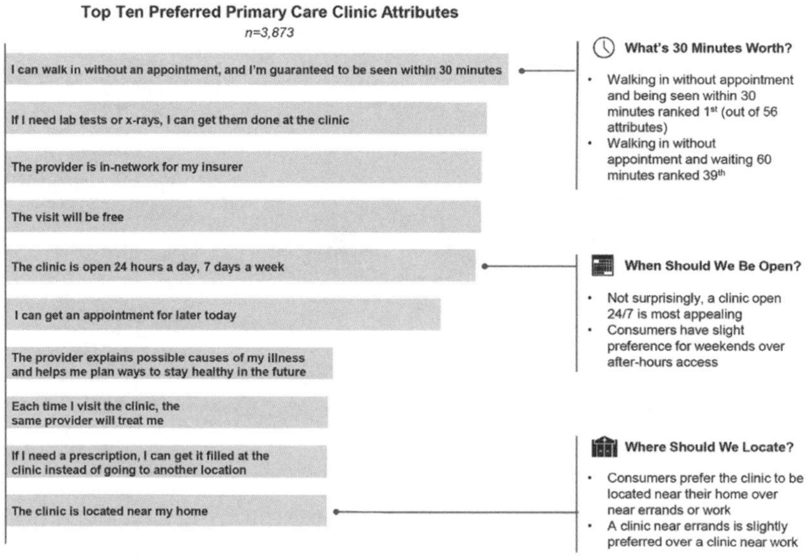

Source: The Advisory Board (2014).

These project types challenge the traditional role for healthcare designers and in some cases reduce it to almost invisibility. However, the retail model does provide opportunity. A large oncology center in New York City recently created a retail chemotherapy suite of its own, not only to reach out to the community but also to implement innovative ideas regarding the quality of environment in which cancer patients could be treated.

Many of these innovations result from analysis of Big Data collections of epidemiological and population health information. Mining social media can reveal usage trends and nascent healthcare issues far in advance of their arriving on the doorstep of an individual healthcare institution. Furthermore, the increase in reliability and speed of the overall connectivity of devices across the country allow patients reliable access to information about the availability and quality of care, as well as the means to acquire personal health insurance. As Gawande (2012) noted,

> Reinventing medical care could produce hundreds of innovations. Some may be as simple as giving patients greater e-mail and online support from their clinicians, which would enable timelier advice and reduce the need for emergency-room visits. Others might involve smartphone apps for coaching the chronically ill in the management of their disease, new methods for getting advice from specialists, sophisticated systems for tracking outcomes and costs, and instant delivery to medical teams of up-to-date care protocols. Innovations could take a system that requires sixty-three clinicians for a knee replacement and knock the number down by half or more. But most significant will be the changes that finally put people like John Wright and Armin Ernst in charge of making care coherent, coordinated, and affordable. Essentially, we're moving from a Jeffersonian ideal of small guilds and independent craftsmen to a Hamiltonian recognition of the advantages that size and centralized control can bring.

Broad application of telemedicine will reinforce the hub-and-spoke model that aligns most closely with the goals of the ACA in which the patient is the hub. Beginning with early adopters, such as Andrew Watson at the Center for Connected Medicine at University of Pittsburgh Medical Center, coordination of care and the overall productivity of providers has increased, moving from episodic reactive patient care toward comprehensive population healthcare.

CONCLUSION

Under the ACA, we as designers have to recognize the new role we play in contributing to the success of healthcare delivery, as well as the new scrutiny that will be applied to each design commission that we undertake. According to Anthony Roesch, AIA, HOK director of strategic healthcare consulting, "The Affordable Care Act for the healthcare industry will improve the quality of care through greater integration of technology, expertise, information and accountability—all under an umbrella of shared risk and reward. This will change the landscape of healthcare from one built around sickness to one centered around health."

Key Takeaways

- Consolidation is being driven by financial pressures and more accountability. While these mergers offer significant patient and community benefits, they require both design innovation and excellence to work well.
- Sustainability should be part of our culture, and therefore every hospital project should address its benefits. It is not necessarily a budget buster.
- The ACA is demanding operational effectiveness. Design can contribute to return on capital investment through systemization of facilities and process, which can lower medical errors.

(continued)

(continued from previous page)

- To bring convenience and speed to the patient, the ambulatory care facilities will be a major part of capital development.
- Evidence-based design has proven that the built environment can improve patient outcome. The ACA, through its value culture and patient satisfaction requirements, almost demands its use.
- The trend toward Lean construction processes already exists, and we will see new partnerships using these processes.

REFERENCES

Advisory Board Company. 2014. "How Do Patients Choose Primary Care Sites?" Published April 1. www.advisory.com/~/media/Advisory-com/Research/MPLC/Expert-Insights/2014/Primary%20Care%20Consumer%20Choice%20Survey%20-%20Top%20Ten%20Clinic%20Attributes.

Cosgrove, D. M. 2013. "What's Happening to Hospitals?" *LinkedIn Influencers.* Published December 11. www.linkedin.com/pulse/article/20131211181952-205372152-what-s-happening-to-hospitals.

Dunn, L., and S. Becker. 2013. "50 Things to Know About the Hospital Industry." *Becker's Hospital Review.* Published July 23. www.beckershospitalreview.com/hospital-management-administration/50-things-to-know-about-the-hospital-industry.html.

Facility Guidelines Institute (FGI). 2014. *Guidelines for Design and Construction of Hospitals and Outpatient Facilities.* Dallas, TX: FGI.

Gawande, A. 2012. "Big Med: Restaurant Chains Have Managed to Combine Quality Control, Cost Control, and Innovation. Can Health Care?" *New Yorker.* Posted August 13. www.newyorker.com/magazine/2012/08/13/big-med.

———. 2011. *The Checklist Manifesto: How to Get Things Right.* New York: Picador.

Guerin-Calvert, M. E., and J. Maki. 2014. "Hospital Realignment: Mergers Offer Significant Patient and Community Benefits." *Center for Healthcare Economics and Policy and FTI Consulting.* www.fticonsulting.com/global2/media/collateral/united-states/hospital-realignment-mergers-offer-significant-patient-and-community-benefits.pdf.

Liss, S. 2013. "You Now Can Receive Chemotherapy at Schnucks." *St. Louis Business Journal.* Posted November 5. www.bizjournals.com/stlouis/blog/health-care/2013/11/you-now-can-receive-chemotherapy-at.html?page=all.

Moler, J. 2007. "Green Healthcare + Common Sense." *Healthcare Monitor.* Spring/Summer. Brentwood, TN: Turner Healthcare.

Phillips, K. 2013. "Will Hospitals Evolve in Time?" *Jarrard, Inc.* Posted November 26. http://jarrardinc.com/2013/11/will-hospitals-evolve-time/.

Weisman, R. 2014. "Hospital Consolidation Benefits Patients, Report Says." *Boston Globe.* Published January 23. www.bostonglobe.com/business/2014/01/23/study-says-hospital-consolidation-good-for-patients-and-communities/F1HiBKyWGUIOAYhBeJH8KP/story.html.

ZGF Architects LLP. 2012. "Memorial Sloan–Kettering Cancer Center, Brooklyn Infusion Center, Brooklyn, NY." *Healthcare Design.* Posted June 30. www.healthcaredesignmagazine.com/article/brooklyn-infusion-center.

CHAPTER 8

Technology Planning for Effective Systems Integration

Debbie Gregory, Scott Johnson, and Julia Whitacre

The Health Information Technology for Economic and Clinical Health (HITECH) Act was enacted as Title XIII of the American Recovery and Reinvestment Act of 2009 and was meant to promote and expand the adoption of electronic health records (EHR). At the time it was considered the most important piece of healthcare legislation of the past quarter century, and it is part of the foundation of healthcare reform.

Part of the HITECH Act involves the creation of "meaningful use," which refers to the use of certified EHR technology in ways that can be measured in quality and quantity and that result in improved quality of care. In the act, this includes regulations and incentives for implementation of the EHRs across hospitals and physicians' offices. The act has three stages. Stage 1 puts in place the systems backbone for broader technology integration and digitally integrated health systems. This includes connectivity and

(continued)

(continued from previous page)

interoperability across information systems, medical equipment, patient monitoring, telecommunications systems, telehealth, building technologies, security systems, and more. This broad integration activity improves workflow dramatically, and providers are awarded with increased reimbursement.

Stages 2 and 3 include the integration of information across providers, speeding care and treatments more safely with lowered costs, fewer repeated studies and services, and reduced medication errors. In this chapter we'll look at the next best opportunities for systems integration and the upcoming exciting improvements in healthcare tied to these accomplishments.

Information technology and business are interwoven. I don't think anyone can talk about one without talking about the other.

—Bill Gates

WHAT IS TECHNOLOGY?

Technology. Think about it for a minute or two, and what comes to mind? Our guess is that five people reading this book will think of 100 different examples of what technology means to them. Apply the healthcare filter to the term *technology*, and the possibilities narrow. Some will think of computer software; some will think of devices such as smart phones, and perhaps others will think of medical and diagnostic equipment (covered in Chapter 9). But no matter your definition, most will argue that technology, as a discipline, has an opportunity to broadly affect outcomes within the new paradigm of the Affordable Care Act (ACA).

Before diving more deeply into this topic, some definitions are in order. For the purposes of this discussion, we are using a relatively narrow definition of technology specifically related to capital construction projects and infrastructure systems that are essential to the built environment. The vast array of supporting software platforms used in healthcare—from electronic medical records to pharmacy, lab, billing, and so many more—are not included. Rather, the focus is on systems typically part of capital development, as listed in Exhibit 8.1. These systems are also known as *low-voltage systems* to those in the design industry.

A quick journey through any acute care facility makes it clear that technology lies at the heart of care delivery and facility operations. Observe, to name just a few options:

- the high density of workstations and mobile devices;
- tracking tags integrated with nurse call for staff location services;
- networked medical devices streaming data to the electronic medical record and related platforms;

Exhibit 8.1 Low-Voltage Systems

- Voice and data networks
- Interactive education and entertainment
- Clock systems
- Wireless infrastructure
- Fixed and mobile devices
- OR integration
- Security
- Clinical systems integration
- Smart rooms
- Nurse call
- Public address/sound
- Audio visual
- Real-time location (tracking)
- Kiosks
- Telemedicine
- Television
- Radio

- interactive/on-demand education and entertainment systems used by patients;
- security systems controlling entry to secure units or secure spaces, such as narcotics storage; and
- nurse call systems, which integrate multiple functions within each patient room.

The amount of technology deployed and used within the care delivery process can be staggering. During a recent observation of a simple clinical process within a major academic pediatric hospital, a nurse interacted with technology systems or devices such as those in Exhibit 8.1 no less than 36 times over the course of a six-minute process. Couple this with the patient's expectations of high-touch, high-service, concierge-like attention, and one can quickly understand that technology is critical to the delivery of care with a broad opportunity to affect patient outcomes in the built environment.

And let's be honest. The technology discipline wasn't exactly standing around waiting for the ACA to materialize. Clinicians and design professionals alike have been reviewing process automation and optimization through technology for quite some time. They have been driven by notable trends that have been developing quickly in recent years. With the increase in smart phones, connectivity, healthcare apps, and the Internet, many early-adopter healthcare professionals are making requests for the increased use in their practice.

TECHNOLOGY DRIVERS

Systems Integration

One of the biggest drivers of technology adoption is systems integration, which means that the whole is greater than the sum of its parts. The yield from systems integration includes enhanced workflow, accuracy, and patient satisfaction. Basic examples include:

- wireless phone integration to nurse call for streamlined communication and alerts;
- real-time location systems integration with electronic white boards for tracking staff, equipment, and patient location; and
- patient entertainment systems integration with electronic medical records to prescribe appropriate educational content for the patient.

Staff Efficiency

The second driver is staff efficiency. The demographics of the nursing population and complexity of care delivery demand easier and leaner workflows, coupled with cost pressures to do more with less. The technology industry is already hard at work addressing streamlined and automated processes to address these issues. The planning, budgeting, and prioritization process is discussed later in the chapter, and it will be evident that efficiency is a core driver for best investment and payback around any given technology solution.

Patient Satisfaction

The third driver is the relatively new landscape of patient satisfaction. As part of the ACA, Hospital Consumer Assessment of Healthcare Providers and Systems (HCAHPS) scores are being factored into the Centers for Medicare & Medicaid Services (CMS) reimbursement levels, but the population at large has already been seeking and selecting providers based on evaluations of customer service. Expectations have risen to hotel-level concierge services in many communities, and technology is front and center in the delivery of those solutions.

In many ways, the new reality and implications of the ACA align with trends and forces already in play in the healthcare technology environment. Pressure on reimbursements means providers will be forced to further streamline processes and improve operational efficiency. Technology resides at the core of this challenge. Further, consumer choices mean more consolidation and competition, so the patient's perception of her experience, both clinically and for hospitality, will be critical. And perhaps most important, measurement of quality clinical outcomes drives the need for high accuracy and effectiveness. Again, technology-enabled workflow that reduces steps, improves the work environment, and drives performance will be at the heart of meeting this challenge.

As discussed later, the planning and budgeting of technology solutions bring expectations of high yield in performance and payback. Interesting, too, is the lens through which different types of institutions see this challenge and the technology environment, and the correlating appetite for investment. Based on a review of recent capital projects across the country, there are distinct differences in priorities for technology spending:

- Greenfield hospital projects and academic teaching institutions are spending between 12 and 14 percent of their total construction dollars on the technology components.
- Community hospitals are spending 10 to 12 percent.
- For-profit hospitals are spending 8 to 10 percent.

In a major metropolitan area where competition is heightened and the choices are many, the playing field is leveled. Owners may conclude that they need to reconsider their choices in their technology spending to find the sweet spot between competition and cost-effective solutions.

We have identified an approach to planning capital projects that will yield that balance. This approach centers on collaboration among historical silos and stakeholders in a new technology governance forum. Looking beyond today's needs to integration, compatibility, and return on investment will guide the way.

THOUGHTFUL PLANNING

For many healthcare enterprises, their existing facilities were built prior to the industry boom in technology. Consequently these institutions have dealt with years of retrofitting technology into existing spaces including:

- bathrooms turned into undersized communication rooms housing servers and network equipment without ample equipment clearances or cooling,
- nurse call panels retrofitted into storage rooms, and
- above-ceiling cabling without any type of cable tray or other support system.

Capital projects offer an opportunity to build with technology systems and all associated infrastructure in mind. But doing it right takes careful planning and budgeting. At the start of a capital project, before ever beginning to assess existing or future technologies, there are several critical steps to guide overarching project success for new low-voltage systems design.

IT Steering Committee

The first planning step is assembling a key group of decision makers as an IT steering committee to drive the technology systems selection. The most successful projects gather a widely diverse group of individuals, all with key decision-making roles within the healthcare system, to mold the technology landscape of a capital renovation or new-build.

In recent years, more and more healthcare technology systems have evolved to become Internet protocol or IP-based: the phone system, cable television, nurse call, and overhead paging systems are just a few examples that can now be managed via a network connection. As a result, hospital IT departments often assume a larger role in the management of systems whose responsibility may have previously fallen to others. Some systems, such as the voice/data infrastructure, are almost always managed by the IT department, but ownership of many clinical-based systems, such as nurse call or patient education/entertainment, can vary widely by facility. Depending on the hospital, a nurse call system can be managed or maintained by the hospital IT department, biomed, clinical engineering, facilities, or even outsourced to a third party. For other systems—such as cable television, time and attendance clocks, or wireless GPS-based clock systems—no overall standard for departmental ownership exists. While departmental responsibility for each low-voltage technology system is unique to each facility, understanding how these systems are managed before beginning a capital project is vital, as are decisions regarding if or how ownership and involvement by key departments may shift as a result of any changes in technology through the capital project technology evaluation.

As you assess the technologies at the beginning of a capital project, it is important to have the appropriate representation at the table for *your specific facility*. Creation of an IT steering committee is essential to making timely decisions that drive project success and align strategic business with IT priorities. According to the Info-Tech Research Group (2010), IT steering committees are used by 62 percent of organizations to ensure this alignment. Best practice supports the formation of an IT steering committee regardless of the size of the organization. While representation from the chief information officer (CIO) and IT department is a given, several other key roles are equally critical:

- *Non–IT administration.* Generally, the hospital CEO, chief operating officer, or the vice president over the construction project—with the CIO—brings a comprehensive look at technology to the facility capital project. He or she has an understanding of what the long-range technology plans are for a facility and how to align these goals with the business operations. Where formal CEO/president-level participation is missing, 51 percent of respondents believe the group lacks the necessary authority to make final IT decisions (Info-Tech Research Group 2010).
- *Clinical leadership.* It is critical to have clinical leadership involved in the evaluation of any and all technology systems. The chief nursing officer (CNO), chief nursing information officer (CNIO), chief medical officer (CMO), or chief medical information officer (CMIO) should be able to speak at an enterprise level about the desired workflow processes and how technology is integrated to increase clinical efficiencies.
- *Additional clinical representation.* In addition to clinical leadership, having additional clinical representation is highly beneficial. This representation is typically best filled by a nurse currently working in a unit who can provide insight to the daily functions—benefits and pain points—of existing technology and its impact on clinical workflow.
- *Other departmental representation.* Representatives from pharmacy and/or lab are also key participants, especially if these services are using or will use electronic notification. Representatives should also be included from any other departments with current or future ownership of low-voltage systems—clinical engineering, biomed, or facilities.

- *Patient or patient family representative.* Consider having a patient or patient family member participate in the high-level planning or initial feedback. The ideal candidate has had an extended stay or multiple stays at the facility in the last year and can provide accurate feedback about how existing technologies improved or hindered their stay and what could be improved from a technology standpoint to result in a more positive overall experience.

The IT steering committee should focus on three main tasks: IT strategic planning, project prioritization and project approval. While the IT steering committee should play a role in IT governance, this group is not intended to do the job of managing day-to-day operations of these systems. Additionally, other teams are best left to focus on activities such as resource allocation. The IT steering committee exists to focus on IT strategy and investment decisions (Info-Tech Research Group 2010).

Building a Low-Voltage Budget

Once the IT steering committee is assembled, the next, and quite possibly most critical, step is to build a sufficient low-voltage budget to meet to the goals of the capital project. Generally, healthcare facilities allocate 8 to 14 percent of their capital budget toward low-voltage systems for new construction. Percentages vary slightly with renovation projects, depending on how much infrastructure (if any) is available for reuse, demolition costs, required network upgrades and so on. Despite living in an age surrounded by technology in our daily lives, many management teams fail to allocate a sufficient amount of the capital budget toward technology systems. By doing so, these teams run the risk of woefully underserving the staff and patients in the facility.

Designing an infrastructure that allows for future growth is a key consideration as well. With today's healthcare environment focused largely on increased clinical efficiencies, improved patient care, patient satisfaction, and the overall patient experience, it simply isn't enough to budget for only the technology basics. Enhanced nurse call features can and should allow nonclinical requests like room temperature to be addressed quickly by routing these requests to a nonclinical staff member. Patient entertainment/education can and should provide the patient with a way to watch movies, access the Internet, review scheduled appointments and watch specifically prescribed clinical education, all from the patient room. These technologies are no longer optional budget items for healthcare facilities looking to achieve top HCAHPS scores and patient satisfaction.

The typical low-voltage technology budget generally covers the purchase/installation of any low-voltage infrastructure, cabling and hardware. This budget also includes all network hardware, peripheral devices—such as computers, phones, printers and multifunction devices—and televisions. Network server storage, software packages and any associated software license costs are generally excluded from this portion of the capital budget and are carried in an owner-provided noncapital budget or operations budget.

Within each project's set of budget challenges, budget prioritization can be the most difficult aspect of creating a low-voltage budget. Some systems, like data cabling or the nurse call system, are non-negotiable and are essential to the project opening. Choosing which nonessential systems to fund can be a challenge, especially when these systems are often the ones that support best practices for clinical efficiency and patient satisfaction. Aligning the budget priorities with technology recommendations from the IT steering committee is important to maximize the return on investment and to think futuristically to support technology systems that may be deployed after the facility opens or as funding is made available.

As budgeting gets tight, there are ways to think creatively and to budget wisely:

- With the cost of copper continually on the rise, don't overcable. Leverage the wireless network for guest access rather than provide a hard-wired cable for guest plug-in. Does your clinical staff use wireless phones? If so, reduce the quantity of wall or desk phones in areas where clinical wireless phones can be used instead.
- Invest in a medical-grade wireless utility for amplified cellular coverage and wireless coverage in your facility, as well as first-responder radio and facility two-way radio.
- Don't overdo system functionalities for day-one deployment. Systems like nurse call and patient entertainment/education generally have an abundance of features and functionalities that can be added on at any time.

The most successful facilities start small and do not overwhelm the staff during training, systematically rolling out new features in the weeks and months following a go-live. This strategy prevents the capital budget from bearing the cost of unused features and allows a facility to provide upgrades as appropriate and as operational budgets permit.

With all these budget constraints, remember the following:

- Strike a balance between not overcabling and still providing infrastructure that supports future technologies that may be deployed following a project opening. While avoiding unnecessary cabling, it is also most cost-effective to pull cabling when a project is under construction. Adding cabling after project completion will come at a much higher cost per cable due to the infection control precautions that must be made when working in an existing facility.
- The facility may not be able to relocate existing peripherals. Especially with new construction, it is likely that the new and existing facilities will have an overlap

in their operational period. Consequently, plan for all anticipated new peripheral devices with the capital project.

- Consider annual system costs, such as maintenance and licensing. Generally a capital budget will cover first-year costs associated with the new systems, but operations budgets will need to support these costs moving forward. Depending on the system and its complexities, some of these costs can be extensive.
- Include patch cords! These items, both at the end-user devices and in the telecommunications/data rooms, are easy to overlook but can add up to a costly gap if forgotten. Typically they are budgeted as part of the structured cabling costs.

Additionally, be sure to identify gaps or overlaps that may exist between different capital or noncapital budgets. Are the TVs covered by an IT budget or by the medical equipment planner? Are data center servers covered in capital network equipment or owner-provided peripherals? Are all software licenses covered by a noncapital budget?

Finally, when capital budgets are highly scrutinized, many facilities get creative to fund systems on their wish list—certainly donor opportunities or sponsorships may exist. Others have applied for grant funding to cover the cost of systems such as distance-learning AV equipment or patient education platforms. A word of caution: planning to pay for systems such as patient education and entertainment by passing the cost along to patients as a fee during their stay tends to backfire as a big point of patient dissatisfaction in HCAHPS results.

In conclusion, ensuring that a sufficient percentage of the project budget is allocated for low-voltage technology is important. These systems drive the staff workflows and patient experiences. Providing a generous technology spend promotes greater clinical efficiencies and patient satisfaction.

FUTURE TECHNOLOGY TRENDS TO WATCH

The HITECH Act, enacted in 2009, set aside funds that sped up the process of EHR adoption throughout the healthcare industry. Additionally this legislation enabled CMS to establish programs that provide for reimbursement incentives or penalties for not adhering to the program standards by the established deadline.

As healthcare facilities began to take on the task of turning every paper record into an electronic record, the meaningful use program was created to help better structure the way that EHRs could improve the effectiveness of patient care. The Office of the National Coordinator for Health Information Technology (ONC) set the following categories for Stage 1 meaningful use standards and requirements that must be met by fiscal year 2015 in order to avoid payment penalties from the CMS.

1. Engage patients and families in their care.
2. Improve quality, safety, and efficiency, and reduce health disparities.
3. Improve care coordination.
4. Improve population and public health.
5. Improve privacy and security of health information.

Stage 2 of meaningful use rolled out in 2014, followed by Stage 3 in 2015, with the focus shifting to advanced clinical processes such as increased requirements for electronic prescribing, incorporation of lab results into the EHR, and greater patient-controlled data, to name a few.

How does any of this relate to the ACA? According to Brooks (2012), "The reform law seeks to accomplish these goals by organizing physicians into accountable care organizations. The meaningful use program gives physicians the tools necessary for operating in a more collaborative environment. The programs may not come from the same piece of legislation, but in a sense they are two separate legs of the same stool."

Ultimately technology investment, through capital healthcare projects, can achieve the goals and standards outlined here supported by both the ACA and HITECH Acts. Because these standards have a large focus on systems integration, there is opportunity to leverage a unified technology systems model that focuses on improved patient safety, increased clinical efficiencies, and greater data accuracy.

Some of these technologies, at the time of this publication, are making the greatest strides to help healthcare facilities achieve these goals through systems integration.

Interactive Patient Care Technology

In today's technology-rich ecosystem, consumers expect information and service to be as accessible as a take-out order or online banking. This technology-savvy generation will also expect the same type of service for its healthcare. Hospitals are embracing the patient-centered system that provides the connection and education patients are demanding. Through integration with other systems like the EHR, nurse call, and locating systems, an interactive patient care system (sometimes referred to as a patient entertainment/education system) does precisely that for the healthcare consumer. According to the American Hospital Association (Wright 2011), "Interactive Patient Care technology can be a valuable extension of EHR, enabling direct patient interaction and providing the proven tools needed to fulfill the criteria in this category that EHR doesn't meet for both inpatients and outpatients."

A variety of patient entertainment/education systems exist. Some work over a data network, some will function over coax, some systems push information to in-room patient televisions or other designated locations from a centralized server, and others require a PC to drive content at the television location. Regardless of infrastructure requirements, all of these systems can provide individualized content to the patient about his treatment, care, care team, and stay. The system is available at the patient bedside or may be accessed at home via a web portal. Content can be accessed by the patient or "prescribed" by a clinician to align with an individual patient's care plan. This system is being adopted by healthcare facilities nationwide to help patients fully comprehend their diagnosis, treatment plan, care providers, and facility processes, such as hospital discharge. The system also allows patients an opportunity to share opinions and data with their care provider, ultimately resulting in a greater quality of care.

There are countless features and systems integrations available through a patient entertainment/education system that help achieve the goals of meaningful use—particularly as it relates to engaging patients and families in their care.

- Follow-up comprehension surveys, recorded back to the EHR, document the patient's understanding of her treatment and offer an opportunity for follow-up questions with a clinician, ultimately improving the exchange of information between patients and caregivers to improve overall patient care.
- Interfaces with wireless phones carried by staff members can allow nonclinical requests to be routed to the appropriate staff member, increasing clinical efficiencies and reducing the number of steps by clinicians for nonclinical requests.
- An in-room food service menu allows patients to order meals outside of regular meal deliveries; by interfacing with the dietary and EHR systems, patients with restricted diets only have access to the foods permitted as part of their care plan, increasing patient safety.

The ability of the interactive patient care system to integrate with other systems, such as nurse call, EHR, wireless phones, or real-time locating systems/radio-frequency identification (RTLS/RFID) needs careful review for compatibility at each specific facility. These interfaces generally share information via HL7 standards, but specific interoperability compatibility should always be verified.

Real Time Locating Systems/Radio Frequency Identification Systems

Technology systems that locate patient, staff, or assets can also help achieve meaningful use to engage patients and their families in their care, support care coordination, and improve quality, safety, and overall efficiency.

RTLS and RFID can be used for locating staff or patients or for tracking assets such as wheel chairs, infusion pumps, beds, or other medical devices throughout a facility. Some facilities are tagging more than 100 different types of equipment! These systems require a set of ceiling-mounted sensors to be located through the facility and staff or assets outfitted with a small plastic tag that is cleanable for infection control purposes.

RFID can locate in real-time any of these assets in a facility, drastically reducing the time nurses or other staff spend searching for these items. Knowing where specific items are can also prevent staff "hoarding" equipment. The interfaces between interactive patient care systems and RFID/RTLS systems allow any doctor's or nurse's information to be displayed on the patient TV when entering the room.

System Integration for "Smart" Facilities

In support of the global objectives for high accuracy, high efficiency, and high patient satisfaction in the acute care facility experience, a growing trend is the broad integration of several components and solutions to create a "smart" environment. Once separately deployed, several systems now combine to form an integrated technology solution in any given patient room, patient care unit, and facility as a whole. The goal is to provide actionable information to the patient or care provider at the right time and place—all in order to streamline workflow, improve outcomes, and enhance the patient experience.

Often called a smart patient room, this ecosystem leverages the many functions and data points shared by several systems that are already familiar and in use:

- Nurse call/code blue
- Real-time location systems
- Patient entertainment/education
- Patient status displays—bedside, entry, and nursing unit
- Data-stream-enabled beds (smart beds)
- Data-stream-enabled clinical devices
- Infection control (hand washing) stations
- Wireless devices—phones, tablets, and PCs
- Integration software and middleware

The resulting integrated environment yields many benefits in support of increased efficiency and effectiveness. A simple, common nursing workflow, such as responding to a routine patient call, capitalizes on the integration, and the following enhanced process emerges:

1. Patient places a call to nurse requesting pain medication via the nurse call system.
2. The nurse receives the call either as a voice call or text alert on a wireless phone.

3. The patient status display outside the patient room door indicates a call alert.
4. The summary status display at the nurse station indicates the call request and its current status.
5. The nurse enters the patient's room, noting the status on the status display.
6. The nurse ID badge is recognized upon entry via the RTLS system, and:
   a. cancels the call,
   b. registers the nurse's use of hand washing protocol via sensor at the infection control dispenser,
   c. introduces the staff member on the patient entertainment screen, and
   d. initiates a login screen on the patient bedside PC.
7. Activity and care reminders are announced on the bedside PC at log-on.
8. Data generated from clinical bedside devices are streamed and documented into the EHR.
9. Patient education that is prescribed by the clinician gets logged as activity in the EHR, with follow up testing/quizzing of the patient likewise documented.

The operative word here is *automation*. Certainly there are too many workflows, integration points, and automated functions to document and elaborate within the confines of this discussion, but the potential is clear. The integrated environment offers much promise for enhancing efficiency and accuracy and increasing patient satisfaction, all primary underpinnings in addressing the ACA in capital projects.

However, there is a significant caution on this particular technology trend. Successful implementation will be highly dependent on the demonstrated compatibility between disparate vendors. The vendor landscape is, for the most part, highly proprietary. For each of the systems listed that participate in the smart environment, vendors have varying approaches to working with others:

- The single-solution vendor, who uses open architecture and is willing to invest in and consider integration with other systems, but is not necessarily proven or established in integration with all other systems and vendors.
- The multiple-solution vendor, capturing the functionality of more than one system, with varying degrees of open architecture for integration. This vendor may be more selective in partnering for integration to gain specific market advantage for a given solution set.
- The comprehensive solution vendor, who captures most functions, with the least interest and motivation for partnering in integration in favor of an all-or-nothing approach.

Thus, one must be highly aware of the compatibility between vendors in achieving a fully integrated environment. A facility cannot simply go shopping for each individual system and expect to easily create an integrated solution. Careful vetting and analysis is required to ensure systems will integrate successfully.

The one-stop shop approach may be appealing, with one call to make and one point of responsibility for implementation. However, there are natural drawbacks as well. First, this one source may not obtain the best-in-class solution for each system included in the integrated product suite. And second, these vendors charge a premium for a comprehensive suite of products.

It is important also to remember that, while integrations exist between many of the systems listed as part of a smart environment, rare is the hospital today that has fully realized this vision. Many claim smart environment deployment, but most are a subset of the potential identified. Adoption data are anecdotal, as concrete industry research to provide firm data points is not yet available.

CONCLUSION

Today's healthcare facility cannot function without extensive use of low-voltage systems. With all the myriad system choices and purchase and implementation strategies, low-voltage technology can no longer be an afterthought in the planning and design process.

> ***Key Takeaways***
>
> - Prior to the ACA, technology was already changing healthcare delivery.
> - Healthcare facilities involve multiple systems, and they are not all integrated.
> - To get the full potential of IT, thoughtful planning is required and is best accomplished with a diversified steering committee at the project outset.
> - Budgets vary by provider, with academic centers investing almost twice as much as investor-owned institutions. Differentiating between required technology and desired technology is important.
> - The meaningful use program from the HITECH Act has had a major influence on technology trends.

REFERENCES

Brooks, S. 2012. "Affordable Care and HITECH Acts Not as Separate as Some Think." *EHR Intelligence Daily*. Published July 5. http://ehrintelligence.com/2012/07/05/affordable-care-and-hitech-acts-are-not-as-separate-as-some-think/.

Info-Tech Research Group. 2010. "Establish an Effective IT Steering Committee, Slide 5." Accessed November 20, 2014. www.slideshare.net/Info-Tech/establish-an-effective-it-steering-committee.

Wright, D. 2011. "Meaningful Use of Health Information Technology: Requirements and Solutions in Patient and Family Engagement." GetWellNetwork White Paper. Accessed November 20, 2014. http://info.getwellnetwork.com/Meaningful-Use-White-Paper.html.

CHAPTER 9

Medical Equipment: Making Prudent Choices for Investing in Capital Medical Equipment

Lisa Charrin

Medical equipment is a unique part of the typical hospital capital development project. It can be a major component of the total project cost—approaching as much as 25 percent. It also requires early attention because the utilities, both underground and in walls, must be defined at the start of the project schedule. However, there may be conflicting pressure from a hospital waiting to select equipment as late as possible to ensure opening its new facility with the latest, most state-of-the-art equipment available.

Additionally, hospitals face the issue of staying with one manufacturer because of systems integration, even if that manufacturer is no longer the manufacturer of choice for a particular system. With consolidation accelerating, the issue is not only hospital specific, but system specific. Having all manufacturers developing an open platform would go a long way toward solving that dilemma, and that may be starting to happen.

INTRODUCTION

Medical equipment is often the second highest cost for a construction project, and it has one of the largest shares of annual capital requests and allocations. The issues surrounding how to prioritize purchases are complex, as equipment touches nearly every aspect of healthcare:

- Physician recruitment
- Staff retention
- Capacity and throughput
- Patient care process
- Patient safety
- Quality and outcomes

The quality of care, especially in inpatient settings, has risen as Hospital Consumer Assessment and Health Provider Systems (HCAHPS) scores, Joint Commission requirements, and other facility guidelines have driven the built environment to support better outcomes and patient experiences.

Many organizations have implemented Lean and Six Sigma principles to enhance operations, to support better workflows, increase quality, reduce costs and improve overall processes. Because design and operations are so closely tied to equipment solutions, new, automated, and integrated technologies are changing workflows. Thus the need to make wise equipment selections is even more critical.

OPERATIONAL AND ACQUISITION TRENDS

As we move to a value-based system, one of the key impacts will be to effectively convert many revenue sources, such as radiology, to an expense. Thus the new goal will be to limit the use of this resource compared to the past goal, which was to create more demand for its use. Even though some have predicted that this shift, higher copays, and changes in malpractice avoidance will reduce the use of certain diagnostic tests, we know that more patients will still have access to and need for care. As facilities expand their hours to accommodate these new patients and maximize use of investments in technology, throughput and utilization become more important. The ability of equipment to maintain longer uninterrupted run times may require bigger investments in maintenance resources and more responsive service agreements.

As the technology advances, so do the options for acquiring that technology. Leasing high-expense medical equipment is becoming more common, despite the fact that leases still must appear as part of capital investments. The benefit remains that leasing can reduce the extent of first costs in a project. And with complex operating agreements, opportunities exist for the equipment to be treated as part of that agreement and not as a lease. For example, equipment may be provided as part of a consumable contract included in a monthly or annual operating agreement. These evolving arrangements are being pursued at both acute care and ambulatory care facilities.

Once relegated to third-world economies or very impoverished US institutions, refurbished equipment is seeing a resurgence. Major manufacturers offer a range of options for refurbished products with warranty and upgrade applications. Using a vendor- or manufacturer-guaranteed program can significantly reduce the cost of equipment purchases while providing adequate levels of technology.

MORE SOPHISTICATED DIAGNOSTICS OUTSIDE THE MEDICAL CENTER

Care is moving into the community, often away from the hospital. The role of the primary care provider has expanded and become more collaborative. Whether tracking a patient's fitness and wellness to redirect him into health or coordinating with multiple specialists to manage diagnostic procedures and medication compliance for a complex condition, the patient's primary physician has become an invested advisor. Today's primary care provider now directs and advises the patient with a team of midlevel practitioners, nutritionists, social workers, patient educators, and care coordinators.

In several states, notably Texas, new facility types are responding to the needs of growing urban and suburban communities. The urgent care center or free-standing emergency department (FSED) is one way in which both for-profit groups and healthcare systems are moving closer to their patients. Texas requires all FSEDs to include radiography and CT scanning as part of the diagnostic capability at every site. So we now have a proliferation of imaging equipment at facilities whose patient volume would have previously never justified such an expense. But the standards of care and demand for patient convenience are changing how we evaluate such expenditures.

More and more sophisticated ambulatory surgery centers are developing away from the hospital mother ship. Some of the most complex cases are now being done less invasively at outpatient facilities. In some facilities even open heart procedures such as valve repairs are done on an outpatient basis.

More collaborations are also occurring between fitness and rehabilitation providers. This sharing of trained staff and equipment minimizes the locations for care for the patient and maximizes the use of expensive resources. Cardio and pulmonary rehab equipment initially used following surgery or for a condition such as chronic obstructive pulmonary disease is comparable to that found in medically based fitness centers.

With the Affordable Care Act (ACA), greater numbers of patients will now have access to various diagnostic studies aimed at earlier detection through wellness-based exams:

- Colonoscopy
- Mammography
- Endoscopy
- Echocardiology/stress testing
- Chest X-ray
- Sleep studies/neurodiagnostics

Many studies are covered under the periodic screening provisions of the ACA. Others are ordered in response to other specific diagnostic findings. Generally these tests are performed in system-affiliated facilities.

Advancements in medical equipment, such as tomosynthesis versus traditional mammography, are also driving consumer choices on where patients go for their exams. Tomosynthesis was approved by the FDA in 2011, and emerging data suggest it is more effective when used in early detection screenings. Patients with dense breast tissue who have already undergone repeat scans or diagnostic mammography are now being referred directly to centers offering tomosynthesis. While reimbursement may lag behind technology advancements, consumers are choosing to pay higher copays for better technology.

And still others are paying for elective tests generally not covered by any insurance. Many of the tests in this last group are being marketed to patients who pay for them out of pocket despite the tests being of dubious clinical value. The tests are often conducted at free-standing centers operated by for-profit groups and located in strip shopping centers. While this approach is definitely one of the ways that care is moving into the community, it may not be sustainable. As education and economic forces cause patients to be better consumers of healthcare technology and better spenders of their own healthcare funds, these test centers for the worried may not survive, especially as patients pay larger co-pays.

The ultimate move into the community is to provide care at home or wherever the patient may be during the course of her day. Wearable monitoring or portable diagnostic equipment is allowing remote monitoring of patient data without requiring a trip by the patient to a provider or diagnostic center. Building on devices and systems developed by the military to monitor the health and status of soldiers in the field, the applications to our civilian world are almost endless. The ubiquitous use of smart phones, watches, and glasses is changing exponentially our ability to be connected to our caregivers. And this technology will only grow.

TECHNOLOGICAL TRENDS IN THE MEDICAL CENTER

Monitoring

In the hospital, both as a means of consolidating functions to reduce the number of full-time equivalents (FTEs) and improve the quality of monitoring, there is increased use of central monitoring. By placing monitoring in one location, fewer highly trained staff can monitor multiple locations in the facility: the intensive care unit, the emergency department (ED), and any other location with critical physiologic status tracking needs. In some instances, proprietary regional centers contract with hospitals to provide this service.

Another trend is to equip all patient rooms with capability for telemetry and vitals monitoring. Primary drivers are integration with the electronic medical record, reducing infection risk by avoiding shared equipment, and saving time by not having to hunt and gather and then set up equipment in a room. These drivers often offset the expense of additional units. Physiological monitors with central monitoring are still the norm in critical care environments; however, centralizing all monitored patients allows better continuity and tracking of alarms, response times, and even preemptive alarms to notify staff of change in patient condition.

When these systems are further integrated with nurse call systems, there is increased alarm management, reduced nurse response wait time, and enhanced prioritization of patient calls.

Laboratories

In the larger clinical laboratories, there is greater use of automation for accessioning and management of specimens. Refrigerated storage towers can automatically retrieve or restock specific specimens. Aliquoting and other specimen handling can also be automated. Automated analyzers are now able to use minute specimen amounts on which to run multiple tests. Industry trends also include point-of-care testing (POCT) and telepathology offering, respectively, extremes of bringing the test to the patient or bringing the specialist to the test. POCT allows immediate results reporting in many cases and obviates the need to take the patient to another location. The majority of POCT devices are handheld and thus portable to wherever the patient is; however, equipment checkout and charging must be well managed and include a process to track staff training and proficiency in the operation of these devices.

With telepathology, a patient having a biopsy no longer needs to wait until a pathologist can be located to determine whether the biopsy specimen is adequate for diagnostic purposes. The pathologist can be miles away and review the image via microscope transmission. Telepathology can also occur between a clinician and lab or between labs and other educational, research, or office locations, much like sharing X-rays via a picture archiving and communication system. However, telepathology is more often used for virtual consultation, with two-way audio and/or video communications between two or more locations or between surgeons and anatomical pathologists for verification of specimen quality or initial findings, including assessment of margins and extent of tumor resection. Equipment will usually include a microscope with digital camera attachment and computer systems that support the transmission of images within defined parameters for speed, resolution, display, and annotation. The weakest link of the various technologies will dictate the quality of the image transmission.

Telepathology is not only applicable to serving remote areas; academic medical centers also use it to expand services and provide patient convenience without duplicating specialists in low-volume areas.

Pharmacy

Automation and robotics are also being used extensively in pharmacies to provide greater accuracy, accountability, and efficiency. Automated medication dispensing stations appear throughout facilities from the patient care units to the ED. The challenge is to keep them adequately stocked. Such dispensing automation is also being used for high-volume supplies.

Anesthesia has also implemented automated medication distribution systems throughout operating rooms and procedure rooms where general anesthesia is required all of the time or for a majority of cases. But these machines require more space in addition to the anesthesia machine and supply cart and require a more robust plan for restocking on a daily basis.

Surgery

We cannot ignore the appearance of robotics in surgery. Minimally invasive, robotic-assisted procedures are being performed routinely, even though reimbursement for these cases is still far less than the cases demand. Savings are being claimed for reduced patient stays, reduced incidence of nosocomial infection, less scarring, less complicated recoveries, and the ability for patients to resume normal lifestyles sooner. Publicity has also focused on greater surgical precision.

The marketing efforts have been so successful that both patients and providers claim that, without such equipment, patients are receiving and surgeons are providing less than optimum care for many procedures. However, several recent studies have indicated no appreciably better outcomes with the use of robotics. Still some facilities, such as academic medical centers with the highest proficiencies, are applying their skills in robotics to newer applications where open surgery may not have even been possible. But with a much higher focus on reducing costs, the challenge to bridge the gap in cost versus reimbursement will be even greater with this technology.

Interventional Procedures

The other major trend is the blurring of lines between previously rigidly defined specialty services. Surgeons and interventionalists are relying on navigation systems and image-guided procedures for preoperative planning tools and intraoperative scanning to improve accuracy and outcomes. While the advent of the interventional platform has created opportunities for sharing pre- and postoperative and procedural staff and space, turf wars still occur over whose procedure room it really is. Many different equipment options still exist, depending on which types of procedures are to be performed and by whom. Major functional considerations include the location of the room and the degree of support for sedation or general anesthesia. Rooms are becoming more like operating rooms with ceiling-hung flat panels, video or power outlets to support a range of tableside medical devices, and columns or booms for anesthesia and medical gases, power, video, and other equipment.

Hybrid rooms also present challenges in terms of reimbursement, which is often a step behind technology capability: how to bill for two separate procedures that can now be performed in a single case or for the two clinicians who must be present for different types of intervention. Collaboration seems to be gaining over traditional politics as more common ground is forged among the formerly separate kingdoms of cardiology, neurosurgery, orthopedics or interventional radiology. Based on the type and volume of procedures, a single interventional suite may or may not be the better option for flexibility. These high-tech rooms are not for every hospital, and at some point physician proficiency demands a volume sufficient to maintain consistent skill and quality in using these types of rooms.

Infection Prevention

With increased awareness of prevention of hospital-acquired infections (HAIs), health systems have made significant investments to upgrade central sterile equipment, acquire instrumentation tracking systems, and improve facilities for the proper flow of dirty and clean material.

The Association of periOperative Registered Nurses (AORN 2010) has recommended minimal use of immediate use (formerly known as "flash") sterilization in an effort to force best practices with centralization of processing among trained and dedicated sterile processing staff. This translates to greater centralized processing capacity but potentially larger instrument inventories to avoid running short during a procedure.

HAIs such as *Clostridium difficile* and methicillin-resistant *Staphylococcus aureus* (MRSA) have caused manufacturers to be major players in reducing the rates of these infections. Airborne sanitizing systems are being implemented in hospitals across the inpatient environment to provide comprehensive cleaning through automated room-sterilization systems. While not universally accepted, these newer technologies use either ultraviolet light or hydrogen peroxide vapor (HPV) to bio-decontaminate patient rooms and other spaces and equipment that are potential sources of HAIs. While HPV is very effective, it runs counter to the green cleaning movement in healthcare. Once again, there are a series of tradeoffs that affect major equipment purchases.

Patient Care Units

Inpatient units are some of the most repetitive areas of a hospital, and while these units are designed similarly, they are often occupied by specialties such as orthopedics or cardiology, depending on the primary reason for admission. However, as patients now present with multiple chronic conditions, the need is growing to bring more resources to the patient where technology permits, such as considering dialysis capability in every room or an EKG on every floor. With improvements in digital and wireless technologies, hospitals have more options of procedures that can be done at or near the bedside:

- Digital X-ray (mobile X-ray)
- Ultrasound/echo/ECG
- CT (mobile or fixed CTs dedicated to inpatient trauma/neuro/neonatal units)
- Fluoroscopy (mobile c-arm)

Several questions need additional research to validate the assumptions about better care. Does the investment really result in improved outcomes? Is there an unsupportable staffing and transportation FTE impact?

While comparatively fewer total hospital replacement projects exist now than in previous decades, there are still projects to provide updated patient care units. But with the relative scarcity of capital for construction, the need for flexibility and long-term adaptability has increased. The patient room has gotten bigger for a variety of reasons: patient privacy, accommodation for family, greater utilization, reduced HAIs, and so on. The amount of equipment at the bedside has also increased.

Repetitive Solutions with Potentially Exponential Costs

The universal room and acuity-adaptable room have provided hospitals with a room capable of providing a range of care, from critical care to discharge, from the same bed. Some essential equipment is standard and ideally is part of the basic room complement. Several new projects have incorporated dedicated equipment closets to house these items. Other items are provided as part of the headwall or even the bed itself. Virtually every healthcare design conference features new opportunities to equip and outfit rooms. And all come with significant costs. But again, the tradeoff appears: spend more to equip all or most spaces, or spend more on staff time and possibly compromised care when an essential piece of equipment cannot be found. While real time locating systems and radio frequency identification can help locate a piece of equipment, someone still needs to move it where it is needed. Knowing the location of an item or tracking the utilization of an asset are critical to managing limited capital resources.

Some of the items that consume large portions of an equipment budget now and can certainly command more include the following:

- Beds—specialty, bariatric, those with advanced monitoring, communication, and entertainment systems built in or able to be added as modules
- Mattresses—specialty types to reduce the incidence of bed sores, blood clots, or pneumonia with rotation or vibration/percussion features and settings
- Patient transport/beds—beds that lift the patient and aid in patient transfer

- Patient lifts—fixed versus portable that can transport the patient into the bathroom, shower, or around the patient room
- Mats and flooring—specialty sensors that alert when a patient gets out of bed or their chair; surfaces that are slip resistant
- Hand wash facilities—sensors that alert if a provider (or other person) enters the room without observing hand washing protocols

The list goes on. There are endless opportunities to assist caregivers and benefit patients through the following:

- Reduced patient falls
- Decreased staff workplace injuries
- Direct integration of patient data into the EHR
  - Patient weight
  - Bed position and incline
  - Bed exits
- Tailored patient education and entertainment

But the benefits must be weighed with the cost. Since the patient room is the most repeated room in an acute care facility, its components can have both tremendous costs and benefits.

Materials Management

As a means of improving care and lowering cost, supply management systems have expanded reporting capabilities and are being integrated with the electronic health record (EHR). Hospitals and systems are implementing inventory management and supply distribution systems that enable better tracking and just-in-time restocking. Planning for capital projects should include discussions around supply concepts early in the planning process to confirm the approach for the new project, as these systems are often undergoing evaluation and change. Use of automated guided vehicles is typically seen in large system hospitals, while smaller facilities use wall panels and plastic bins to maximize storage.

The responsibility for supply purchasing and management is being consolidated into a centralized function in many institutions to replace previously fragmented purchasing, storage, and distribution processes.

Satellite materials management centers are being constructed on campuses to optimize dock and distribution activities separately from the main facility. Some large system medical centers already serve as satellite providers to their smaller community hospital affiliates. All of these supply systems and approaches can be a combination of capital equipment and leased operational costs.

INTEGRATION OF MEDICAL DEVICES AND INFORMATION

The medical equipment community is quickly following the consumer electronics industry by creating:

- multiple platforms, some open and others proprietary;
- wireless-enabled technologies;
- remote diagnostics; and
- tracking systems and interfaces to the EHR systems.

Manufacturers continue to improve systems to respond to demands for increased workflow and integration with the EHR. Healthcare systems are balancing the idea of single manufacturer relationships with best-in-breed for each medical device. As a result, manufacturers are moving away from proprietary closed systems to open platforms that defy the old sandbox mentality and begin to see the world as the new playground.

But an added challenge has surfaced: keeping up with technology integration. Every time a device is upgraded or replaced, new or modified interfaces with the EHR or other compatible systems are needed. However, even with more software upgrades and fewer physical product replacements, hospitals and systems still need to look closely at specifications and allocate adequate time to update these related systems and conduct training in their use. Such technology integration can be a significant barrier to overcome if not proactively planned and assessed as part of the equipment purchase.

The portals to access information come in multiple formats—the computer on wheels, the bedside computer, the laptop, the mobile device, the physiological monitor, the integration control desk, and so on. These devices are all designed to bring information to the forefront, completely customized, and geared to improving patient care. With workforce shortages a reality, many of the equipment systems are aiding care through alarm management and enhanced protocols to alert caregivers to subtle changes in the patient's vitals that could signal the advent of sepsis.

Technology has enabled virtual consults and, as consumers and physicians have grown accustomed to finding anything using an Internet search or with a handheld app, the medical device community is working to keep pace. Social media plays a role already in increasing patient awareness of treatment options. Interest is growing in how medicine can begin to connect the data coming from consumer market devices tracking, for example, patient exercise and how that data could become a part of monitoring patient compliance with prescribed care plans. But this raises the issues of whose equipment the patient is using and what interface is required. Equipment and items classed as medical devices, as opposed to consumer electronics, will be more likely to support a more connected, virtual world of healthcare and wellness.

CONCLUSION

While the evaluation of technology investments is initially focused on the benefits to the patient, correlating the reality of improved outcomes with the potentially huge capital investments will be important. Unbiased research is critical to making informed decisions with such impact on care and finances. ECRI Institute has historically been one group to provide analysis of equipment safety and efficacy. Other groups, such as the Radiological Society of North America, also provide valuable insights into proven equipment performance and value. With decisions of this magnitude, more information is essential.

As the setting shifts from treating patients in hospitals and clinics to home, there will likely be a rise in the technologies that aim to connect the patient's day-to-day activities with his medical record and/or care providers. Again, an expensive approach.

We know that equipment technologies are evolving with key features and functions that move these decisions from commodity-based cost decisions to value-based care delivery decisions. Until we have an entirely value-based delivery system, equipment will remain as market drivers, recruitment lures, and consumer satisfiers. And tough decisions that are not solely about optimum outcomes will also remain.

The responses really haven't changed from the time of almost unlimited construction at the first part of the twenty-first century. There are now just many more possibilities.

With these ideas in mind,

- plan early and often;
- assume that technological advances will require replacement of some equipment that still has a useful life, and budget accordingly;
- choose for efficacy, interoperability, and integration;
- consider partnering with specific manufacturers to maintain access to technology advances and dependable service; and

- provide adequate time when acquiring new and upgrading existing equipment to accommodate changed interfaces.

Medical equipment, like the technological infrastructure and the cadre of healthcare professionals, is an essential part of any healthcare facility's operational backbone. Its complexity, capabilities, and cost are ever-changing and increasing. The challenge is to choose the right equipment with the right integration and the right adaptability to meet both today's patient care needs and tomorrow's.

Key Takeaways

- Just as technology is changing our personal lives, it is changing the entire medical equipment landscape.
- Touching virtually every part of a healthcare facility, medical equipment is an integral influence on the delivery of healthcare.
- By increasing patient satisfaction, reducing medical errors, and enhancing wellness components of the ACA, medical equipment is now influencing the noncapital development aspect of healthcare.
- Medical equipment and technology are emblematic of the classic conflict caused by the ACA: do we make huge investments in equipment, hoping to lower hospital utilization as a result of the wellness aspect demanded by the law?
- Because of the amount of equipment coming into a hospital and the growing interdependency between the modalities, the interoperability of the equipment becomes a major challenge.

REFERENCE

Association of periOperative Registered Nurses (AORN). 2010. "*Recommended Practices for Sterilization in the Perioperative Practice Setting.*" *Perioperative Standards and Recommended Practices.* Denver, CO: Association of periOperative Registered Nurses.

CHAPTER 10

Privatization: Better Value for Money Through Innovation, Discipline, and Risk Transfer

John Kemper

The massive real estate property that goes into the average-sized health system is mind-boggling. Often, in cases like the Texas Medical Center in Houston or New York Presbyterian Hospital in Manhattan, it is like driving though a city. The monetary investment, as well as investment in staff to oversee and manage that real estate, is overwhelming. But as mentioned in Chapter 5 and Chapter 6, just because hospitals are big users of real estate doesn't mean they have to own that real estate.

An argument can be made that the hospital or healthcare system would be better served if it expended all of its energies and capital improving the delivery of healthcare—and not in worrying about roof drainage and repairing air handlers. This chapter addresses the concept of privatization. The concept started in England more than 25 years ago

(continued)

(continued from previous page)

> with its private financing initiative (PFI), and then moved to Canada about 15 years ago with its public–private partnerships (PPP). The approach has been growing in the United States in non-healthcare areas such as convention center hotels, parking garages, student housing, and infrastructure projects such as roads and bridges. In fact, the state of Virginia is now building 100 percent of its new roads through privatized toll roads.
>
> With the pressures on reimbursement that have been identified in this book, it is inconceivable to us that more and more projects, especially those of larger capital development, will not be done through privatization.

IN THIS CHAPTER we explore how privatization has been and can be utilized to provide better value for the scarce capital resources available to healthcare owners through innovative delivery models. We examine how and where these models have been utilized throughout the world and how they might be utilized in the US healthcare market.

FINANCIAL REALITIES

The Affordable Care Act (ACA) is having a tremendous impact on healthcare providers, especially on reimbursement structure. Because of declining reimbursements, healthcare systems are trying to stabilize margins by realizing economies of scale any way they can.

Another factor affecting providers is the consolidation and merger of many systems. These new arrangements often result in a large number of facilities being acquired. But the long-term strategy for the use of these facilities is not being developed as part of the acquisition process. The result in the not-too-distant future will be a large, pent-up demand for repositioning of these facilities.

At the same time, healthcare leaders are focused on reducing operating costs. Currently cash is king for healthcare providers, and the demand for this limited cash will drive organizations to explore new and innovative ways, such as the privatization model, to deliver much-needed capital improvements.

"Long term structural change in the sector has favored a minority of larger, well managed hospitals and systems, while creating ever tighter competitive conditions for the majority of smaller, especially free-standing, hospitals. While some years of robust economic growth have stabilized the outlook for the sector, credit trends have been negative and will remain so until the next wave of regulatory and business model changes are more clearly established in the coming years." Moody's Investor Service provided this assessment of the healthcare market in January 2012. With the need for capital growing to meet meaningful use requirements, replace aging infrastructure, acquire new partners, and develop a more robust ambulatory care network, healthcare organizations must develop a flexible delivery strategy that uses all sources of capital available. The lack of a strategic financial plan and swift execution to enable growth and improve defensive position in the market will put an organization in a perilous position.

While capital markets have become a club for those AA and A-rated healthcare organizations that enjoy more financing options and some very low tax-exempt debt at today's rates, that club is not totally exclusive. All investment-grade healthcare organizations have a myriad of options available, but some take more time than others to syndicate.

ALTERNATIVE FINANCING OPPORTUNITIES AND ASSESSING FINANCIAL HEALTH

More often than not, healthcare organizations let the development of capital needs lead while the development of a plan to finance them lags behind. Given the sensitivity of time to market in such a tightly competitive and regulatory environment, alternative financing strategies are often abandoned and become lost opportunities due to the lack of time to perform the required due diligence. Prior to embarking on a capital project or program, the healthcare organization should complete what is known as a launch gap analysis, as shown in Exhibit 10.1. A critical part of this analysis should be the exploration of alternative financing options.

In order to position a healthcare organization to be able to access the lowest cost options for capital these organizations should do the following as a minimum:

- *Monitor and measure.* Set up tools and account codes to closely monitor financial performance at a service-line level and measure that against available benchmarks. The ability to get good data from within your organization can allow for the maintenance and strengthening of the organization's financial position.
- *Open up to financing alternatives.* Many alternatives can be syndicated together to provide capital to address current needs. Identify one person within the organization to be responsible for identifying all options within your jurisdiction and developing a decision matrix to evaluate options as needs arise. Continuously updating this decision matrix is imperative as local, state, and federal funding grants can have a limited shelf life.
- *Think about partnerships differently.* The past featured a majority of partnerships between hospitals, physician

Exhibit 10.1 Launch Gap Analysis Process

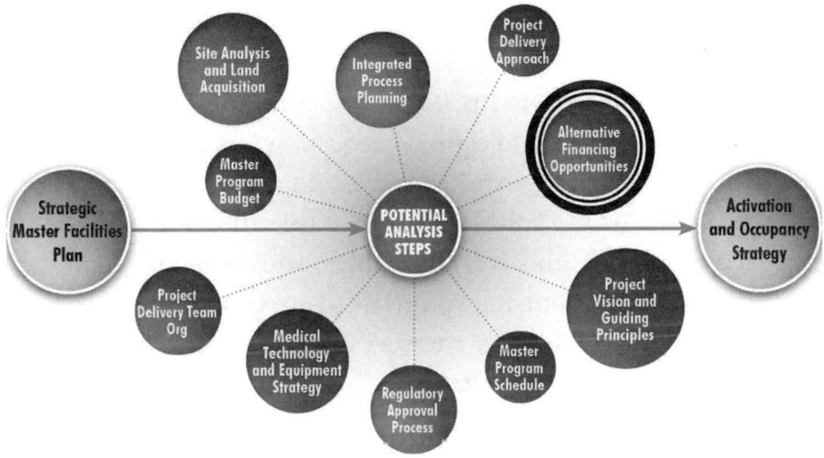

Source: CBRE Healthcare

groups, long-term care providers, and the like. The future will also feature partnerships with insurance companies, private equity groups, large corporations, research and pharmaceutical companies, technology firms, and academic institutions at all levels. This transition seems logical, as healthcare affects the lives and balance sheets of our entire population. As healthcare continues to transform, partnerships that never would have been considered in the past will arise. These new options can help to increase available capital and improve an organization's long-term financial position.

While many details surrounding these three strategies need to be pursued by a healthcare organization, following this approach will ensure that the financial plan is leading the development of capital needs and a look at alternative financing options.

PRIVATIZATION

Many options are available to healthcare organizations as they develop sources for capital uses. The feasibility of each of these options varies based on an institution's credit rating, tax treatment, and the timing and type of capital need. For years, healthcare organizations have primarily worked with medical real estate developers to provide turnkey solutions for medical office and ambulatory care facilities. While this is still a viable option for non–acute care facilities, it is important to explore third-party solutions for acute care facilities that typically are more capital intense. One approach with great promise is privatization.

What Is Privatization?

Privatization generally refers to private enterprise—business activities unregulated by state ownership or control. Privatization is not new to the healthcare market. The nation's for-profit systems have operated as private enterprises since they came into existence. It is estimated that about 59 percent of the nation's hospitals are private not-for-profit hospitals (AHA 2014).

Not-for-profits are exempted from federal income taxes (and often other taxes as well) and can issue tax-exempt bonds.

A for-profit or investor-owned hospital or system is either owned by private investors or is owned publically by shareholders and is part of a company that issues shares of stock to raise revenue to expand healthcare activities. Depending on economic conditions, for-profit hospitals can have better access to capital than not-for-profits that often fund construction by issuing debt through tax-exempt bonds.

When discussing the privatization of healthcare facilities, especially the large acute care facilities, understanding how other countries and organizations have approached this subject is helpful.

Throughout the European Union, Australia, Canada, India, Japan, and Russia, public–private partnerships (PPPs) have been used widely to deal with the economic stressors that have plagued the financial marketplace in general and the construction industry in particular.

Let's explore the origin and history of PPPs. A PPP is a government service or private business venture that is funded and operated through a partnership between a sponsoring organization and one or more private sector companies. In the United States, PPPs have a long history dating back to the Virginia Company, founder of the Jamestown Settlement. The Virginia Company was really a PPP dating back to the early 1600s!

PPPs usually have two fundamental drivers:

- They enable the sponsoring agency to harness the expertise and efficiencies that the private sector can bring to the delivery of certain facilities and services typically procured and delivered by the sponsoring agency.
- They are structured so that the sponsoring agency seeking to make the capital investment does not incur any borrowing.

Limited forms of public–private collaborations have existed since the Middle Ages in various forms. Most credit the United Kingdom as the birthplace of modern-day PPPs. The most common form of PPP used in the United Kingdom, the private finance initiative (PFI), was introduced in 1992 by the Conservative government of Prime Minister John Major to rebuild its aging healthcare infrastructure. As then-Minister of Health Alan Milburn said (Parliamentary Debates 1998), "As part of a modernisation programme, there is more investment in London's front-line health services. Moreover, that money for front-line services is backed by capital investment, as we cannot build a twenty-first-century NHS [National Health Service] in London in nineteenth-century hospitals."

The main driver of the PFI program was to involve the private sector in the design, construction, financing, operation, and maintenance of public infrastructure, and to secure the delivery of well-constructed, well-maintained infrastructure at a good value to the taxpayers.

The typical PFI structure is illustrated in Exhibit 10.2.

The special purpose entity (SPE) was typically led by a large construction management firm, and the SPE owned the real estate. The public sector entity was the National Health Service (NHS), usually represented by the local health trust.

The SPE paid to the NHS a yearly "availability fee" once the construction was completed. The PFI approach was considered a real estate transaction, which would be known as a *lease back* deal in the United States. Since 1992, the United Kingdom has experienced many successes in the 700-plus PFI projects it has brought to financial close, many of which were healthcare related. However, many also questioned the PFI approach.

Exhibit 10.2 Typical PFI Structure

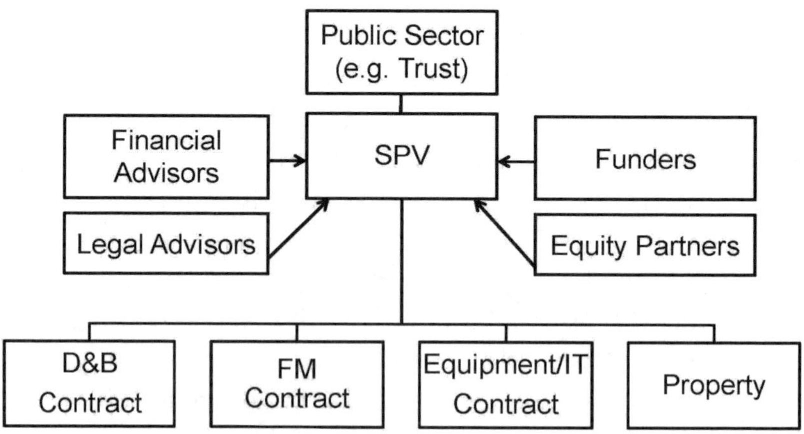

Source: CBRE Healthcare

As in the United Kingdom, Australia and Canada have long histories with PPPs for infrastructure and healthcare projects. Many observers claim these projects have been more successful. But why does the PPP model work successfully in some cases and not in others?

That question was debated in the United Kingdom and was the basis for a 2011 government study (HM Treasury 2012). The study identified several issues:

- The process is often slow and expensive, leading to reduced value to taxpayers.
- The PFI contracts are often inflexible, making changes difficult during the operational period.
- The process has not been transparent enough in the areas of future liabilities and returns to investors.
- The risks transferred to the private sector have resulted in higher risk premium charges to the public sector.
- The perception of windfall gains to equity investors has led to concerns about the true value for money of the projects.

To address these concerns, the UK government's new initiatives include the following key components:

- Include the government as a minority public entity coinvestor.
- Introduce funding competitions for a portion of equity to attract long-term investors.
- Accelerate project delivery by, among other things,
  - strengthening the mandate of Infrastructure UK and supporting departmental centralized procurement units,
  - shortening the tender process, and
  - standardizing procurement documentation.

- Introduce additional treasury oversight.
- Improve transparency by publication of more information throughout the process.
- Return more risk management to the public sector.

For healthcare owners considering the use of the PPP structure to deliver major facilities in the future, it might be time to copy the Canadian approach. In Canada, offices such as Partnerships British Columbia have been established and charged with helping the provinces navigate the world of PPPs to make sure the transactions are structured properly so the sponsoring organization (healthcare provider) gets the best return on its investment. This approach has an impressive record of delivering projects on time and at significant savings.

These offices such as Partnership British Columbia are not government agencies, and they function more like consulting firms. They are able to hire staff with expertise to navigate the legal, financial, and technical complexities of PPP transactions. In the United States, a handful of states such as Virginia, California, and Michigan have established dedicated PPP organizations.

In recent years, the growing sophistication of performance contracts has allowed private developers, localities, and, in some cases, states to structure the roles of partners in PPP transactions with improved certainty and ability to measure performance. These performance-based transactions hold great promise for implementation in the US healthcare marketplace.

In a typical performance-based transaction, a private entity would be charged with planning, designing, building, financing, and maintaining the facility and it would receive a flat fee, typically called an *availability fee*, from the sponsoring organization for doing so. If the costs come in higher than expected, the private sector company and not the sponsoring agency is on the hook to pay the difference. An excellent example of the potential of this delivery method for a large healthcare project is the Abbotsford

Regional Hospital and Cancer Center, a 300-bed facility just east of Vancouver, British Columbia, opened in 2008 as a replacement for an older facility.

Under the terms of that transaction, the private partner agrees to certain performance standards over the duration of the 30-year, $424 million contract. The private partner can earn more if it exceeds those standards, and it will earn less if performance falls short. Partnership British Columbia officials estimate that by transferring risks associated with construction, maintenance, and operation to a private entity, they saved approximately $39 million over the term of the contract.

This type of transaction is being used extensively in Canada to rebuild the country's healthcare infrastructure, and it holds great potential to be a more innovative and creative way to deliver major healthcare facilities in the United States.

Such projects, known as performance guaranteed facilities (PGFs), have the following characteristics:

- An independent third party accepts responsibility to design, build, finance, maintain, and, in some cases, operate a single project or bundle of similar projects (new construction, renovation, or expansion) for either a private or public healthcare organization.
- The agreement covering this relationship is longer term, usually 25 to 30 years, driving the parties to invest in the best net present value or life-cycle costs, not first costs, with predefined hand back conditions.
- There is a firm price for the term of the agreement for capital repayment, operating and maintenance, and refurbishment—not only for the base building, but for all improvements; this price can also include all furniture and equipment.
- There is no charge on title required by the third party, as the project is financed with the sponsor's (healthcare

organization's) promise to make the monthly payments, understanding that this will be conditional on the facility being available and performing to agreed standards or key performance indicators (KPIs). In other words, the operational risk is transferred to third party, and if the KPIs are not met, the monthly availability payments are adjusted.

This is a performance-based contracting arrangement, where

- payment from the sponsor only begins upon completion of construction, and
- ongoing payments are subject to deduction for failures in service delivery of the facility or parts thereof being available for use.

The partnership model is structured as illustrated in Exhibit 10.3.

Although financing is fundamental to the PGF approach, this should not be considered as simply an alternative financing

Exhibit 10.3 Performance Guaranteed Facility Structure

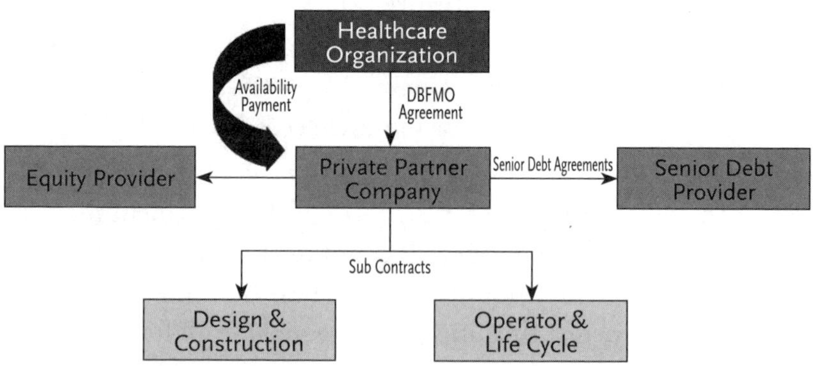

Source: Plenary Group

mechanism. The financing in the PGF model is the catalyst that drives the value proposition stemming from the risk transfer and the optimization of whole-life costs or life-cycle costs. It keeps the private partner company's interests aligned with those of the sponsor.

Although the cost of financing through vehicles such as tax-exempt debt issues and other corporate/government debt issues can be initially less, the benefits derived from the performance-based approach far exceed the incremental costs. Exhibit 10.4 illustrates the key financial metrics that need to be in place to make a PGF model work.

Value for money reports for healthcare facilities in Canada indicate savings in the range of 12 to 18 percent on the net present cost of facilities where PGF has been applied. Additionally, there are approaches to incorporating the less expensive debt into the structure to increase the overall value proposition. Exhibit 10.5 highlights the differences in risk allocation compared to the most common procurement approaches.

The following is a comparison of these three approaches.

Traditional approach. Under the traditional approach of facilities procurement where the sponsor uses its own source of funds (typically raised through tax-exempt debt or other financing), the sponsor may get lower-cost financing but retains most, if not all, of the construction and operations risk for the facility. It is exposed to cost and time overruns during the construction phase in a traditional procurement and operating, maintenance, and rehabilitation risk during the operating term for any of the procurement models other than PGF. One of the more significant exposures is to deferred maintenance, which often results in premature and costly deterioration of the asset.

Capital lease. Under a typical single credit tenant scenario, the sponsor transfers risk for design and construction (base building

Exhibit 10.4 PGF Financial Metrics

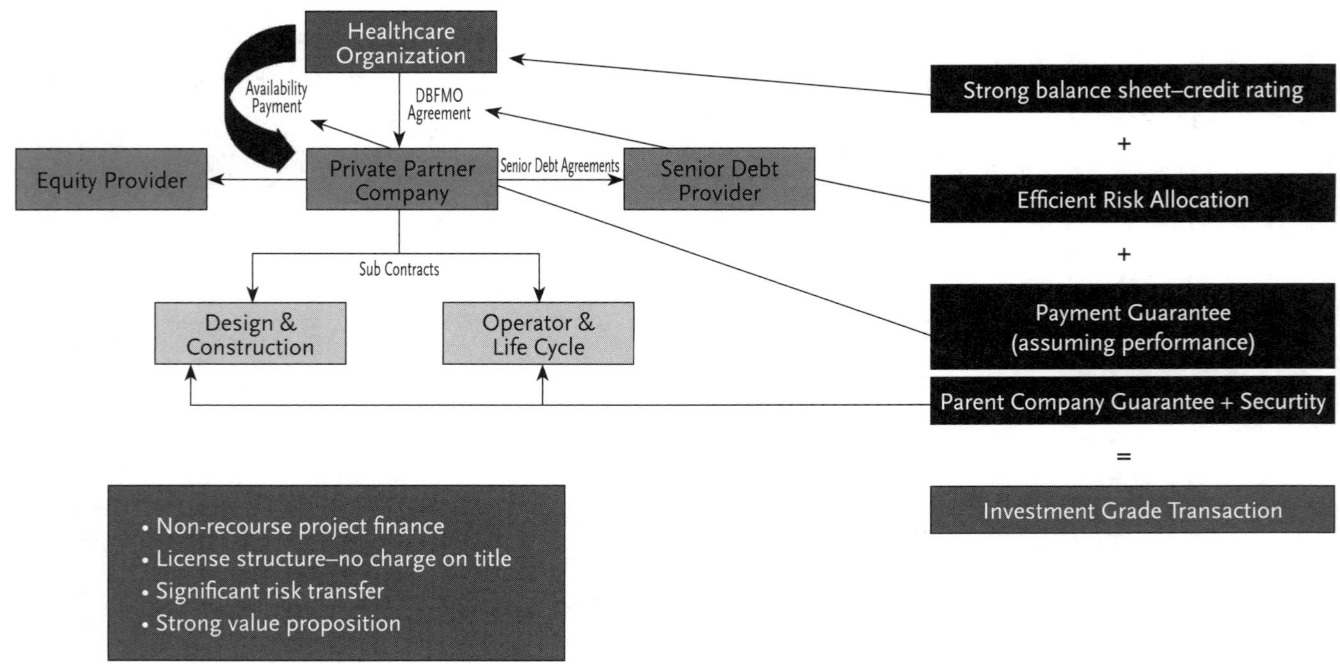

Source: Plenary Group

Exhibit 10.5 Risk Allocation by Procurement Type

	Risk Element	Traditional	Capital Lease	PGF
Procurement	Program operations	Sponsor	Sponsor	Shared
	Design and construction	Sponsor	Shared	Private
	Finance	Sponsor	Shared	Private
	Land/building ownership	Sponsor	Shared	Sponsor
Operating Term	Rights retention	Sponsor	Private	Sponsor
	Operation costs above plan*	Sponsor	Sponsor	Private
	Cost of operations	Sponsor	Sponsor	Private
	Availability/abatement	Sponsor	Sponsor	Private
	Life-cycle replacement	Sponsor	Shared	Private
	Condition at end of term	Sponsor	Shared	Private
	Operating performance	Sponsor	Sponsor	Private

*Plan set during procurement phase, prior to commitment to proceed

Sponsor	Shared	Private

Source: Plenary Group

only), and perhaps some operating costs for a short term as defined in a capital lease agreement. Life-cycle refurbishment costs may be carried in a sinking fund held in trust. However, shortfalls (or surpluses) would be to the sponsor's account. The ownership of the underlying asset belongs to the private developer.

An issue with this model is the misalignment between the design–build phase and long-term operations. Cost pressures during construction can lead to scope reductions that lessen the quality of the building but protect the developer's preferred equity return. The sponsor also loses its rights in real property as they are transferred to the developer through either the sale or long-term lease of the underlying real estate. This means that the developer (landlord) has approval rights to changes in use limiting future flexibility for the sponsor. As noted above, although the developer may take some building performance risk, it is typically limited to the base building and often results in a pass through of expenses over and above a base year benchmark. Payments to the developer are due regardless of building performance and availability for use by the sponsor.

PGF model. The sponsor retains its property rights but transfers full design and construction, operations, and life-cycle refurbishment risks to the private partner, including tenant improvements, not just the base building, and can also include equipment and furnishings. Most important, unlike the other approaches, the private partner only gets paid back if the facility is available and performing as specified; otherwise an abatement regime kicks in, and the payment is reduced accordingly.

Equally important, the private partner provides a firm price for these costs for the term of the agreement, creating certainty and ensuring efficient operations to optimize building performance. It is also common to find energy guarantees, where the private partner will guarantee energy consumption on the basis of the intended use—again promoting optimization of building performance and alignment of interests. The value proposition that comes from the optimization of whole-life costs is likely the most significant but undervalued benefit of this approach.

From the perspective of a facility's entire life, the early work of design, construction, and transition is estimated to be less than

13 percent of the total facility cost over 40 years. The low-hanging fruit clearly comes from focusing on the whole-life costs during the design and construction phases of the contract. Making small investments in facility efficiency and durability during the design and construction phase will result in significant dividends in the form of long-term operational savings.

Although this example refers to a hospital, other facility types, such as ambulatory and outpatient centers, would likely have a similar ratio. While operating and maintenance costs may be lower, so are construction costs. Regardless, the general conclusion will not change. This optimization is often attempted with traditional approaches under the banner of integrated project delivery (IPD). The challenge with IPD is that more often than not it becomes an exercise of well-meaning people who are brought together to identify the design and construction elements required to optimize project delivery and whole-life costs, but who may then be asked to value-engineer many of the elements out to achieve a capital cost target.

The financing component of the PGF model shifts the paradigm as it moves the focus to the net present value of the monthly payments for the term of the agreement, rather than the first-in costs. In addition, the optimization is guaranteed because the payments are fixed for the same term at agreed-on rates based on the proposed design.

The value proposition is further enhanced through the provision of an energy guarantee that is developed during the design process on the basis of an energy model that reflects the design loads at the time of the initial design. As equipment or use changes over the term, the energy model is updated. The energy guarantee is for consumption, not cost, as passing risk for commodity prices for a long term would be inefficient.

Exhibit 10.6 illustrates how the PGF delivery process works from start of planning to when a fully functioning facility is turned over to the sponsoring agency.

Exhibit 10.6 The PGF Delivery Process

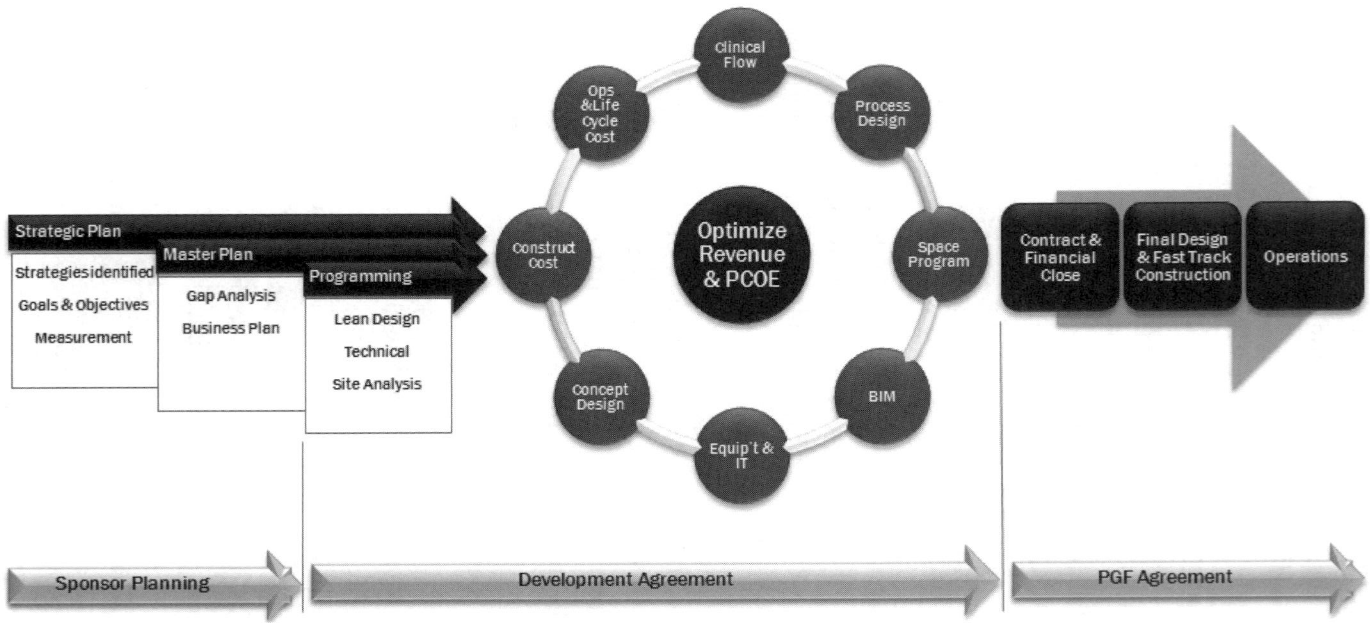

Source: CBRE Healthcare

CONCLUSION

The PGF model can deliver a superior value for the money than traditional approaches, including sponsor-contracted design and construction (traditional) and developer leases (capital lease). This value is achieved through the performance-based approach to risk transfer and the optimization of whole-life costs that are guaranteed through the payment mechanism. The major benefits that can be derived by a healthcare owner when considering the PGF or some other form of privatization include:

- speed to market;
- laser focus on clinical process efficiency;
- ownership of the asset retained by the healthcare owner;
- emphasis on a clear and well-defined risk allocation;
- certainty of whole-life costs;
- guaranteed facility condition;
- private sector expertise, innovation, and discipline;
- delivery on time and within budget; and
- healthcare owner focus on core services instead of procurement, contract management, construction oversight, and facility operations.

The need for building, renovating, and replacing critical infrastructure continues to grow in the United States and in the healthcare industry in particular. To address these needs, organizations must explore and enhance programs for the financing and delivery of capital projects through innovative approaches such as PPP. Properly structured partnerships can conserve an organization's financing capacity, leverage private dollars, and tap into private marketing and management skills that traditional procurement discourages.

Key Takeaways

- Hospitals are big users of real estate, but they don't have to be owners of real estate.
- Lack of accumulated cash, caused by ACA reimbursement headwinds, is a major driver of PPP. This alternative ownership model will grow just as it has in other non-healthcare areas.
- PPP is a major shifting of risk, as availability payments will include not only buildings but medical equipment; furniture, fixtures, and equipment; delivery of non-healthcare services (e.g., dietary), and, in some cases, operational performance guarantees.
- The pursuit of these projects can be expensive, as the minimal amount of money that is provided to the finalists is insufficient. The best situation is when an owner contracts with a planner and architect to do bridging documents before solicitation takes place.

REFERENCES

American Hospital Association (AHA). 2014. "Fast Facts on US Hospitals." Updated January 2. www.aha.org/research/rc/stat-studies/fast-facts.shtml.

HM Treasury. 2012. *A New Approach to Public Private Partnerships.* Accessed November 10, 2014. www.gov.uk/government/uploads/system/uploads/attachment_data/file/205112/pf2_infrastructure_new_approach_to_public_private_parnerships_051212.pdf.

Moody's Investor Service. 2012. "US Not-for-Profit Healthcare Outlook Remains Negative for 2012." Published January 25. www.carelogistics.com/media/52520/120125_moody_s_2012_nfp_healthcare_outlook.pdf.

Parliamentary Debates, Commons. 1998. Volume 313, 3 Jun Column 322. Accessed December 1, 2014. www.publications.parliament.uk/pa/cm199798/cmhansrd/vo980603/debtext/80603-13.htm.

Epilogue: A Little Daylight

Georgeann B. Burns and Robert D. Levine

I'd rather be vaguely right than precisely wrong.

—John Maynard Keynes

It has been written that there are ten disruptive forces in healthcare today as a result of the ACA (Bina 2014):

1. Transitioning to value-based reimbursement
2. Shifting volumes to ambulatory care and lower reimbursements
3. Moving from caring for the sick to managing population health
4. Advancing health information technology
5. Accelerating the introduction of digital health tools and medical technology
6. Shifting demographics—older and more diverse population and larger income disparities, yet with greater access to care
7. Projected provider shortages
8. Informed and involved patients
9. Increasing government regulation
10. Shrinking availability of capital

This book identified and discussed these disruptive forces. But when you take a step back and look at all of these forces together, it's easy to see the dramatic changes that are taking place. When you look at that list and think about it carefully, every single item can affect or be affected by capital development, in both direct and indirect ways. As mentioned in the prologue, it's clear that we need new ways to deliver healthcare, and therefore, new buildings in which to deliver it. Those buildings will have to be delivered quickly and competitively, yet made flexible for future changes as healthcare delivery needs change. We need buildings that are inexpensive to maintain and manage, yet durable and functional.

But most of the solutions are already right in front of us. We don't necessarily need to invent totally new policies, as in "blue ocean" thinking (Kim and Mauborgne 2005). We just need to embrace and incorporate policies that are already available but not fully integrated into our culture. It's been said that becoming proficient (even expert) in something doesn't take knowledge of everything, it just takes knowledge in several core parts, and that everything else is just an offshoot of that core. Those core solutions are discussed here.

CULTURAL CHANGE

Culture in an organization, by definition, involves shared habits and expectations and is hard to change. And that's why it works—because it lasts. But culture can strangle innovation in the crib. Culture continues because it's the default setting that defines an organization. Things are done because things have always been done that way. But the ACA flies in the face of our existing healthcare culture.

It took years after computer aided design (CAD) was developed before all architectural firms began to embrace it. Even today, with essentially all architectural work being performed on the computer, famed architect Michael Graves (2012) was critical of CAD as he felt that it stifled innovative design, the same way an audio book robs the reader of the full depth of the reading experience. Yet the architectural profession has been transformed with the use of CAD.

Debbie Gregory, in Chapter 8, suggests that technology can be a spark to create a culture that supports innovation and transformation. With new opportunities to work and deliver care created through new tools, our ability to transform can be accelerated.

PLANNING AND PROGRAMMING

We have an idea. If you want to save money on operating a new building, why not build a smarter, smaller, more efficient building? If you really want to save money, have fewer staff. The challenge is getting the right staffing complement while delivering the right care. And that means really understanding how care needs to be given, where it needs to happen, and who needs to deliver it. The answers to these *how* and *where* questions are changing and will continue to change. It is our responsibility to be as well-informed as our clients and the users of these buildings about how to frame these questions and then how to answer them.

INTEGRATED PROJECT DELIVERY

Gillian Tett (2014) discusses the General Motors ignition switch recall (or lack thereof) and makes the argument that the GM failure wasn't an unlawful policy of hiding their problems, but more a result of a company culture of building silos. Some people knew of the problem, but not the right people.

The same could be said of the BP failure that occurred in the Gulf of Mexico in 2010. The company knew a decade before the accident occurred that there was a safety problem with its deep sea rigs. But at BP, just as with GM, the wrong people knew.

We saw a similar situation with the financial failure of Lehman Brothers in 2008. The company wasn't hiding the fact that its collateralized debt obligations were on its balance sheet, and that its leverage was approaching 50 to one (instead of ten to one). It knew of the dangers, but the wrong people knew.

All of these companies worked within silos, with little communication between them. Our own industry of capital development has been building silos for decades. The owner doesn't share the true budget with the design team, the contractor doesn't see the documents develop until they are "ready," the industry's lump-sum bid (low bid wins) mentality keeps the subcontractor out of the room until the documents are 100 percent done. Change orders to correct design flaws and claims regarding extended schedules are what results when everyone is pulling in different directions.

But there is a solution to all of this, and it's called integrated project delivery (IPD). Bradley Taylor described it in Chapter 2, as did Dawn Naney and Clay Goser in Chapter 4. In a true IPD, all parties to the project (owner, architect, and contractor, referred to as the OAC team) sign a single contract agreement and are all pulling in the same direction. The early thinking about IPD started with the Sutter Healthcare System in Sacramento, California. Sutter was undergoing a major capital development program and saw the value of a collaborative relationship among the entire team.

An IPD contract has some ongoing issues, in that the risks are shared in an industry that prides itself on keeping risks in separate silos: architects take design risks, and construction managers take construction risks. And you can make the argument that the risk belongs with the entity that can best identify it and then mitigate it. But therein lies the problem. The OAC team spends all its time posturing for the good of its members' own risk mitigation and not for the benefit of the overall team. But in the long run, what is good for the team, and more specifically the owner, is also good for the architect and contractor and, through them, the vendors. It has been clearly shown that projects using this integrated approach benefit greatly, and the argument against signing the IPD contract comes more from the perspective of a culture change than from the legal issues.

A good resource for IPD is *Integrated Project Delivery: A Guide* by the American Institute of Architects (2007).

BUILDING INFORMATION MODELING

We talked briefly in the book about the lack of productivity gains in the construction industry over the past 50 years. This problem is caused by many factors. For example, the industry has a low cost of entry and is made up of many small contractors building a large portion of work exposed to weather. Much of the work is remodeling and not new and requires coordination of dozens of subcontractors that can be underfunded and understaffed. It could read like a horror show.

But within that environment, why was it that Providence Medical Center in Portland, Oregon, in 2008 was able to build a more than $100 million dollar new facility, under budget, within schedule, with minor change orders, no claims, and few safety issues? The project was one of the first in the nation to use the digital process known as building information modeling (BIM).

By first building the entire project digitally, the team was able to coordinate all of the mechanical piping, ductwork, electrical conduit, plumbing fixtures, walls, steel beams, ceiling heights—all areas of conflict in the field—before they put a shovel in the ground. As a result, there was more off-site prefabrication, which led to less labor in the field, which led to higher safety and quicker installation. Requests for information from the architects, normally a source of project delay, were reduced from 500, which would be normal for a project of this size, to 15. That led to shorter schedule, lower staff costs, lower general conditions, and therefore lower project costs. Pretty easy to connect the dots.

BIM has been around for more than a decade, yet many projects either don't use it or use it sparingly. That's because it does add to the early cost of the work, and when competing for work, no one wants to stand out with higher costs. But that cost pales in comparison to the cost benefits. BIM also requires a close collaboration, not only between the OAC team, but between all of the subcontractors as well. Until our industry views BIM as embedded in the cost of the work and not an "extra" program to be "considered," we will never benefit from its full value. That acceptance as "cost of the work" must begin with the hospital owner.

A good resource is the BIM Special Section of McGraw Hill Construction, found at www.bim.construction.com.

LEAN

Hospitals and health systems have been seeing the values of changing the way they deliver health services through a process called Lean for years. How healthcare is delivered affects staff, hours worked, safety, medical errors, readmissions, and ultimately costs.

The construction industry has also been embracing Lean, but not with the same success. That needs to change. We know that the whole Lean process came out of the automotive industry, specifically Toyota. In fact, a tour of the Toyota factory in Lexington, Kentucky, is well worth the visit. They welcome visitors.

But automobiles are built in a secure, controlled environment. This is not the case with the construction industry. Additionally, because of our low-cost bid mentality, most subcontractors are bidding their work with the expectations that they're only interested in their own productivity and work. But Lean looks for more collaboration, and the last planner schedule is predicated on that concept. The last planner schedule (which is at the heart of Lean) is a collaborative schedule that engages the main project suppliers from the start. It is focused on pull schedule techniques (to counter the fact that work normally expands to fill the time allowed) and team commitments. It takes a change in mindset and behavior. It's working smarter, faster, better. It means asking questions and creating a collaborative team environment among all who manage or perform the work. Lean construction eliminates unnecessary tasks, keeps excess materials off of job sites, creates a safer work environment, and accelerates the workflow of a project. Lean construction is just good common sense.

Let's take a look at a typical example of what occurs on a construction site. A drywall subcontractor will want to store his drywall and studs on all of the floors while the building is still open enough to do so inexpensively. But storing materials on the floors while other trades are trying to navigate with rolling scaffolding is not to everyone's best interest. So collaborating with other trades on what is to the best interest of the overall project, not just an individual subcontractor, is what defines Lean.

One way of overcoming that tension is to incentivize the subcontractors to cooperate. Randy Keiser, project executive for Turner Construction, describes a project in Tennessee in which he advised that a "savings pool" be established by the owner, and that all of the subcontractors participate, not just the large ones. Keiser was told by the drywall contractor at the end of the project that his share of the pool increased his fee by more than 100 percent. We would guess that subs with rolling scaffolds didn't have any problems on that project.

A good resource is The Lean Building Institute, www.leanconstruction.org.

SUSTAINABILITY

We can hear the groaning on the subject of sustainability, LEED certification, and anything to do with the Green Building Guide, all because of the perceived cost of getting involved. There wasn't a developer that we talked to, and we talked to a vast cross-section geographically, that didn't advise that you couldn't get competitive lease rates if they included "green construction." We disagree. Well, sort of.

As Rossi and Lent (2006) observed, "Every year hospitals consume huge volumes of materials. In 2004 alone, the healthcare sector consumed $23 billion worth of durable medical equipment and $32 billion worth of nondurable medical equipment, while investing another $86 billion in structures and medical equipment. This scale of consumption creates both concerns and opportunities. The concerns stem from how the plastics, metals, fibers, and minerals used in healthcare construction and medical devices affect our health. Materials matter, as Kenneth Geiser wrote in his book by the same title, because as 'we mine, synthesize, process, distribute, use, and, finally dispose of materials, we generate worrisome threats to the sustainability of the ecological systems upon which we depend.' As one of the largest economic sectors in the United States, healthcare is a major contributor to the impacts of material consumption."

As noted in Chapter 7, we knew that cigarettes caused cancer many years before we printed warnings on cigarette boxes and developed smoke-free public spaces.

We know today that fossil fuels are adding to global warming, yet we continue to design buildings that don't mitigate the need for those fuels. It's not so much money but intellectual energy that's needed to be energy efficient and sustainably compliant. If we don't take the lead in the healthcare industry, who will? What better advertisement for a hospital than to open its new building with a LEED certification? Of the 69 credits that are required for certification, 37 of those credits are required by code anyway, and of the remaining 32 requirements, half are free. So, no, we don't accept the argument that it's "too expensive to go green."

Yet, of the 5,500 or so hospitals that exist today in the United States, less than 5 percent are LEED certified. Because of lower reimbursements, hospitals need lower operating costs, and sustainability is part of the answer.

A good resource for sustainability is the US Green Building Council's (2010) *LEED 2009 for Healthcare*.

FLEXIBILITY

We've made it pretty clear that healthcare reform will be a work in progress. Much of the law was intended to be developed over a multiyear period through both committees and commissions. So the desire for a flexible building and program that can adapt to changing conditions is important. But hold that thought. As with everything, flexibility must be measured against cost.

A great and classic example of that is taught in Structures 101. We can design a bridge with a safety factor of 2.0 such that the bridge will withstand all types of storms, traffic, and potential terrorism and disasters. But the cost will be so prohibitive that it will never get built. Or the bridge can be designed properly with a safety factor of 1.3, be affordable, and (this is the important factor) can be safe, within the context of the definition of the word.

We've been adding flexibility to building design for years. We've been enlarging foundations to allow for vertical expansion; designing heavier steel structures to dampen vibration for future equipment; and increasing corridor widths to allow for patient occupancy, electrical, and mechanical capacity for future expansions, all with a cost to the budget. Today, with pressure on reimbursement, building in that flexibility must be measured against the cost, and therefore possible loss of program. But with information technology being such a major part of the ACA and clearly the future of healthcare, nothing is more important than building in flexibility for technology, and that is best done through wireless technology. A good wireless technology program can do the following:

- *Continuous auto-optimization from the cloud.* Tunes the network for optimal performance under changing conditions.
- *Standards-based security for HIPAA compliance.* Virtual isolated networks are deployed to reduce security issues and improve ease of use.

- *Internet access for patients and visitors.* Serve multiple constituencies with a single wireless network.
- *Browser based multisite management.* Manage centrally over the web with no limits.
- *Improved response time and streamlined processes.* When healthcare institutions know where their staff, patients, and assets are at any moment, they can improve workflow, reduce costs, and increase patient and staff safety.
- *Connect remote specialists to clinics from remote locations, and all within a wireless environment.* With cloud-based solutions, networks can be extended to remote specialists.

By using the cloud, future renovations for updated equipment and newer information technologies are no longer required because the routers are all offsite. All that is required is the installation of a wireless spine. Wireless technology provides the ultimate flexibility.

DESIGN–BUILD

There are many variations of the process, but the most important feature of design–build is that design and construction are performed by one entity under one contract with the owner. That entity can be a company that provides both services under one roof, or an affiliation of two firms (one design and one build) that have come together for this project. In either case, it's important that the design–build team offers to the owner the independent and varied cultures of both the architect and the contractor.

Advantages of design–build include the following:

- *Stabilizing and reducing cost.* This occurs because allowing one entity total control over project design, scope, and budget means less opportunity for scope-related change orders. Additionally, the close relationship between the

design team and the contractor in a design–build team tends to reduce liability issues associated with increasing project costs.
- *Establishing schedule.* By allocating all responsibility to one entity, owners find that time-consuming issues—such as poor communication, requests for information, design errors, design omissions, and so on—will be minimized.
- *Reducing claims.* Implicit in the design–build process is the shelter of the owner from liability. Because the architect will no longer be acting as an agent of the owner, design errors and omissions will be the sole responsibility of the design–build team. It inherently promotes a nonadversarial relationship between the designer and the contractor.
- *Reducing complexity.* Many owners have neither the staff nor the experience to manage the traditional triad of owner-designer-contractor. Taking one player out of the game lessens managerial tasks.

Not all projects lend themselves to this delivery method, and a project should have certain characteristics for design–build to be considered in the first place, including:

- a well-defined scope of work,
- shared understanding of that scope between the owner and the design–build team,
- educated owner staff,
- construction sophistication by owner,
- a formal and clearly established budget, and
- a formal and clearly defined schedule.

Although design–build offers many advantages, dangers abound if the team is not selected carefully. It's important to make sure that the team selection is qualifications based, not fee based or commodity driven.

As is true of all delivery methods, the best way for an owner to reduce his risk with design–build is to be an active participant in the process. This will include recognizing and understanding the inherent legal issues relating to insurance, surety products, contract language, and other details of the process.

A good resource for design–build is the Design Build Institute of America (www.dbia.org).

BEING AN EDUCATED OWNER

The following are the five most dreaded comments an owner can make about a capital project.

1. "I want to work with an architect and construction manager that have the lowest fees."

   Fees are not indicative of qualifications. The healthcare design and construction industry has moved from being fee-based to being qualifications-based, and fees are but a minor component that should not drive team member selection.

2. "If I don't lump-sum bid, how do I know I'm getting the best price?"

   Contractor input is needed during the initial development process, not at the end of the document development. A critical component of value analysis is lost by excluding the experience and knowledge of qualified contractors and subcontractors as the program and budget are being developed.

3. "I don't want to take any risk, so I need strong contract language to protect me."

   Onerous contract terms are passed on to the subcontractor community and affect budget, not risk.

Risk mitigation is done through involvement and communication, not contract terms.

4. "I don't need a project manager or owner's rep—that's what the architect is for."

   Truthfully, the architect does have some fiduciary responsibility to the owner. And on many projects, the owner can be properly represented by the architect. But on sizeable healthcare projects, the owner can be well served by an independent project manager that breaks down silos and supports good owner–team communication.

5. "I'll buy the equipment (medical and mechanical) myself. That way I save the contractor's mark-up."

   Whatever may be saved in bypassing the contractor or distributor, the risk to the owner is dramatically increased if the purchase of the component parts is not correct, or if the delivery is not on time, or if the warranties and guarantees are not intact. The services of experienced contractors, distributors, and equipment planners are invaluable. Excluding them is the wrong place to look to save money.

Being an educated owner makes you a better capital project development team member.

CONCLUSION

Two major factors influence the adoption of cost-effective project development. The first factor is performance—getting a capital project done. We've heard many construction people say that Lean principles are nothing more than good construction practices that they've been doing for years. Yet these principles don't show up on most of the work. That's because no formal program is in place.

Companies with those programs as part of their culture tend to do it on all projects. Same goes for sustainability and also for BIM. Otherwise, their inclusion is hit or miss.

And the second factor is the tendency to avoid adding extra components and cost to the early capital budget. A wall has often been built between the capital budget and the operating budget. While we know these additions will yield major benefits to the project and its downstream operating costs, so vital in today's environment, major opportunities are often passed over. We constantly do cost–benefit analyses on mechanical systems and exterior enclosures that clearly show a quick three- to five-year payback, yet these proposals are never accepted because of the lack of funds in the capital budget. Privatization projects, especially with a 501(c)(3) entity responsible for operating costs, do often include these longer-term beneficial components; their inclusion is simply included in the lease rate. The private sector must follow that example.

One of the main reasons the Obama administration was able to get the American Medical Association and the American Hospital Association behind the passage of the ACA was the implicit agreement that although the ACA was going to reduce reimbursement by almost $1 trillion over the ensuing ten years, the law was meant to expand the covered population by 32 million people, half of whom—almost 16 million—were to come from the Medicaid expansion. Those additional covered lives were assumed to more than compensate for the lower reimbursement.

Even though one of the main objectives of the ACA was to remedy the growing lack of access to healthcare, the 2010 Supreme Court decision allowing states to opt out of Medicaid expansion makes it likely that a significant portion of the population will remain uncovered. Unless an equal proportion of the $1 trillion cutback in reimbursement follows, there are bound to be continued major pressures on reimbursement to hospitals and health systems, and therefore a limit on their ability to direct funds to capital development projects. We are already seeing significant reductions in the number of hospital admissions and in the lengths of stay.

These reductions are further affecting traditional revenue streams at all reimbursement rates. The concomitant relocation of diagnostic and treatment procedures to hospital-based ambulatory care sites (often with higher charges per procedure than non-hospital-based care) is still based on treating these procedures as revenue sources. Some systems are clearly hoping to offset the acute care losses with the increased ambulatory care revenue. However, as we move to accountable care and bundled payments, we believe that the cost differentials between sources and sites for the same care will diminish or disappear. And that the focus will shift inevitably to determining where and how to provide the most efficient and cost effective care.

As a result, looking for opportunities to reduce and contain cost in the delivery of healthcare and, to the extent possible, in the buildings that deliver it becomes ever more important. That has been the whole purpose of this book.

As a further resource for all of the topics in this book, please check out the Suggested Resources on page 243.

REFERENCES

American Institute of Architects. 2007. *Integrated Project Delivery: A Guide.* New York: American Institute of Architects.

Bina, S. S. 2014. "10 Disruptive Forces in Healthcare." *Becker's Hospital Review.* Published May 12. www.beckershospitalreview.com/hospital-management-administration/10-disruptive-forces-in-healthcare.html.

Graves, M. 2012. "Architecture and the Lost Art of Drawing." *New York Times.* Published September 1. http://www.nytimes.com/2012/09/02/opinion/sunday/architecture-and-the-lost-art-of-drawing.html?pagewanted=all&_r=0.

Kim, W. C., and R. Mauborgne. 2005. *Blue Ocean Strategy: How to Create Uncontested Market Space and Make Competition Irrelevant.* Boston: Harvard Business Press.

Rossi, M., and T. Lent. 2006. "Creating Safe And Healthy Spaces: Selecting Materials That Support Healing." The Center for Health Design. Accessed January 6,

2015. www.healthdesign.org/sites/default/files/Creating%20Safe%20and%20 Healthy%20Spaces.pdf.

Tett, G. 2014. "A Fragmented Corporate Culture is the Villain of the Piece." *Financial Times.* Published June 12. http://www.ft.com/cms/s/0/1ed7e096-f099-11e3-8f3d-00144feabdc0.html#axzz3LzBLBOs6.

US Green Building Council. 2010. *LEED 2009 for Healthcare.* Accessed December 15, 2014. www.usgbc.org/Docs/Archive/General/Docs8878.pdf.

Suggested Resources

Although it has been said in healthcare that Google is not a second opinion, we know the Internet has helped millions of patients become better informed.

The Internet can get you better informed about many other aspects of healthcare as well, whether it's systems, hospitals, and providers, or any of the capital projects disciplines involved, such as planning, design, construction, vendors, and so on. This list of resources is just a small sampling of what's available.

- The Hill (www.thehill.com). This site covers Congress on all issues as well as covering political campaigns. Because healthcare is such a regulated business, this site is a good way to stay plugged into the conversation.
- The Center for Health Design (www.healthdesign.org). This not-for-profit group is at the heart of evidence-based design (EBD). Its Pebble Program is well known for its EBD research.
- *Hospitals & Health Networks* (www.hhn.com). H&HN is a daily digital magazine with topical and timely healthcare articles by industry leaders.
- Kaiser Family Foundation (www.kkf.org). This site is a major source of topical articles regarding all aspects of healthcare. Many people have suggested that the Affordable Care Act (ACA) was modeled after Kaiser

Healthcare, although this site contains the entire gamut of opinions on implementation of reform.

- National Conference of State Legislatures (www.ncsl.org). NCSL gives a nice review of the status of Certificate of Need applications and outcomes as well as healthcare legislation on a statewide basis.
- Health Care Policy and Marketplace Review (www.healthpolicyandmarket.blogspot.com). This healthcare reform blog is run by Bob Laszewski, a reporter for the *Washington Post*. Its material is timely, educational, and all relevant to healthcare reform.
- *Healthcare Design* (www.healthcaredesignmagazine.com). This monthly magazine covers all aspects of the industry, from interior design and architecture to construction and operations, as well as white papers and blogs.
- *Medical Construction and Design* (www.mcdmag.com). This is one of the first healthcare magazines to feature construction, along with design articles relating to the industry. Its editorial board is equally weighted with experts from facility, construction, and design.
- *Modern Healthcare* (www.modernhealthcare.com). Long the standard for weekly reading, this magazine covers a broad range of articles and is known for its editorial comments as well as timely coverage of healthcare. Its companion newsletter, *The Daily Dose*, provides daily updates.
- InformeDesign (www.informedesign.org). This site is a major resource for EBD and is filled with research publications and tutorials regarding EBD and sustainability.
- Clinicate (www.clinicate.com). This site explains clinical communications and provides patient education solutions, access to colleagues and patients, and major reference access.

- The Centers for Disease Control and Prevention (www.cdc.gov). An excellent site for articles on diseases and conditions, environmental health publications, healthy living, mobile apps, and emergency preparedness, all of which are applicable to capital development.
- KevinMD (www.kevinmd.com). This blog provides a weekly inside look at the healthcare profession from the physician's perspective.
- *Becker's Hospital Review* (www.beckershospitalreview.com). *Becker's* is a major source of white papers, webinars, and articles by and relevant to CEOs, CFOs, and CIOs.
- The Mayo Clinic (www.mayoclinic.org). This site is an excellent resource for articles and research on all things healthcare. Mayo stands out for its collaborative model for delivering healthcare, a methodology that is at the heart of healthcare reform. The site is great for research and education.
- The Cleveland Clinic (www.clevelandclinic.org). The site is well known for its information on diseases and conditions as well as treatments and procedures, just as Cleveland Clinic renowned for its research and innovations.
- The Digital Health Corner (www.davidleescher.com). The author gives an excellent look at the influence that digital technology is having on the healthcare industry. He covers all issues that are relevant to designing and implementing digital health technologies.
- *Journal of Ambulatory Care Management* (www.journals.lww.com/ambulatorycaremanagement). This publication focuses on all topics related to ambulatory care delivery.
- The Agency for Healthcare Research and Quality (www.ahrq.gov). This government entity's mission is to improve the quality, safety, efficiency, and effectiveness of healthcare for all Americans.

- Nursing Institute for Healthcare Design (www.nursingihd.com). NIHD fosters inclusion of nurses and healthcare providers in all phases of the design process, provides education, and disseminates information on major design and care issues.
- Healthcare Financial Management Association (www.hfma.org). HFMA focuses on financial issues facing healthcare institutions, including operational and facility effectiveness.
- *Health Environments Research and Design Journal* (www.herdjournal.com). This peer-reviewed journal enhances the knowledge and practice of evidence-based healthcare design by disseminating research findings, discussing issues and trends, and translating research into practice.

Index

About the Contributors

CHAPTER 1

Alan R. Yordy, FACHE, is the president and chief mission officer of Peace Health, an integrated healthcare system in Washington, Oregon, and Alaska. The system includes ten hospitals, an 850-provider medical group, and a health plan. He has served the healthcare industry for more than 33 years as a senior healthcare executive. Yordy is the recipient of numerous awards, including Executive of the Year, United Way of King County; Oregon Hospital Political Action Committee Leadership Award, Oregon Association of Hospitals and Health Systems; AHA Political Action Committee Leadership Award, American Hospital Association PAC; and the Regent's Award, American College of Healthcare Executives. A frequent speaker at national and regional conferences, he is highly respected for his opinions on Lean design, patient safety, and clinical integration.

CHAPTER 2

Bradley Taylor is project team manager, Design and Construction, Oregon Health & Science University in Portland, Oregon. Taylor is responsible for the programming, design, and construction of all capital construction projects and manages a project delivery team of space programmers, architects, project managers, project coordinators, and project team assistants. His education and background in architecture have given him a unique perspective on capital development, as he has designed and detailed numerous commercial projects primarily for regional hospitals and clinics.

CHAPTER 4

Dawn M. Naney is the cofounder of Symphony, LLC, in St. Louis, Missouri. She has more than 16 years of experience managing teams responsible for the successful planning and execution of projects, programs, and portfolios of varying size and complexity in a variety of fields, including design and construction, information technology, clinical excellence, and process improvement, primarily in the healthcare industry. Her accomplishments include establishing portfolios, creating and implementing program and project management frameworks, facilitating business process reengineering, developing earned value management, monitoring risk management, and managing processes and tools for a 13-hospital health system.

Clay W. Goser is a principal and cofounder of Symphony, LLC, in St. Louis, Missouri, where he provides project, program, and portfolio management; organizational management; and consultancy for process and procedure. He previously served ten years with the US Army as a health facility planner, providing planning, design, and construction services for military hospitals both nationally and internationally, and was the director of community hospitals for BJC Healthcare, an 18-hospital system. Goser has presented at various professional organizations, such as the American Society of Healthcare Engineering, Construction Management Association of America, Healthcare Facility Symposium, Lean Construction Institute, Association of General Contractors, International Group for Lean Construction, and the Texas AEC Leadership Forum.

CHAPTER 7

Paul J. Whitson is senior vice president and regional leader for healthcare at HOK in St. Louis, Missouri. He has more than 20 years of professional experience in the planning and design of healthcare facilities. He has received numerous awards, including the Unbuilt: Honorable Mention (*Modern Healthcare*) and Best Sustainable Development Award (Cityscape Abu Dhabi) for Sheikh Khalifa Medical City (2012). He is a frequent speaker at national conferences.

CHAPTER 8

Debbie Gregory, RN, BSN, is a senior clinical consultant at Smith Seckman Reid, Inc. She has been a registered nurse for 30 years with a clinical focus on critical care, medical–surgical patient care, surgery, and obstetrics. Gregory is cofounder and past president of the Nursing Institute for Healthcare Design, a not-for-profit nursing association dedicated to educating and inspiring nurse leaders about their role in healthcare design and construction. The organization provides research, education, mentoring, and collaboration among nurses working in the healthcare construction industry. She has written numerous publications about healthcare technology and nurse leaders in healthcare design. She received the *Nashville Business Journal* Healthcare Heroes Innovator Award in 2011. Gregory is currently pursuing her DNP in health innovation and leadership from the University of Minnesota.

Scott Johnson is former senior principal at Smith Seckman Reid, Inc. His expertise includes systems strategic planning and budgeting, detailed design, and implementation project management as part of an integrated project design and construction team. He is a frequent speaker at major national conferences, such as the

American Institute of Architects, Academy of Architecture for Health Annual Conference, American Society of Healthcare Engineers Planning, Design & Construction Annual Conference, and the GE National VAR Conference, Trends in Technology.

Julia Whitacre is a technology consultant with Smith Seckman Reid, Inc. She has nearly a decade of low voltage planning, design, and project management experience for major academic medical centers and top healthcare system organizations across the United States. Her recent awards include Nashville Emerging Leaders Class of 2013 Honoree and Nashville's Top 30 Under 30 Honoree in 2011. She is a graduate of Vanderbilt University's School of Engineering and is a member of the Healthcare Information and Management Systems Society (HIMSS).

CHAPTER 9

Lisa Charrin is the vice president of Mitchell Planning in Houston, Texas. She has more than 24 years of healthcare experience and is one of the nation's most recognized industry experts on the future of medical technology. She presents regularly at national healthcare design conferences on technology trends, hybrid room designs, cancer centers, and research labs. She has also published several articles and white papers on planning for trends in surgery and imaging. She has served as a grant reviewer for the National Institute of Health, providing expertise on reviewing laboratory equipment requests.

CHAPTER 10

John Kemper is CEO of John E. Kemper, LLC, in Richmond, Virginia. He previously served as senior managing director of CBRE Healthcare and as CEO of KLMK, one of the nation's leading project management firms. He is experienced in all aspects of project delivery, including project organization and launch; professional services procurement; scope, cost and schedule control systems; and coordination with regulatory approval authorities. He has a comprehensive understanding of the formation and collaboration of project delivery teams that form the foundation of successful projects. Kemper earned a bachelor of science degree in civil engineering from Virginia Military Institute. He has written numerous publications, including *Launching a Capital Facility Project: A Guide for Healthcare Leaders*, second edition (Health Administration Press 2010).

About the Editors

Robert D. Levine is president of Robert Levine Consulting, LLC. He has more than 50 years of construction industry experience. As senior vice president of Turner Construction Co.'s Healthcare Group, he was responsible for effective management and development of healthcare projects throughout the United States. In that position, he provided extensive and focused understanding of the industry and healthcare trends for more than 25 years. In his career, he has been involved in completing nearly $3 billion worth of healthcare projects.

In 2007, Levine received the first Russ Coile Lifetime Achievement Award from the Center for Health Design, which recognizes individuals who dedicate their careers to the advancement of the healthcare design industry. Levine is a frequent speaker at local and national conferences and has written extensively on industry trends, building development, and senior living. He has been published in *Medical Construction & Design*, *Healthcare Design*, and *Commercial Building*. He serves on the board of directors of the Health Care Institute, an affiliate of the International Facility Management Association.

Georgeann B. Burns is president of Health Facilities Planning Partners, LLC. Burns has devoted her career to working on healthcare projects, beginning with one of the nation's leading architectural firms, SMP, in San Francisco. Her projects there ranged from research studies for the Veterans Administration to master plans for leading academic medical centers. In addition, she has worked with other national and international firms, such as HKS, RTKL, The SLAM Collaborative, and Anderson DeBartolo Pan. She also led GPR Health, Inc., and later the Austin Group, Inc., both consulting firms focused on healthcare planning and programming. She has served as a board member and president of the AIA Academy of Architecture for Health, was a founding trustee and president of the Academy of Architecture for Health Foundation, and is a current member of the Academy's Leadership Council.

With a growing interest in Lean principles and their application to healthcare delivery and the process of healthcare project delivery, she formed Health Facilities Planning Partners, LLC. She has also been a contributing author to several industry journals and a frequent presenter at national conferences.